Jacob T Child

The pearl of Asia

Reminiscences of the court of a supreme monarch; or, Five years in Siam

Jacob T Child

The pearl of Asia
Reminiscences of the court of a supreme monarch; or, Five years in Siam

ISBN/EAN: 9783742891440

Manufactured in Europe, USA, Canada, Australia, Japa

Cover: Foto ©ninafisch / pixelio.de

Manufactured and distributed by brebook publishing software
(www.brebook.com)

Jacob T Child

The pearl of Asia

PREFACE.

During many leisure hours, while absent amid the sunny glades and emerald vales of Asia's most favored kingdom, Siam, I made numerous notes concerning that land of mystic lore and ruined fanes, a section novel to all who have been so fortunate as to have visited its walled city with its hundred glittering spires, whose temples and palaces are marvels of architectural beauty, whose wide-spreading rice-fields feed untold millions, its groves of waving palms ever ready to minister to man's wants, its rivers and canals plethoric with fish, its fruits and flowers lavishly luxuriant, an Eden of loveliness, the land of the lotus. To the general reader Siam is a *terra incognita;* much has been written concerning it by superficial observers, who came on one steamer and left on the next. What has been gathered for this volume has been carefully condensed and concisely told. It was my intention when appointed Minister to the Court at Bangkok, by President Cleveland, to prepare a work on this faraway and marvelous land that might prove of interest to many who may desire to know something of a people that live under a supreme monarch and follow the teaching of Buddha, and in doing so I have endeavored to hold the mirror up to nature, in fact, to " tell the truth."

Respectfully,
JACOB T. CHILD.

RICHMOND, Mo., June 14, 1892.

CONTENTS.

	PAGE.
I. Siam Proper—The Pearl of Asia................................	9
II. Arrival at Bangkok—Scenery on the Menam..................	22
III. Reception by His Majesty King Chulalongkorn............	35
IV. Characteristics of the Country and Habits of the People......	40
V. Ayuthia, The Ancient Capital...................................	73
VI. Dining with the King..	86
VII. Wonderful Ruins of Angkor and Nagkon Wat................	91
VIII. The Supreme Palace and Royal Temples.....................	102
IX. Peculiar Manner of Scaring Away the Dragon...............	113
X. The Water Rite..	117
XI. Ceremonies of Hair Cutting....................................	122

v

XII.
Wat-Sa-Ket and the Siamese Golgotha............................ 129

XIII.
A Siamese Execution... 136

XIV.
Paddy (Rice) and its Cultivation.................................... 142

XV.
Excessive Taxation of the People.................................. 147

XVI.
The King's Instructions to His Son................................ 153

XVII.
Funeral of a Chinese Mandarin..................................... 161

XVIII.
Royal Palaces at Bang-Pa-In and Ratburee..................... 164

XIX.
The Legal Oath Administered to Witnesses..................... 173

XX.
Installation of The Crown Prince................................... 176

XXI.
Prominent Temples and Pagodas................................... 184

XXII.
Buddhism in Siam.. 194

XXIII.
A Translation from the Pongsawadan, or History of the Kings of Siam.. 224

XXIV.
"Taut Katin," or Wat Visiting....................................... 235

XXV.
Grand Display of the Royal Flotilla on the Menam.......... 239

XXVI.
The Marriage Ceremony Among the Affluent................ 247

XXVII.
The Attap Palm, Tong Yang and Other Trees................ 252

XXVIII.
Holidays and Festivals....................................... 260

XXIX.
Customs of the Siamese for the Dying and the Dead—Cremation, etc... 272

XXX.
Practice of Medicine—Native Doctors........................ 296

XXXI.
Siamese Ploughs, Ox-Yokes, and Harrows.................... 310

XXXII.
Brief Synopsis of Siamese History—A Translation............ 314

XXXIII.
Fac Simile of Copy of His Majesty's Speech with Translation... 320

XXXIV.
His Majesty's Birthday Festivities........................... 321

XXXV.
The Money Standard of Siam................................. 326

XXXVI.
The Press of Siam... 329

XXXVII.
A Visit to Petchaburee; Its Palace—The Holy Mountain and Laos Village... 333

ILLUSTRATIONS.

		PAGE.
1.	His Majesty, King Chulalongkorn	Contents.
2.	Temple at the Mouth of the Menam	22
3.	The King's Garden	32
4.	River View of Portion of Bangkok	35
5.	Native House in the Interior	40
6.	Scientific Class at Sandalay College	44
7.	Her Majesty, the Supreme or Celestial Queen	49
8.	Fruits of Siam	63
9.	Floating Houses on the Menam	73
10.	Ruins of Nagkon Wat	91
11.	The Supreme Palace of the King	102
12.	Wat Pherce Kea, or Temple of the Emerald Idol	104
13.	Imperial Altar and Emerald Idol	113
14.	Wat Sa-Ket, or Gold Mountain	127
15.	Court-Yard of Bangkok's Golgotha	136
16.	Residence of the American Minister in Bangkok	161
17.	Ruins in Ayuthia	164
18.	Prisoners Working in Teak Lumber Yard	173
19.	The Crown Prince, Heir Apparent to the Throne	176
20.	Golden Temple and Flotilla on the Menam	180
21.	Prabat or Temple of Footsteps of Buddha	184
22.	Brass Idol in Temple, Bangkok	187
23.	Grand Temple at Phra Pratom	191
24.	Elephant Procession in Stone	194
25.	The High Priest of Siam	224
26.	Bird's-eye View of the Palace Grounds and Wall	235
27.	A Nobleman and his Family	253
28.	Royal Premain, or Cremation Building	272
29.	Native Bullock Carts and Ox Yokes	310
30.	Scene on the Canal	314
31.	Fac Simile of his Majesty's Speech	321
32.	Interior of the Throne Room	326

THE PEARL OF ASIA.

I.

SIAM PROPER—THE PEARL OF ASIA.

By reference to the map it will be found that Siam is an extensive kingdom of southeastern Asia, containing an area of about 250,000 square miles. In the north the country is mountainous, but it stretches toward the south into well-watered fertile plains on which are raised large crops of paddy (rice), the principal article of export; the next article of importance is teak wood, obtained from the forests in the interior and rafted down the river. Sugar cane, pepper, teal seed and fruit trees are also largely cultivated.

The government is an absolute monarchy, nominally hereditary, but the sovereign H. M. Phrabat Somdetch Phra Paramendr Chulalongkorn is invested with the power of appointing his successor. A Council of Ministers (Senabodie), with the King at its head, exercises the legislative power. There is also a Council of State which consists of the Ministers, ten to twenty members appointed by the King and six Princes of the royal house. For administrative purposes the kingdom is divided into forty-one provinces, each presided over by a Governor appointed by the King. The prevailing religion is Buddhism, the King being at the head of the church, but perfect freedom is allowed to Christian missionaries, Mahometans and all others. The King's revenue has been estimated at about $10,000,000 a year, derived chiefly from land tax, spirits, opium, gambling, customs, tin mines, fruit tree tax, fisheries and many others, a full list of which will be found elsewhere. With the exception of custom duties all the taxes are farmed, sold to the highest bidder. The expenditures are stated to be less than the receipts; also, the exports less than the imports, hence the country is prosperous and it has no public debt. The population is estimated at about ten millions, but no census has ever been taken. There is a small standing army, as also a militia; every male inhabitant, with certain exceptions, above the age of twenty-one, is obliged to serve in the army for three months in the year. The navy consists of a few steam-corvettes and gun-boats under the command of Commodore De Richelieu, a Dane. The king's yacht, the Vesatre, a handsome vessel, was lost a short time before I left the Kingdom.

Trade and industry are in a backward condition, owing to the state of serfdom in which the people are kept by the feudal owners of the land. The natives are liable to forced labor (corvee) for several months during the year, and this prevents much of the land being put in cultivation, probably not over one-twentieth of the available land being utilized for agricultural purposes; many broad acres of the very best are held by the priests for religious purposes, the wat grounds being considered the choicest in the kingdom and are to be found in every available spot. There is a Postal and Telegraphic service in Bangkok. In 1885 Siam joined the International Postal Union, and these affairs are well managed. The foreign trade of Siam, in the hands of foreigners, mainly centers in Bangkok, but considerable tin is now being shipped from the

Malay peninsula. Two telegraph lines connect Bangkok with the outer world, one with Burmah and the other via Saigon, both in good order, but the latter was for some time rendered useless, as the Cambodian insurgents pulled down the wire and cut it up for slugs for their rifles.

The export of rice is yearly increasing, but for the past two years the crops, owing to excessive drouths, have been partial failures notwithstanding considerable new land has been brought under cultivation in the delta of the Menam. The teak trade has not been profitable for the past two years, as the demand for it in Europe has been limited. Numbers of cattle are annually shipped to Singapore from Bangkok, and the export to Burmah is very large, exceeding 50.000 head a year. Immense numbers of fine cattle can be found throughout Siam, and the prices in the interior are very low, the value of a good cow with its calf being five ticals or three dollars. When the road to Khorat is completed, opening up the interior, this will cause an advance in price and an increase in the industry. The platu, Siamese herring, has heretofore been an article of export, but their scarcity the past few years has been coincident with the lowness of the river, and they now fail to congregate in immense shoals at the head of the gulf of Siam, as has been the case heretofore during the last three months of the year. It is supposed that the rivers, when in full flood, bring down vegetable matter especially attractive as food for this species of fish. An abundant supply of salt is always procurable, obtained by evaporating sea water, and on the coast is principally used in the preparation of platu for export; it also forms an important article of the up country trade. The Chinese population of Bangkok, numbering about one-third of its citizens, use large quantities of flour which is imported from San Francisco, via Hong Kong, also American canned goods. Lines of steamers ply between Bangkok and Hong Kong, and from Bangkok to Singapore, which carry the mails and do a prosperous business.

To Maj. James McCarthy, whose Siamese title is Phra Wibharg Bhuvadal, Superintendent of the Survey Department, we are indebted for much of the following information concerning this magnificent kingdom, he having traversed most portions of it, visiting parts that no white man had hitherto penetrated, for the purpose of preparing a correct map of Siam and its tributaries. Occupying the heart of Indo-China and nearly the whole of the Malay peninsula, it has a seaboard sweeping round the Gulf of Siam from about the 4th degree of latitude on the Malay side to about the 11th degree of latitude on the Cambodian side, a distance of nearly 1,200 miles. The great feature of Siam proper is its magnificent system of rivers, the principal of which is the Menam Chow-Phya, on which Bangkok is located thirty-five miles from the gulf. This river is commonly called the Menam, which is a generic name for all large rivers, Me meaning mother, and Nam water. About one hundred miles from the sea there is a bifurcation of the river, both branches flowing through rich alluvial soil devoted to rice cultivation, the banks being well studded with thriving villages. Toward the delta, formed by the bifurcation of the river, two large streams converge, the Meklong, from the Burmese frontier on the northwest and the Bangpakong from the hills on the Khorat plateau; both empty themselves into the head of the Gulf of Siam. All these rivers are connected by navigable canals, thus enabling the Siamese to travel by boat to Bangkok. The rivers and canals are always alive with boats and rafts of teak wood and bamboo. The country is subject to a yearly inundation, and unless the rivers overflow their banks a short rice crop is expected, as the planters rely on irrigation. The May-Nam-Kong flows through the Northern and Eastern parts of the kingdom, receiving the waters of many affluents, but the channel of this mighty river is so blocked with large rocks and cataracts that its navigation is difficult and in some parts impossible even for the light native crafts. From the northeast of Chiengmai two ranges of mountains branch off, one running south in an unbroken chain through the Malay peninsula to Singapore; some of its peaks between Siam and Burmah rise to the height of 7,000 feet, one in the Malay peninsula reaches 8,000 feet; the other range follows the course of the May-Nam-Kong, first running east and west and then in a southerly direction toward Cambodia. Siam proper is mostly flat, diversified by isolated hills and broken and jagged ridges of limestone mountains. Its population is a mingling of all Eastern nationalities: Siamese, Cambodians, Burmans, Annamites, Malays and Chinese; the latter swarm all over the country and seem to the manor born. The portion of the country that is administered by the Central government includes the greater part of the Malay peninsula and the larger portion of the Menam and the May-Nam-Kong valley. Some Malay, Lao and Cambodian States are only tributary, that is, they make offerings of gold and silver flowers to the King at Bangkok. Each ruler of these States is appointed by the King and he exercises considerable power in his own province. The most important of the tributary States are those of the Lao, which are now under the complete control of the Bangkok government; they occupy the mountainous country to the North and have a fine climate. Those in the valley of the Menam are known as the Lao Phoong Dam (black-bellies), because they tattoo their waist to the knee, and those in the valley of the May-Nam-Kongare known as Lao Phoong Khao (white-bellies), as they do not tattoo themselves. The Lao very much resemble their brethren of Siam proper, speaking the same dialect, and those of the valley of the May-Nam-Kong bear a strong resemblance in every particular; many of the words peculiar to the Lao in ordinary conversation are said to be used in Siamese poetry, the accent being different.

Lying between the parallels of 4 deg. and 23 deg. north latitude, Siam has but two seasons, distinctly determined by the monsoons. The southwest monsoon, bringing with it rain, prevails from May until September, but the high mountain range running on the west, from north to south, prevents the excessive rainfall experienced on the Burman coast. From September until February the northeast monsoon blows, and from November to February dry weather proper and cool breezes prevail, rendering traveling all over the kingdom enjoyable and pleasant. From the middle of February until the rain sets in the heat is oppressive, but even at this period the thermometer seldom rises higher than 97 degrees in Bangkok; though, once or twice, I have seen it up to 100 deg. In the winter it occasionally falls to 60 deg. In the interior of the country, at places of low elevation, the heat is intense, sometimes rising to 110 deg.; while, on the other hand, at the same places in winter the mercury falls as low as 45 deg. The annual rainfall in Bangkok is about sixty inches, but in the interior of the country, judging from the inundations of the river, it must be a great deal more. Malarial fever is a common complaint. Cholera is more prevalent in Lower than Upper Siam, being rarely absent. Small-pox is common and His Majesty sends native physicians throughout the kingdom to vaccinate the people, believing in its mitigating influence, and much good has been effected thereby. A small-pox ward has been established at the Wang Lang hospital. The Siamese use principally herbal medicines, some of them very effective. Among the Laos superstition attributes much of the sickness to the influence of evil spirits. The different classes of Lao take opposite views of the influence of the spirits. When a person falls sick among the Phoong Dam the spirit doctor is sent for who questions the patient, frequently in a raging fever, as to who caused his sickness, and woe be to the unhappy individual, whether man or woman, whose name may be mentioned. He is expelled from the village community as being possessed by the evil spirit who has caused the sickness, his house is burnt down and he is forced to live at some distant village expressly set apart for all possessed. With the Phoong Khao it is different; to be possessed by a spirit is a great privilege. The Governors and everyone who can afford it has his spirit man; nothing important is undertaken without consulting him. He usually begins by working himself into a fit, then asks for a substantial meal and drink of samshoo, rice whisky, and is then prepared to answer questions, drinking enough to put him to sleep and when he awakes pretends to a total ignorance of all that has taken place, a practice in vogue with our clairvoyants.

The inhabitants of Siam are for the most part agricultural, their towns merely clusters of villages and hamlets, consisting of wooden and bamboo houses and huts thickly settled on the river banks. The capitals of Siam have always been noted for the beauty and magnificence of their palaces and temples. From Chieng Sen in the north, the southward march of the Siamese is traced by the magnificent ruins of the temples of the capitals of different periods. Bangkok, the present capital, is the site of the eighth capital since Chieng Sen, which, to some extent, supports the Siamese in their claim to a history extending many hundred years back. In Bangkok the royal palace and temples surpass all other buildings in richness and grandeur, as can be seen by illustrations.

When Ayuthia was abandoned Bangkok became the capital, and it was here that the present dynasty made it the seat of royalty, and it is here that the king presides over his councils and became one of the great reformers of the East by issuing his famous edicts abolishing slavery, thus placing Siam on a footing with the more advanced nations. Outside the palace walls and within the city, besides the numerous temples and glittering pagodas, are many excellent buildings. The foreign representatives live on the right bank of the river and have handsome residences generally. The river itself presents a busy scene. The population of the city is variously estimated from seven to eight hundred thousand inhabitants. Khorat is the next most important city; it is a crenelated walled place, the walls crumbling down, about three miles round, built at an elevation of 750 feet above mean sea-level, and is one of the most important places in the valley of the May-Nam-Kong. The district is famous for the stupendous ruins of stone temples, the same in design and construction as those found in Cambodia and Borroboodur in Java. Nothing, as is the case at Ankor, can be discovered as to the builders, all knowledge of them seems to have been lost in the past. Outside the city walls is a colony of Chinese who carry on all the trade of the district. Chiengmai, or, as it is called in Burma, Zimme, is one of the most important towns in the Lao Phoong Dam country, a walled city, about five miles round, situated at an elevation of 1000 feet on the Me-Ping, or northwestern branch of the Menam, a place of considerable business and the headquarters of the Presbyterian missionaries in the Lao states, who are accomplishing considerable good with their schools and hospitals. An English vice-consulate has been established there. It is in direct communication, by boat, with Bangkok, but the journey is a tedious one, taking under ordinary circumstances as many as fifty days; its daily market is an interesting sight, mostly managed by women, of whom at least fifteen hundred are employed. Salt is very scarce and it is gladly taken instead of money. Among those who throng the market, besides the usual Burman traders, found all over Indo-China, may be seen Llwas and Moosars, members of interesting hill tribes, the supposed aborigines of the country. The former occupy themselves peacefully in iron smelting; the latter are more retired and live by their bows and arrows on almost inaccessible mountain tops, having but little to do with their neighbors. Luang Phrabang is the principal town of the Lao Phoong Khao country, and is on the May-Nam-Kong, at an elevation of about one thousand feet above sea-level. A short time since, during the late troubles, this once powerful city was almost entirely destroyed by Black Flags, who had to be driven back over the border. It is very picturesquely located at the junction of the Nam-Kan, and May-Nam-Kong, and surrounds a small hill. The river, which is a thousand yards broad, is closed in on all sides by high hills and presents the appearance of a lake, the scenery being very romantic.

From the Malay peninsula tin, lead, gold and rubber are exported. The gold, worked only by Chinamen, is found in alluvial deposits near the heads of the largest rivers in the peninsula, all rising near the same mountain, the highest in Maloga, about 8,000 feet above the sea-level. This mountain is now the chief home of the few remaining groups of Oorang Utan, or wild men, the aborigines of that section, after which a species of long-armed apes have been named. The Lao country is that portion of the Kingdom with the greatest trade resources which are in no way developed. The principal drawback to the development of trade is the want of improved communications; the chief means at present is by the river, a comfortable enough method for holiday seekers, but not sufficient for this pushing age. In the Lao country elephants, bullocks, mules, donkeys and carriers are to be met with in all directions carrying the produce of the country; the mules and donkeys come from Yunnan, usually ladened with opium. The carriers accompany the Burmese peddlers, who, with their wares spread all over the Lao country, have made the Indian rupee the current coin nearly to the gulf of Tongking. They mostly carry raw silk and gum benjamin which they exchange for European goods at Maulmain. Me Ung, a tea that grows indiginously all over the Lao country, is an article of local traffic. To improve the communications of the country by railways has been the life-long idea of the King and the Government, and at last His Majesty has entered into a contract with an English company to build a road from Bangkok to Khorat, a distance of about three hundred miles, at his expense, which will be extended to the frontier should business justify it. Another road is also under construction, from Bangkok to Chanta Boon, a thriving place on the coast of the gulf.

Buddhism is the national faith and by many considered merely a religion of philosophy, while some of the more advanced and learned Siamese claim that the late Professor Darwin and many of the liberal Professors of the present day are real Buddhists. In the Lao country, however, spirit worship has crept into their religion to a considerable extent. Spirits disport themselves everywhere, but the tops of trees are the favorite haunt, and one very often sees all manner of offerings placed at the foot of gigantic forest trees to propitiate them. There are numerous temples, monasteries and excellent rest houses (salas), built from motives of charity for weary travelers. The monasteries contain scores of yellow-robed priests or monks; they keep their heads shaven, even their eyebrows, and eat but one meal a day, which they must go out and beg for in the early morning. They practice celibacy, but are at liberty to leave the monastic life when they feel so inclined. Every man in the Kingdom, including the King, must, after the age of twenty-one, enter the priesthood for at least a short period. With the numerous monasteries in the country no one need starve, and thousands of indolent men and boys seek the wats for rice, and the priests always supply them with food. A man going to sleep hungry in Siam is unheard of, except under extraordinary circumstances, such as being confined in prison or lost in the jungle.

To the Governors and Judges appointed by the King are delegated the administration of justice, such as it is. The laws are now being codified and many of them excellent, especially in regard to the sale and transfer of property. If interest is not collected on a mortgage for six years the interest then ceases and persons holding property for ten years without paying rent become the owners. There is no usury law and money brings what a person can get for it, but the regular rate of interest is from ten to twelve per cent. Disorder is of rare occurrence among the Siamese proper, the people being noted for a love of peace and quiet; but when they become aroused, as was the case lately near Changmai, they can become decidedly belligerent, but the Government crushed the movement with a strong hand, beheaded several of the leaders, and the people returned to work. In Nan, one of the Lao provinces, the punishment for theft is death, and one's property can literally be left on the highway without the slightest danger of anyone interfering with it. In support of this rigorous law the Governor of Nan informed me that it was only about once in three years the services of an executioner was needed, whereas in other states, where such a law is not in force, many lives were annually lost through robbery, as the people were powerless to protect themselves, having no firearms.

As a general thing, the Judges and officials are ignorant and incompetent, frequently corrupt, no one having any confidence in their decisions; "squeezing," as it is termed in the East, having been reduced to a fine art. At times prisoners are tortured, to make them confess, by mashing their fingers till the nails come off, applying a bamboo band around the head to which is attached a handle which, being struck, the vibration causes the most intense agony, the Siamese term it "death," whipping with a bamboo, the victim being stretched out on the ground, face down, with a man holding his arms and another his feet, stretching him out his full length, and then the executioner almost flays him alive, his weapon a piece of bamboo about four feet in length and three inches in width, which cuts like a knife when it strikes the tightly drawn skin. With the advance of western ideas this is rapidly being abolished, though at times the jailers treat their prisoners brutally.

II.

ARRIVAL AT BANGKOK—SCENERY ON THE MENAM.

A gentle zephyr swept over the sparkling waters of the Siamese gulf as the Taichow gracefully steamed across the bar that guards the mouth of the Menam Chow Pyah, the main river of the last of the oriental kingdoms, Siam, to most of the world a *terra incognita*. It was a lovely evening; the sun was slowly sinking into a bed of crimson, canopied by clouds of gorgeous coloring, rimmed in with pearliest of skies, while emblazoned on the eastern heavens hung a perfect rainbow, spanning the river that seemed to spring from groves of palm which laved their roots in the fast-flowing stream; an hour and a scene in keeping with the end of a voyage from the occident to the orient, from land of pine to land of palm. Sweeping round the bend of the river, about five miles from its mouth, a panorama of supernal loveliness burst upon the view, riveting the attention of the most stolid, and making a deep impress upon all on board. In the midst of the river and near a large fort, rose majestically from the water one of the most unique and artistic temples or wats (as they are termed in Siam), in the realms of Buddhistic worshipers, a poem of architectural sublimity. The structure, which covers at least one acre of ground, is as white as if hewn from Pentellicus, and its airy spire and lace-like halls and corridors, as seen in the gloaming, seemed to be

Temple at Mouth of the Menam.

the work of genii. It completely covers the island on which it is built, and thus has the appearance of springing from the flood, while around its walls the waters ever chant a requiem for the ages fled. This wat was erected by the father of the present king, to propitiate the spirits of the stream, and is worthy of its position at the portals of this nature-dowered, sun-emblazoned land of ancient lore, the pearl of Asia, a temple fit for the abode of the lorlei of the Orient. The fort that guards the entrance to the river is one of the best in the kingdom and is of considerable strength, built on an island and mounts some heavy modern guns, among them several Krupps; it has complete command of the stream, while on either side are strong fortifications which could be speedily manned should necessity require. Here, also, is located the village of Packnam, and now for the first time one gets an idea of Siamese architecture and the habitations of the people. The palaces and residences of the princes and nobles are, many of them, handsome and palatial, built of brick and stuccoed with hard white cement, which gives them the appearance of having been built of marble, with large wide verandahs, upon which open innumerable doors and windows to allow free ingress of air; the roofs are of various colored tiles and add no little to the appearance of the building, as they are highly ornamental. The palaces are generally two stories high, with large rooms and corridors; the ceilings, which are handsomely frescoed and elaborately gilded, are about sixteen feet in height, which adds no little to the appearance, as well as comfort, of the rooms; the floors are, in many instances, inlaid with various kinds of wood in the most elaborate pattern, and as no carpets are used they are kept highly polished and display to advantage the skill of the native designers. The main entrance is by flights of marble, or stone steps, to a portico on the second story, thence into a handsome corridor; the lower story is only used for the servants and slaves, who are innumerable.

As a general thing, the palaces are handsomely furnished, especially the drawing-rooms, pictures adorn the walls and rare articles of bronze and porcelain add additional interest to the surroundings and show the artistic taste of the occupant; the grounds are kept in admirable order, and on all sides the serpentine walks are bordered with crotons and other rare flowers, gorgeous in coloring and as fragrant as the breath of morn sweeping over a bed of violets, amid which spring, at intervals, the graceful palm and feathery bamboo making an admirable framework for the white-winged edifice thus held in the clasp of nature's choicest treasures. The Siamese are natural gardeners, are imbued with an idea of the beautiful, which they display in laying off the grounds in the best of taste, and thus the parterre of many a palace is an artistic picture, brilliant with coloring and musical with birds. But there is another side to the picture. While the nobles thus live in splendor, the vast majority reside in dwellings built, in the frailest manner, of teak covered with the attap palm, a thatch that answers admirably, which are reared up on poles about six feet high above the ground or over the water of the rivers or canals. But, as the weather is always warm, they answer all the purposes necessary for the native, whose sole idea is to enjoy life as indolently as possible, doing but little work, and that under compulsion. As his necessities are but few, requiring but little clothing, wearing neither shoes nor hat, his food rice, fruit and fish, his only luxury betel, he sleeps, gambles, fishes or works as the spirit moves him; the women taking upon themselves the task of caring for their progeny, which run as naked over the fields or through the streets as Eve found herself before the typical fig-leaf became a fashionable garment.

Passing Packnam and taking on custom-house officers, the Taichow anchored; then when morn's first rosy blush coruscated the eastern sky the steamer breasted the current, and as its grand proportions opened out in the early dawn an ever-changing panorama greeted the eye: its surface dotted with boats of various kinds, many of them rowed by yellow-robed priests who were in search of their daily rice, as they live exclusively on charity; its banks lined with palms and tropical verdure, while at intervals was passed wats embowered in greenest of foliage, whose gilded spires and tiled roofs flashed back most royally the beams of the rising sun; villages with houses built out in the stream, and wide stretches of rice fields upon which were grazing herds of buffalo and cattle. It was a scene truly oriental and worth a trip half round the globe to witness. In a couple of hours the shipping at the wharves, the junks anchored in the river, the innumerable floating houses and rice mills, residences and boats, denoted that Bangkok, the city of olives, the capital of Siam, had been reached, that our voyage was ended. Here the Menam is about half a mile in width; for twelve miles it flows through a densely populated city, while upon its waters float myriads of boats, from the smallest canoe to large rice and cargo boats, aquatic habitations of thousands, which ply on the rivers and canals throughout the interior, thus bringing in the produce of the country for hundreds of miles, the only means of reaching market.

Upon landing, a new civilization meets one; the scantily-clad Siamese, the almond-eyed son of Confucius, the swarthy Malay, the tattooed Laos, stalwart Burmese, fine-featured Hindoo, Parsee and Mahometans, mixed up with yellow-robed priests of Buddha, greet the eye, and the white man is welcomed with a politeness and courtesy truly Asiatic; but he soon realizes that he is in a strange land, a land of mysticism, whose legends run back to the genesis of time, whose traditions come down from the dim past as poetical as the songs of Solomon, photographed on the plastic memory of generations. Here Buddhism rears its gilded wats, here Mahomet has his worshipers, the Parsee daily turns his face to the rising sun; and here the followers of the son of Mary, the lone Nazarine, have planted their altars and the voice of many descended from parents of a different faith now mingle together and breathe forth fervent prayers to the martyr of Calvary, for the labors of the missionaries have been productive of good work; though but now in the bud, it must necessarily flower forth in all of its beauty and be productive of a golden harvest. They have sown their seed in fertile soil.

The city of Bangkok, the capital of Siam, situated thirty-five miles from the gulf, has well been called the Venice of the East. Its main thoroughfare is the Menam Chowpea, Menam meaning mother of waters. It is the largest stream in the kingdom and is navigable to Raheng, some five hundred miles in the interior; into it pours a number of tributaries that take their rise in the mountains, but it is only during the rainy season that it is navigable that high up; then the merchant and native avail themselves of the high water, which at times overflows the country for miles, to raft down the teak that has been hauled by elephants to the river, and to ship the paddy (unhulled rice) to the capital city. Bangkok is also permeated with innumerable canals, many of them running far into the interior and connecting the other rivers that empty into the upper waters of the Siamese gulf, so that there is an unbroken chain of communication by waterways over this portion of the kingdom for the transportation of produce to this central market. As the country is perfectly level, or nearly so, the canals do not require locks, but are always open and easily navigable for the largest sized boats; at all times the canals are thronged with boats transporting cattle, rice and other products of the country from the interior, and they are well stocked with fish. Along the margin of the river can be seen the large paddy mills, twenty-four in number, where the rice is hulled and prepared for shipment in sacks holding about two bushels, vast quantities of which go to China, India and Europe. The mills are run by steam-power, and the fuel used is the husk of the paddy. Many of the mills are lighted with electric lights and have all the modern improvements, employing hundreds of Chinese coolies at two salungs a day, about twenty cents American money. They work hard for that, unloading and loading vessels, but they work with great willingness and seem contented. After their work is over they can

be seen sitting in front of their houses, half clad,
smoking opium; that appears to be their sole idea
of dissipation, save when they resort to the gambling
dens, licensed by the government, as they are inveterate gamblers, and they occasionally indulge in drinking samshu, a villainous liquor made from rice,
which is highly intoxicating. Most of these rice mills
are owned by Europeans and Chinese, but the first
one erected was by Americans, and is still known by
the name of American mill. The city proper lies
along the river and the canals, and is thickly built up
on both sides of the stream for nearly fourteen miles;
but the palaces and substantial and handsome residences of the princes and nobles are hid by a fringe
of floating houses, which in some places are two deep,
and are owned and occupied by traders who pay
a small sum for the water privileges, and who sell everything needed. Some of the houses are handsomely fitted
up and finished, built of teak, while others are built
of bamboo; many of them are covered with attap, a
species of palm that only grows in Siam and the
Straits settlements, while others are covered with cor-
rugated iron. The floating house is one of the prominent features of the city, and the natives regard them
as more healthy than those on land, as they can thus
easily get rid of all their debris by tumbling it into the
river, and have all the water they want without having
to carry it; which, as they bathe once or twice a day, is a
great convenience. The city proper is confined within
white walls, forming a circuit of four and a half miles,
about twelve feet high, with sixteen large gates
opening out on the main thoroughfares each fifteen feet high; these walls are built of brick,

stuccoed with a white cement, which is as hard as marble and is made by mixing palm molasses with the plaster when it is applied; at the base they are ten feet thick, and at the top they are so arranged that persons can walk along them; at certain distances towers are erected with lance-like windows, so that rifle-men can command the approaches. Inside the walls is a road or street, running parallel thereto, laid with brick and covered with sand, which extends around the entire distance, about six miles, making a good drive, and from each gate a road leads to the palace which is enclosed within similar walls, as seen by illustration, and is situated on the right river bank, presenting a handsome view both from there and along the esplanade. It is enclosed with double walls pierced by massive gates covered with iron, which are closed at night; the inner walls enclose the palace proper, where the King and his wives and servitors reside; outside, but within the outer walls, is the royal wat in which is enshrined the emerald idol; the golden pagoda containing the sacred relics of Buddha; a handsome wat in which, in an elaborately carved cabinet of ebony and mother of pearl, are the books of the great teacher, the floor of this temple is covered with a carpet of woven silver; the magnificent porcelain pagoda in which are placed the golden urns that hold the ashes of the Kings and Princes of Siam, the foreign office, the mint, the stables of the white elephants and the new court of justice, besides innumerable residences of servants of the various queens and barracks for the guards; also a market, as it is reported that over five thousand persons reside within the enclosure. The court-yard of

the palace proper is very handsome. About two acres
in extent, paved with blocks of black and white marble,
ornamented with statues and dwarf China trees in handsome porcelain pots. The entrance to the building is
by two pair of stairs that lead up to a magnificent
portico, also of marble, with marble pillars that can
not be less than thirty feet high, and at the base of the
stairs are two elephants heavily gilt, nearly of
life size. The interior of the palace is in keeping
with its entrance, and the reception room of
his Majesty is one of the handsomest extant
and literally crowded with works of art of the
rarest description; among others a number of onyx
tables, which Prince Devawongse, Foreign Minister and brother of the King, informed me that he
purchased in New York. Inside the walls Bangkok is
laid out at angles centering on the palace, and the
streets are well paved and kept in good condition
lighted at night with gas and oil lamps; on each side
are built rows of two-story houses mostly of brick, and
covered with tile, nearly all of which are owned by the
King and Princes, bringing them in a handsome revenue, as rents are very high; the houses are principally
occupied as stores and workshops, the occupants living
upstairs. One of the main thoroughfares is known as
the New Road, running parallel with the river, about a
quarter of a mile back, and connected therewith by
smaller avenues. It extends from Bankolem Point, at
the lower part of the city, a distance of seven miles, to
the city gate, and is closely built up with a heterogeneous
mass of houses, brick, teak and bamboo. A vast amount
of business, in the retail way, is done on this avenue,
as it is always crowded with natives and along it runs

a tramway that extends to the palace, and the cars are always crowded, the fare being eight ats, equivalent to eight of our cents. Other avenues, well and substantially built, lead to the city walls which are pierced by large gateways, closed with heavy iron-covered doors, at each of which is posted a sentinel, always on guard, seemingly more as an ornament than a necessity, as no one ever heard of any one having been arrested for passing through. Most of the Princes have palaces inside of the city walls, but the elder brother of the King, Prince Ong Yoi, has his palace, a rather modest building, on the west bank of the river, nearly opposite the royal residence; the Crown Prince's palace, a magnificent structure, is a short distance from the main portion of the city; it is a modern building, ornamented with towers and turrets, built of brick and stone; it is a very imposing structure and is surrounded by handsome grounds. The esplanade, south of the palace walls, is about three-quarters of a mile in length, and over two hundred feet in width, handsomely laid out and flanked on the south side by the arsenal, a large, handsome building, and rows of houses occupied by officers and employes of the government; the road is solidly paved with hard brick, covered with sand, and on each side is wide stretches of grass kept closely mowed and in splendid order, making a magnificent boulevard. The King's garden, a short distance from the palace, is a lovely spot and worthy of the admiration it always receives from visitors. It is handsomely laid off in walks, and scattered over it are the rarest tropical plants and trees, all of which are carefully cared for; the orchid house is about two hundred feet in length,

two stories high, the upper story having no roof, so
that potted plants of all kinds are placed therein and
grow to perfection in the sunshine that simmers down
on them in a shower of molten gold. One of the
features of the garden is a gothic aisle of lofty bamboos
three hundred feet in length and thirty feet in height,
as perfect in form as any to be found in the old min-
sters of England, a marvel of artistic skill and an
object of rare beauty, entirely unique. In the center
of the grounds is a handsome Italian monument,
erected by the King in remembrance of the death of
his Queen who was accidentally drowned several years
since, and it is a worthy tribute to a most esti-
mable lady, her death being deeply deplored
by all his subjects. Throughout the grounds are
fountains, ornamental summer houses and band-
stands, the King's band playing there every
Saturday, at which time the gardens are thrown open
to the public and on the lawn the Europeans and
nobles play tennis, croquet and other games. At one
time the King had collected a number of animals with
the intention of establishing a zoo, but nearly all of
the animals have died and the cages are rapidly falling
into decay. Though not so large as some of the parks
in the East, this garden or park is decidedly one of the
handsomest and is kept in good order; the drives and
walks are well rolled, the grass closely mown, the
shrubbery and bushes well trimmed, and no more
pleasant place can be found in the city to spend an hour
of pure and unalloyed enjoyment. The canals, or
klangs, as the natives term them, are the main feature
of the place; along them live a dense population and
for many miles can be found stores filled with goods

The King's Garden.

of all kinds and workshops, a hive of industry. A number of the canals are over one hundred feet in width, along which pass a steady stream of boats of all sizes, and as the canals rise and fall with the tide in the river they act as sewers to carry off the filth that necessarily accumulates in such a crowded community; but at times it is almost unbearable to pass along them caused by the stench arising from the decaying carcass of a dog or other animal floating in the water, as everything is thrown into the river or canal, it being the easiest way of disposing of them. At all hours of the day can be seen numbers of the natives disporting themselves in the water, as they know that frequent bathing is conducive to health; the children, as a natural consequence, are taught to swim early, and as they go as naked as a Greek statue it is no novelty to see a shoal of them not two feet high gamboling in the water like so many porpoises, and from a look at their merry faces you can see that they enjoy it, and no more cheerful people live than the children of "the land of the afternoon," where the lotus blooms and nature is lavish in her productions.

The stories told by travelers about the overflows of the country are but partially correct, and that in regard to Bangkok being a city built on poles over a continually flowing river is veritable bosh. Only twice in the five years that I was a resident at Bangkok did the high tide in the Menam get out into the city, and that was only in a few low places where the back-water overflowed from the canals. In the interior considerable land is overflowed at times, during the months of November and December, the spring tides, but then only for an hour or two daily,

which benefits the soil. There is no more solidly
built city than Bangkok; the large majority of the
people live in good houses with solid floors, where the
rise from the river never reaches them, the floors being
level with the ground, their houses being built of brick,
two stories high. Large numbers of houses are built
on pile, especially along the canals and out in the
interior. The reason for this is that they are but frail
bamboo structures, and many of the natives believe
that it is wicked to live in the lower story of a house
if the upper is occupied, especially by females, hence
the lower part is devoted to the dogs, pigs, cows and
other scavengers who clean up all the debris thrown
through the cracks in the floor; also it may be for the
purpose of being out of the reach of toads, snakes and
the multitudinous worms that infest the lower floors.
On the high lands the natives have these long-legged
houses, which they reach with a ladder about six to
eight feet in length. They say it keeps tigers and
thieves out, as the ladder is drawn up every night for
protection. The palaces, temples, warehouses, hotels,
colleges, residences of the merchants, mills, etc..are large
and substantial buildings built in modern style, and
the water of the Menam was never known to encroach
on them.

River View of Portion of Bangkok.

III.
RECEPTION BY HIS MAJESTY KING CHULALONGKORN.

The first official act that a minister performs when he reaches Bangkok is to call on the Foreign Minister, now H. R. H. Prince Devawongse, and request an audience with the King, at the same time presenting an office copy of the letter of the President to Chulalongkorn I. Duly armed with a copy of President Cleveland's letter and a copy of the remarks to be made in presenting it, in company with the Vice Consul General, Dr. McDonald, I was driven to the palace of the Foreign Minister, who gave us a most cordial reception. After an exchange of pleasantries the Prince informed me that it would give him great pleasure to let me know at what time it would please His Majesty to accord us an audience. Much pleased with the courteous and affable manner of my reception, I returned to the Legation to await the action of the Siamese officials. In this instance they acted promptly. Next morning Prince D. called with the information that His Majesty would be pleased to receive us that day at 5 P. M. at the supreme palace, and that one of the state carriages would be placed at our disposal. At the hour named a handsome open carriage, drawn by four Australian horses, with outriders and driver dressed in scarlet livery, drove up to the entrance of the Legation, and a leading official, who spoke English fluently, informed me that he had been deputed to convey the

Doctor and myself to the palace, whereupon we entered
the carriage; the outriders galloped in front, the driver
cracked his whip and away we went at a rattling rate,
scattering pedestrians on all sides, dashed through the
gateways in the city walls, the sentinels saluting us,
and after a drive of about three miles turned from the
main highway into the esplanade that skirts the palace
walls. As soon as our carriage made its appearance a
battery stationed near the main entrance to the palace
grounds commenced firing a salute of forty guns.
Reaching the eastern walls we drove through a massive gateway and found ranged on each side
of a broad paved avenue, a distance of over
two hundred yards, a double line of soldiers,
armed with repeating rifles, standing at a salute.
Passing down the line our driver halted at the portals
of the second wall, that which encloses the palace,
when we alighted and were conducted into the court
where more soldiers were stationed, who presented
arms as we advanced. To the right, as we entered,
were the royal white elephants dressed out in Asiatic
splendor, their howdas and trappings sparkling with
gold and jewels, their keepers in barbaric uniforms.
A large body of native musicians, dressed in scarlet,
saluted us with a weird kind of music, beating on
peculiar shaped drums with their hands. In front of
the palace was placed the King's band of musicians,
lead by an Italian, who performed the Star-Spangled
Banner, a compliment to the American minister.
Crossing the handsome court we were received at the
steps of the portico, which were covered with carpets,
by the King's body-guard, a picked body of men, who
presented arms, and we were escorted into the palace by

one of the Princes who was waiting to receive us. It was a scene of Asiatic pomp and power; the flashing steel of the military, the gorgeous trappings of the elephants, the music of the native drummers, the strains of the King's band with hundreds of spectators squatting around, with the white walls and gleaming roof and towers of the palace made a picture worth a visit to the Orient to witness, one that would have immortalized an artist could he have placed it on canvass. It seemed as if it was a scene eliminated from the Arabian Nights. I could not help remarking to the Doctor, "This is indeed grand." Entering the antichamber we were received by Prince Devawongse and other leading Princes and officials. As soon as we were seated tea was handed round and I was requested to write my name in an album, which I did, then in another with the date of my birth. I suppose that the latter was for the purpose of allowing the court astrologers to cast my horoscope and see whether I would be antagonistic to their government. While conversing pleasantly about my trip and other matters a blare of bugles rang out; the Prince informed me that His Majesty was waiting to receive me, and I was at once ushered into the throne room (see engraving), in which was assembled most of the Princes and nobles of the realm in full costumes, the buckles of their gold belts flashing with gems of priceless value. Advancing to the center of the room I beheld the King standing under the royal pagoda umbrella, on a dais about four feet in height, dressed, as his picture represents, in a white Prince Albert coat, plum-colored panung and white stockings, and low quartered shoes; across his breast he wore a broad yellow sash and a number of orders,

and held in his hand a sheathed sword, its scabbard
encrusted with jewels. At first sight he impressed me
with the idea that he was every inch a king. Bowing
three times to His Majesty, who returned the salutation,
I laid the letter of President Cleveland on a silver
tripod and waited for the court interpreter to introduce
me, which he did in an oration of considerable length,
in Siamese; the letter of President Cleveland was then
handed to the King, who welcomed me to Siam and
spoke feelingly of the warm friendship that existed
between the two countries, to which I responded in a
similar manner. The King then asked me a number of
questions in regard to my trip, which was interpreted
to me, and he then bowed gracefully and retired; the
audience was over and I was then introduced to a
number of the brothers of the King and Governors of
provinces. Next day a copy of the King's speech with
the translation was sent me. Leaving the palace we
were again escorted through the ranks of the soldiery
and returned to the Legation. It was one of the most
impressive and imposing ceremonials that I had ever
witnessed. The scene in the throne room was gorgeous
beyond description; the rays of the sun, streaming
through stained glass windows, a royal tint of soft
purple, fell like a benison on the coats of cloth of gold
and silver worn by the Siamese noblemen. They were
in full dress to do honor to the representative of the
great republic, and I looked, in my plain suit of black,
like a crow among a flock of tropical birds.

This reception by the King was an epoch in my life,
and the impression I then formed of the supreme ruler
of Siam was borne out by his actions during my five
years stay in his dominions: that he was a wise, humane,

prudent and brainy monarch. Under his sway many of the ills hitherto borne by his people have been ameliorated; he has abolished slavery in its worst form, is protecting the people from the squeezing of avaricious governors, has made inquiries in the reported corruption of the judiciary, aided and assisted education, is paying personal attention to the carrying out of the laws, encourages all kinds of progress and throws no stumbling blocks in the way of the labor of the missionaries; in fact, allowed his son, the Crown Prince, to lay the corner-stone of the magnificent Catholic college, besides subscribing a considerable sum in aid of its erection. No foreigner who has been accorded an audience with King Chulalongkorn I. but leaves his presence impressed with the belief that he is the foremost man of his nation and that his people are blessed with a ruler, unlike most Asiatic monarchs, kind and humane. Under his rule the kingdom has grown into wealth and power; Bangkok has become a city of great commercial importance, fast becoming one of the noted metropolises of the world.

IV.
CHARACTERISTICS OF THE COUNTRY AND HABITS OF THE PEOPLE.

The natives of Siam, the peasants, are virtually peons; they attach themselves to some master and have his name tattoed on their wrist, called sak, otherwise they are liable to be arrested and placed in the army for life. For the privilege of becoming a retainer of a nobleman the servant gives one month service during the year, which he can work out, or he can pay from five to ten ticals for his time. If he should get into difficulty with any of the many tax collectors his master sees that he is not squeezed, he standing between him and any attempt to take advantage of his surroundings. His wants are few, a bamboo hut and a few cooking utensils, but little furniture, scarcely any clothing; a small amount of rice, a fish or a piece of meat and a pinch or two of salt, together with fruit, goes to make up his bill of fare, but at times he indulges in canumb (sweet cakes) or preserved fruit, and spends the best portion of the day chewing betel; all are inveterate chewers, from King to peasant. Men and women are clothed alike, wearing a panung around the loins, which extends from the waist to the knee. It is made of cloth, cotton or silk, according to the rank of the wearer, and is about three yards in length and one yard in width, which is wrapped around the body with the ends drawn between the legs and then tucked in the fold, looking, when on, like a pair of knee breeches.

Native House in the Interior.

The women, also, wear a cotton band around the breast, leaving the shoulders exposed like a decollete dress, sometimes a white linen jacket across which they throw a broad silk scarf, yellow being the most fashionable color. But few of them wear shoes or hats, their dark hair shining with cocoanut oil, with a flower fastened in it. The nobles dress neatly, wear Prince Albert coats, panungs, hats and shoes and stockings. Having small extremities they look neat and attractive in low quarter shoes and silk stockings. When in attendance at the palace or on holidays they dress gorgeously, their coats made of a damascene cloth of silver and gold, over which at times they throw a lace or gauze robe. All wear flexible gold belts, some of which are very handsome, the buckles set with precious stones; many of the wealthiest use large diamonds for buttons, among others I noticed that the ex-Kromata, Chow Phya Bhanuwongse Maha Kosa Dhipati Thi Phra Klang, had his coat buttoned with five diamonds of the purest water, about the size of hazel nuts.

The male Siamese peasant is indolent; he lets the women do most of the work while he fishes or gambles or chows a boat. The mania for gambling pervades all ranks; men, women and children can be seen engaged in it, from throwing coppers up to horse racing and cock fighting, the Malay breed of chickens being proverbial for their fighting propensities. In every village is a regular cockpit, around which the villagers congregate and bet on the rival chickens. They also fight kites by crossing the strings of two or more while flying, and the one that breaks the string of the other is the victor. Thousands of persons can be seen of an evening at the Lotus gardens watching a kite fight.

Small fish about an inch and a half in length, reared for the purpose, are placed in a transparent jar filled with water, when they fight till one kills the other; they are the gamiest little things extant; when angry they expand their fins and swell up like a rooster, assuming the most brilliant colors. A species of beetle is also taught to fight; in fact a Siamese will bet on anything, and licensed gambling houses can be seen in every part of Bangkok and other cities throughout the kingdom. The royal lottery is very popular with all classes, it has two drawings daily. At noon and midnight boats ply up and down the river calling out the lucky numbers, and hundreds of purchasers can be seen watching for the boats to appear so that they may learn what their ticket has drawn. Thousands of tickets are sold, the Chinese investing largely. Wheels of fortune can be seen in all the bazaars at their fairs, which are held at the various wats; the handsomest Siamese girls are selected to preside at the booths where they have glass jars filled with tickets, on which is named an article on exhibition, and by paying a small sum you are allowed to draw a ticket. Like similar lotteries at home, it is seldom that one gets back the value of the coin invested. Raffles are also very popular with the Chinese residents. Chess is played by the nobles and princes, some of them very expert, particularly Prince Devawongse, who is considered one of the best players on the coast. For three days, the Siamese New Year, gambling is allowed to be carried on free, at other times it is licensed and under the control of the farmer who has purchased the exclusive right of the city. Saturnalia then reigns supreme, and gambling devices can be seen on every side.

The houses of the mass of people are built of bamboo, with attap palm roofs, raised on poles about five feet above the ground, with one or two doors and a couple of openings with shutters for windows. Glass is unknown, and fire for comfort is never needed; what little they have to cook is done on a clay furnace, and they use but a small quantity of wood or charcoal, as fuel is scarce and expensive. The houses are built generally near a river or canal, and frequently the building extends out over the water, so that all the filth or debris can be easily disposed of. Dogs, cats, ducks, chickens, children and pigs all live together. As the natives squat down to rest they require no chairs to sit on, in fact the only furniture they have is a mat and a mosquito net, a water jar, some cooking utensils, a chest or two, a clock and a small mirror, sometimes a few pictures. Everything denotes indigence, but I have been informed that in many instances the inmates have valuable jewels and heavy gold chains, which, should they need money, they can easily pawn, the city being full of pawn shops, the curse of the place, owned by Chinese, in which can be found rare curios that have been stolen. A large class live in boat houses; they are principly merchants and traders, and some of them have their houses furnished neatly and others elaborately; their furniture is made of ebony, rose, padoo and other rare woods inlaid with mother of pearl and lacquer, the ceilings gilded, from which hang innumerable lamps and chandeliers, it being their belief that light keeps away evil spirits. During an epidemic of cholera hundreds of tall poles are raised, on the top of which are suspended lanterns which are kept burning to scare away the bad angels that are supposed to be hovering around in search of victims. At night the Menam is a blaze of light from the houses, the ports of the ships are all open, and as you slowly drift down with the tide it seems like a glimpse of fairyland, a chapter culled from the Arabian Nights.

The youth of the country are taught to read and write and instructed in mathematics by the priests in the temples, the boys serving as acolytes; but now that the King has put the educational department of the government in the hands of Prince Dumarong, he is doing all that lies in his power to encourage education by giving it his personal attention; that he is succeeding can be seen from the photograph of the scientific class at Sandalay College, the Siamese high school, now under the charge of Rev. Dr. McFarland, an American, who has spent over a quarter of a century in the Emerald Kingdom; he is an eminent educator and is succeeding admirably. No brighter young men can be found in any of our colleges than these pupils of his, who are destined to fill responsible positions in the Siamese government. The latest and most improved text-books are selected for the schools, English and American preferred. Having attended several examinations of the scholars, I was astonished at the proficiency manifested by all. At the last examination of the students at Sandalay College the Crown Prince distributed the prizes of merit, a number of handsome books, all of which were in the English language. The Presbyterian mission have several schools in Bangkok, one at Wanglan, for girls, where the ladies in charge have accomplished much good, among their scholars being a young Princess, the daughter of Prince Dumarong. Unfortunately, after passing through the school and

Scientific Class at Sandalay College.

being thoroughly instructed in the tenets of our religion and learning the English language, many of the pupils do but little good, becoming the mistresses of foreigners, but few of them devoting their time to teaching. The school at Sam Ray is for boys, and quite a number of young men have been educated there who are now filling lucrative positions. Some are ostensibly Christians, but the old leven of Buddhism clings to them. As it is unpopular among the Buddhists to become a Christian, these young men have no religion and will eventually drift back into the belief of their parents. This is not the fault of the missionaries, no people work harder than do these devoted followers of our Lord; they are sowing seed for future usefulness; they are teaching the Siamese the necessity and benefit of education; their schools in Bangkok, Petchaburee and in the Lao country are but so many landmarks on the highway to permanent success. Like the gentle fall of dew upon the parched herbage, it tends to a golden harvest, and in the years to come they will realize that their labors have not been in vain. Many of these workers in the cause of their Master now sleep beneath the waving palm of that land of sunshine and flowers, others have returned with impaired health, but the coronal of worthy deeds belongs to them—they, at least, have done their duty.

All of the inland traffic is done by boats that ply on the rivers and canals, the Menam at Bangkok being covered with them, ladened with produce of every kind, cattle, horses, rice, fruit, fish, wood, water and rice jars, groceries, dry goods, silks, lamps, china ware, lime for betel, chickens, ducks, eggs, onions, coal oil, hides, liquor, and, in fact, everything that is marketable. The boats are built of large teak logs, hollowed out, with cabins covered with attap or bamboo in which the owner lives and rears his family. These boats are propelled by long oars, the women as well as the men being adepts in rowing, while the bright eyes of a brood of little ones can frequently be seen peering through crevices in the cabin. Produce is thus brought down a distance of from four to five hundred miles from the interior when the water is at the proper stage, the canals having to depend on the rivers to flood them, as they have no locks and are on a level with the streams. The canals connect with all the rivers that flow into the upper gulf, so that the waterways of Bangkok are the most elaborate and far reaching of any city in the world, and each year they are extended farther and farther into the interior, which, while it adds to the mileage of the waterways, increases the acreage of rice fields, the law being that all land reclaimed and made tillable shall be exempt from tax for a certain number of years. This is a great inducement to open up land, and many Burmese and Chinese are availing themselves of the privilege, as rice is a staple product and finds ready sale at the capital.

Unlike other portions of the orient, the women of Siam are not trammeled with caste or required to keep themselves secluded. While polygamy is indulged in by the King and many of the nobles, the chief wife is considered the head of the family, her word is the law of the household, the others are termed lesser wives. Should a Siamese head wife, or wife proper, refuse to allow her husband to take a lesser wife, he could not do so; should he persist, against her protest, she can then demand a divorce and the property belonging to the family must be divided equally between the husband and wife. Such divorces are very rare, the chief wife looks upon the lesser wives as so many appendages to her rank, and when she goes abroad they all follow, and she is as proud of showing them as the stately dames of European courts their jewels. The King has forty-seven wives; his chief wife and mother of the Crown Prince is his half-sister; the law of Siam making it incumbent on His Majesty to thus marry in the family, so that when his heir is born he thus preserves the pure blood, celestial, as it is termed, none other being eligible to succeed him. His other wives are members of the leading families, one of the last being the daughter of the King of Changmae, a handsome Lao princess. As the output of so many wives it was reported that the King had ninety-six children and that he was a very affectionate father. It is seldom that the lower order have more than one wife, and from what I have observed of the natives the women rule the ranch, the husbands being afraid of their active tongues, and no more outspoken viragoes live than the women along the Menam. The Siamese language is one well adapted to invectives and indecency, and the tirade that they pour forth in a moment of passion is terrible, and they are easily aroused. If well treated the Siamese women make good wives; they are industrious, love their children, and are not as immoral as one would suppose, considering their surroundings. No regular marriage ceremony is observed among the peons; two young persons are brought together by an old nurse or member of the

family, the young man sees the girl and if he likes her
he pays the parents or guardian from one hundred to
five hundred ticals, one-half of which is used in giving
a feast to the family and friends of the contracting
party, the other to the girl for the purpose of going to
housekeeping. When the feast is prepared the bride,
arrayed in silk panung, white linen jacket with gold
buttons, a bright silk scarf thrown across her shoulder,
and her black hair dressed with flowers, gold chain and
bracelets, waits for her lord and he comes forward,
takes her by the hand and presents her to his parents
as his wife, both prostrating themselves with their faces
to the floor; the priests sprinkle them with holy water,
read a few lessons from the writings of Buddha, and
she is then received and acknowledged as the wife of the
bridegroom. I have been assured that the taking of a
second wife requires no ceremony, the fact of so many
ticals having been paid for the girl and she having been
taken to the house of her purchaser being considered all
that was needed. Notwithstanding this state of affairs,
immorality is not so prevalent in Siam as in most
Asiatic kingdoms. Strict followers of Buddha, they
obey his tenets and believe in his code of morals. Prostitution exists to a great extent in the large cities, the
bawdy houses in Bangkok being licensed; but the
revenue derived from this unholy traffic is not placed
in the general treasury, but used for the purpose
of repairing and opening up new roads. The women
are finely formed and as graceful as a Greek statue,
with small hands and feet, but they are not handsome;
exposure to a tropical sun without bonnets has bronzed
them, their dark hair and sparkling eyes redeem their
flaccid features, but their mouths are horrible, the chew

Her Majesty, the Supreme or Celestial Queen.

ing of betel has ruined their shape and their gums and teeth are as black as ebony. During my stay in Bangkok I saw only a few handsome women, my observation being mostly of those I met on the road, principally peons. The wives and daughters of the nobles are refined and handsome, but they are nearly all small and diminutive, as will be noticed by the likeness of the Supreme Queen. At a garden party, given by His Majesty, he was present with a number of his Queens, all of them handsome women, tastefully dressed and sparkling with magnificent jewels; none of them wore hats, their hair was ornamented with flowers, their velvet jackets fastened with gold buttons. On another occasion I noticed eight of the Queens on their way to Wat Sa Ket to attend a cremation, four each in open carriages. They were handsomely costumed, wore magnificent gems, heavy gold chains, and were escorted by a squadron of lancers; they chatted merrily as their carriages swept onward to the cremation grounds, their bright eyes taking in the busy scene, bearing themselves as high-born dames and wives of a supreme monarch. They were a type of the Siamese seldom seen abroad, lithe of limb, fashioned as superbly as was the dark-browed Cleopatra when she held the Roman Cæsar in her meshes, but they, too, chewed betel, and lips parched by this astringent are never kissed; that is a part of the love-making of the Siamese that is neglected. Mothers never kiss their children, lovers their sweethearts, husbands their wives; instead, they rub their faces together as if they were smelling, and those that are addicted to eating capit in their curry or indulging in a durian smell to heaven. Capit is made by pressing salt and prawns together, allowing the mixture to stand until it becomes putrid and it is then used to flavor curry. The durian is considered the best fruit on the coast. It is shaped like a melon, green, with huge spikes on the hull, which has to be cut open with a knife or hatchet, inside of which is a creamy substance of the consistency of a custard; this is eaten with a spoon, and those that have a cultivated taste for it assert that it is the most delicious fruit that grows, but the smell is terrible, outrivalling Limburger cheese.

A curious custom prevails among the women, dusting themselves with powered saffron, which they also sprinkle over their children, giving them a golden appearance. The reason given for this practice is it keeps them cool and is an antidote for mosquito bites; but it is their great desire to have light complexions, and this aids them to do so. The lacon girls, that posture in the theatres, rub lime juice on their faces which gives them a white appearance, but, with their black mouths, renders them hideous.

The lacon or Siamese theatre is peculiar to the country. The actors, with the exception of a few clowns, are females, the principal performance consists in posturing, though they have a number of plays in which the Siamese are always victorious. The performers squat at one end of the room, which is fitted up as a stage, and they have but little scenery. When they wish to represent a forest a performer brings on a couple of trees painted on canvas, when cavalry is needed three or four of the girls appear with little tin horses which they hold by their sides and gallop round the stage. During their battles, when a person is killed she lays on the floor for a minute or so, then gets up and walks away. At times the clowns get off witticisms and vulgarisms that please the crowd squatting round, most of whom are women. The girls are handsomely costumed, all barefooted, well trained and are as lithe and graceful as the human form will permit. They posture in every imaginable shape and bend the fingers of their hands, which are tipped with gold nails, back until they rest on their wrists. Dressed like nats or angels, they wear tall, peaked crowns similar in shape to that worn by the King on state occasions; some of them sport costly jewels, having lovers who lavish presents on them like their western sisters of comedy, the leading lady at the Prince's theater being quite an artist. Their performance is not in the least immodest, and well worth seeing once or twice, after which it becomes monotonous; but I was informed by those that understand the language that the witticisms of the clowns and many of the lines spoken by the girls would have disgraced Billingsgate in ancient days. During one of the evenings that I attended a brass band performed various airs, among them "The Star-Spangled Banner" and "Dixie;" others kept up an ear-splitting noise by beating two sticks together. The King has a company of lacon girls in the palace, who perform in the palace grounds during state ceremonials. While traveling in the interior I witnessed performances at Ratburee and Petchaburee which were intended for merit, the companies having been hired to perform by some one who had made a vow while sick to give a lacon to celebrate his recovery. They were held on the public square, where a stand had been erected out of some rough teak planks, decorated with colored tissue paper, on which was placed a roasted hogshead dyed purple, canumb, fruit, rice, flowers, joss sticks, lighted lamps, and other trumpery, before which the actors postured to the edification of the squatting crowd who will set for hours on their heels watching the performers. The food and other things were placed there for the spirits to partake of, and if it was not eaten by them before the performance was over, which lasted till sunset, it was taken home and eaten by the girls. Nearly all of the Princes have companies of these girls, and it seems as if the natives never tire of witnessing their performance. Entering the wat at Petchaburee I noticed a large pile of toys, three or four figures of lacon girls made out of baked clay, pasted on a piece of wood, also some hanging on bushes, and was informed that that was the way some of the natives took to cheat the gods, that when a lacon was promised by a man when he was sick he compromised the matter with his conscience when he became well by purchasing one of these clay lacons and then hang it up on a bush or place it in a wat remarking "that is the way to fool him," meaning the god whom he had supplicated when sick. Others purchase a small statue of Buddha and place it on the altar in one of the temples, where it remains until it becomes old and dingy, when the priest throws it into a corner. I have seen several hundred of them thus piled up, having been cast aside.

Traveling between Bangkok and Petchaburee the boat is rowed across an arm of the gulf to the mouth of the Petchaburee river, a beautiful stream fringed with ferns and palms. Reaching there just as the sun was setting we ran our boat ashore and our servants

commenced preparing dinner, when all of a sudden the
boat was surrounded by several hundred monkeys and
apes of all sizes, who kept up an incessant chattering,
fighting and quarreling. A gray-headed old fellow,
about five feet in height, seemed to be the leader and
had a special spite at one nearly the same size. We
threw bananas, potatoes, rice and various things to
them as they swarmed down to the boat, apparently
under the charge of the leader. Soon the lesser ape
secured a half of a cocoanut and ran off with it up a
tree; the leader missed him and, seeing the culprit
seated upon a limb enjoying his meal, made a rush
after him and then they had it, very much to the delight
of the boat boys who were watching them. After a
severe tussle they both fell to the ground clawing one
another in their rapid descent. It was remarkable
how the mother monkeys cared for their little ones,
which they carry between their fore legs with their
small black faces sticking out and clinging fast for dear
life. After eating all that we could give them some of
the monkeys trotted off to the beach and washed their
hands and faces and ran their paws through their hair
as cunningly as if they had been human beings. The
Siamese never injure a monkey, they believe that the
spirit of the dead go into them ; hence they are tame
and some of them very intelligent. A native christian
preacher, who resides near the mouth of the river,
while passing along heard a peculiar noise as
if some one was in distress, and hastening to the place
from where the noise proceeded discovered a monkey
holding on to a bush, with his tail immersed in the
water, uttering the most mournful cries. The poor
animal turned on him a look of entreaty, and catching

hold of it he found that its tail was clutched fast by a large crab. The monkey had been in the habit of switching its tail in the water, to induce a crab to take hold of it, then it would jerk it out with the crab attached, and thus secure a meal; but in this instance he had caught more than he had bargained for. Passing along one of the canals my attention was called to a number of monkeys crossing the waterway. They had formed a bridge of their bodies across the canal, by catching hold of hands and swinging over from the top of a tall tree. The bridge once formed, the others scampered across; the leader on the side they had crossed to ran up the tree as high as he could go, carrying the chain or bridge with him, then the monkey who had clutched the tree on the side that they had left let go and swung across. As our boat approached they sat in the trees and chattered, wanting us to throw something out for them to eat. Monkeys of all kind abound in Siam, from the orang-outang to the tiny black monkey, only a few inches in height; but the rarest of all is the white ape, found in the deepest solitudes of the jungle and looked upon by the natives as sacred, the tabernacle of some great nobleman's soul or possibly a Buddha; in fact, all white animals are held in high esteem, white being their emblem of purity.

The vast jungles abound in all kinds of tropical animals, ranging from the royal tiger, which is as large as an ox, down to the most ferocious wild cats and bears. Cheetahs, leopards, deer and other animals can be found close to Bangkok, and afford sport to the adventurous hunter who is willing to brave the miasma of the forest in pursuance of his sport.

Among the dank vegetation of the jungle venomous and other serpents abound, the largest of which are the python and the boa, many of them over forty feet in length, and are killed by the natives for their skins, which are taken to China and tanned, the leather being used in the manufacture of musical instruments and fiddle strings; the flesh is also regarded as a dainty, the natives having an idea that it gives them strength and is a remedy for the many ills that they are heir to. The hooded cobra is one of the most venomous, but there are scores of them lurking in the shade and slime that would prove deadly if they should strike a person with their fangs, among them one about a foot in length; beautiful to look at, whose bite is so fatal that death almost follows instantly, and it is dreaded by all, as it is frequently found coiled up in a basket of fruit; among the most curious is one that has a head at each end, but the most singular is the bull snake, a small reptile about four inches long with a head shaped like that of a bull, which lies in the grass unobserved, and its bite is more like the pricking of a thorn than anything else, which, if unheeded till next day, will cause the victim to swell rapidly; then, if heroic measures are not at once resorted to, death will soon follow. I do not think that there is another spot on our planet that can discount the jungles of Siam or her gulf and rivers in snakes, nine-tenths of which are venomous; but, notwithstanding such is the fact, but few of the natives are bitten, and it is seldom that one hears of a death from their sting. To realize the number of these reptiles, a visit to the King's palace at the mango gardens will suffice, where there are many preserved in alcohol, others dried.

In some parts of the kingdom alligators abound, specimens of which can be seen at Wat Po and at the King's garden, where they are kept by the priests to exhibit to the curious who pay a small amount to see them fed. They are very much like the alligators of our Southern lagoons, but are looked upon by the natives as something remarkable and with great dread. It is their belief that they subsist on children, and I was told of many instances where children were taken out of their cradle by these hideous monsters, but found that there was no truth in them.

There are more than forty kinds of snakes, some few of which inflict deadly wounds with their tails, but the most venomous is one from ten to twenty feet in length that has the power of reflecting prismatic colors, and another, about seven feet in length, it is reported, is so poisonous that it kills every living thing it touches when excited, such as trees, grass, etc., and when dead the poison which was imparted to them will dart into the hand or foot of any one that may come in contact with it. Boas frequently come into Bangkok. Early one morning I heard a great outcry in front of the Legation, and upon inquiring the cause learned that a large boa was coiled up in the branches of a banyan tree, trying to catch a peacock, that the noise was occasioned by the boys in attempting to capture it. After firing at it several times it uncoiled slowly from the limb and fell with a terrible plunge into the river, nearly capsizing a Chinaman's boat who was looking on. It could not have been less than thirty feet in length. It is said that the boas found in the city are but puny fellows compared with those in the jungle, which are from fifteen to thirty cubits in length, with a girth around the middle, when not particularly filled, of from thirty to fifty inches. They feed on deer and other large animals which they charm, crush in their coils and swallow whole. According to the natives they are amphibious, live also on fish and have the power of dipping canals and shallow ponds dry when seeking food. They also believe that in all the great rivers there is an animal they call Nguak-ngoo, similar to a snake, but having a head like a woman, with long hair, a regular mermaid. It ranges in length from thirty to fifty feet, and its bite is fatal, not poisonous, but it has the power to suck all the blood out of the body of a man or animal when they drag them to their subaquatic caverns; hence, when a body disappears and does not rise in the river and float they say a Nguak has got it. All kinds of spirits are supposed to dwell in the rivers, and offerings are frequently made to them.

Birds of the rarest plumage abound throughout Siam, but few are songsters. High in air fly innumerable gulls, on airy pinions, flashing like brilliant jewels in the dazzling sunlight. When evening comes and the shadows fall the air is filled with crows wending their way to their roosts in the tall trees that embower some wat. Myriads of little sparrows fly through the verandahs and nest in the ceilings and curtains of your home; parrots and paroquets flash their gorgeous plumage amid the foliage of the banyan and tamarind trees; humming birds, with tremulous wings, suck the sweets from fragrant flowers, pelicans sit moodily on the banks of river or canal with pouch filled with fish, and the miner bird, the rarest of its species, with ebon plumage and gold band around its neck, talks as fluently as if of humankind. Hanging on trees can be seen hundreds of curiously fashioned cones, about a foot in length, woven from straw and bark by a small bird about the size of a swallow, their nests, into which they enter at an aperture near the bottom so as to protect the inside from rain or the depredation of hostile birds, who would otherwise rob their dwellings. Along the coast and islands is a small swallow that makes its nest out of sea-foam, which it gathers with its bill and blows on a rock in a cave or crevice and keeps at its weary work until it forms a perfect nest, in size and shape of that of a sparrow, in which it lays its eggs. These nests seem to be made of gelatine and are eagerly sought for by the denizens of the coast and sold in Bangkok and China for several dollars an ounce, being worth more than five times their weight in silver, some of the nests weighing three ounces. The Chinese esteem them a great delicacy, but they are tasteless and when converted into a liquid can be flavored to suit the taste. Out in the jungle are hundreds of birds not to be found in the groves in and around the capital city, such as the adjutant, a gigantic crane, which stands on his legs six feet high; the bird of Paradise, white and blue peacocks, jungle fowl, the progenitors of our chickens, geese, cranes, snipe, and a demi-crane, about the size of a raven, dazzling white, with yellow legs and bill; tukans, cockatoos, owls and many others quaint and curious, living rainbows in color and animated gleams of glory. A collection of the birds of Siam would be invaluable, many of them unknown to the naturalist.

No portion of the world is more plethoric with fish than the waters of this favored land, its gulf, rivers and canals teeming with them, many rare and curious. One of the most valuable is the platoo, a fish about the size of our herring, which is caught in immense quantities in the gulf, and after being cured by the peculiar process of steaming and salting they are shipped to Singapore and the islands south. It is one of the most delicious pan fish ever cooked and is very popular in Bangkok. Pla tapeng, a large fresh-water fish, is also much sought after, as is the pla chado. The Siamese smoke and dry a good many fish, and boats filled with them can be found on the river and along the canals where they are retailed to the natives. As they are very salty purchasers use them for seasoning their rice. For this purpose the pla hang is most in demand, similar to our herring, also the pla kooron and the pla chalamet. Large numbers of prawns and crabs are sold cheap, as in fact are fish of all kind. Most of those disposed of in Bangkok are brought up from the gulf in row boats, a distance of thirty-five miles, which the fishermen make in a few hours. Oysters abound in the gulf, but they are small, about the size of a nickle, yet, when cooked, are finely flavored, in some of which pearls are found; muscles and other shell fish are gathered in abundance along the shores of the gulf and islands, the bottoms of vessels soon becoming covered with them. While on the coast I was shown many curious and rare specimens of fish, some as round as a ball with spikes like a porcupine, others with heads like a cow, and had a chance to notice the antics of the climbing perch, a medium-sized fish, which will climb up a bush or plank to catch a fly. When the tide falls it makes a round basin a foot or more in diameter, by throwing up mud with its mouth, which will hold water sufficient for its wants till the tide rises; during the interval it skirmishes round in the mud for food and when it meets a fellow a battle royal takes place, fighting fiercely, frequently injuring one another. I have seen thousands of them at a time making their little reservoirs. Another curious fish is the spitting perch, about two inches in length, and when a fly or other insect lights near it it shoots a drop of water from its mouth with great accuracy and rarely misses its mark, thus securing its food. The fighting fish I have spoken of elsewhere. In the aquariums of the nobles can be found some very rare fish, brought from Japan and China, gold fish with six and seven tails beautifully marked, and when swimming in a glass globe or in the basin of a fountain seem more like the creation of fancy than a reality. A very peculiar fish is found in the rice fields, when they are flooded, with skin and color similar to a cat-fish. They are very numerous and boat-loads are brought to market. The musical fish is unknown outside these waters; it is smaller than a minnow, and hundreds of them will fasten themselves on the bottom of a boat or other hard substance and keep up a noise like drumming, to the uninitiated it sounds like weird music coming up from the depths of the waters. Many of the gulf fish weigh from ten to fifteen pounds, and no banquet is considered complete without a pla chado or a pla tapong. Prawns, also, enter largely into the diet of the Siamese, especially for curries and the manufacture of capit; in fact, the finny tribe is one of the essentials for the sustenance of the people, as many have but little else but fish and rice to subsist on. Frogs of all kind abound, from the tiny toad to the mammoth bull-frog, and the nights are made hideous by their croaking; the natives consider them good eating and catch large numbers. One of the rarest of the species is the whistling frog, which always pipes his notes before a rain and whistles melodiously. It is very rare, and the only one that I ever heard was in the banyan tree in the American Legation grounds. Many were skeptical in regard to this frog till they heard it whistling.

Insects and reptiles find a Paradise in this sun-kissed land of verdure, every bush and shrub is a habitation for them; but a strange thing is to be noted, that save during the durian season but few flies can be seen, no lice, scarcely any roaches or fleas, but a world of ants, red, black and white, the latter the most destructive of the species. Wherever they find a lodgment they destroy everything that comes in their way, books, clothing, furniture, wood of all kinds. Many valuable articles have been destroyed by these pests before it was known that they had made an inroad, and every one is on the lookout for them; they are the curse of the country. To new comers the chin choke and tokay are very annoying, but harmless. They are lizards and infest every dwelling; the first is about six or eight inches in length, the latter a foot and over and derives its name from the way it utters its cry "tokay," which can be heard a long distance. They are beneficial about a house, when one becomes accustomed to them, as they destroy mosquitos and insects. On one occasion I saw a tokay capture a bat, after a long struggle, and eat it with much gusto. Chameleons run up and down the trees, changing color as they come and go, peering at you with their sparkling eyes. Butterflies and moths flit about and some of the latter are of immense size:

one that I saw measured, from wing to wing, was
found to be over nine inches, a thing of beauty, brilliant with gold and purple and emerald. Among the
rarest of the insect kingdom is the leaf fly. It is a
perfect leaf, green as if just plucked from the parent
stem, about the size and shape of a green briar leaf,
and it astonishes the beholder when he goes to pick one
up to see it glide away, and it is only by catching one
and examining it that you realize that it is one of
nature's strange freaks. Another is called the bamboo
bug, resembling a small section of bamboo so perfectly
that when you stoop down to pick it up and feel it slip
through your fingers and hide itself in the grass
you find yourself wondering what kind of creation
it is. Shortly after a shower, when the rain
first sets in, the air is filled with winged ants, that come
up out of the ground, and they remind you of flying
snow-flakes during a storm, pouring in streams through
doors and windows, choking the lamps, as sometimes
do the millers and candle flies, at night, but the greatest nuisance is the festive mosquito. He sings most
loyally the same song in the valley of the Menam that
he does on the Jersey flats and runs his bill in the
liveliest manner. For a year or two he fattens on
strangers, then one becomes inoculated with mosquito
virus and he seeks daintier food; but he is a bloated
aristocrat and frequently contains some of the best
blood of Bangkok in his corporosity. Spiders innumerable and of gigantic proportions spread their
glittering webs on all sides and find their way to every
portion of the dwelling houses, all colors, kinds and
sizes, many of them poisonous, but the natives pay but
little attention to them.

Fruits of Siam.

The fruit of Siam comprises everything that grows in a tropical climate: Oranges, limes, pampelmos, citrons, pomegranites, bananas of all kinds, cocoanuts, tamarinds, bale fruit, makroot or fragrant lime, jack fruit, mangoes, linchee, maprang, a grape-like fruit; pine apples, water and musk mellons, rose apples, durians, bread fruit, satawn, mangosteens, look sala, custard apples, guavas, klooi kei, champoo daang or red rose apples; look lamoot, a sweet plumb; lookk cheeop, Rochelle fruit and many others that are daily offered for sale in boats and in the bazaars. The illustration of fruits gives but a few of the many fruits of this prolific section, in which should be included the betel nut and palm fruit. The betel to the Siamese is what tobacco is to the western nations or opium to the Chinese. Fruit is very cheap, especially bananas, which go largely to make up the daily food of many families. Vegetables of all kinds are raised in the gardens adjacent to the city, which are irrigated during the dry season, and the markets are thus daily supplied in abundance, but the best cabbage and white potatoes are brought from China. Indian corn, small ears, is plentiful and roasted on furnaces is sold on the avenues by vendors; turnips, radishes, tomatoes, onions and garlic, beans, peas, etc., grow in profusion. Tobacco is raised in small quantities in various parts of the kingdom and would be more extensively cultivated were it not for the excessive tax demanded by the government, ten per cent. on the crop. Cotton is gathered from large trees, forty and fifty feet in height; the fiber is short but is used in filling mattresses, pillows and cushions, but the natives spin considerable of it into cloth and use it for other purposes; the finer sort, vegetable cotton, is also cultivated in the Lao states and parts of the lower country and called paw. It also pays a tax of ten per cent. Cattle and hogs are raised in great numbers, and butcher shops can be found in various parts of the city, as meat is sold in all of the bazaars; mutton is expensive, the sheep are imported from China and it retails at 35 cents per pound, while other meat sells at eight and ten cents. The beeves are small with a hump on their shoulders and are exhibited in the menageries as the sacred cattle of Burmah; they are about the size and color of a Jersey, but are never used for milk, the natives being too indolent to milk them. The hogs are large, of all colors, sway backed, and their flesh is superior to any other pork, according to western taste. Chickens and ducks are cheap, hatched by the thousand in paddy (rice) husks, and the duck farms are worthy a visit from the curious in such matters, the owners feeding their large broods on fish and other offal. Some turkeys are raised, but the price asked is so high, $10 apiece, that it is only on state occasions that they are served up; but a banquet is considered incomplete without one or more to grace the board. Peacocks are also eaten and are better than turkeys, but not so expensive.

The Siamese are adepts in moulding statuets from clay, which they burn and color. I have seen some very handsome, the equal in design to those manufactured in Italy. They also mould and make large numbers of statues of Buddha, from an inch in height to those of mammoth proportions, of bronze, which they gild. For over a mile along one of the klongs can be seen numerous workshops used exclusively for the manufacture of these idols or statues. Porcelain is manufactured in many parts of the kingdom, some very handsome, and the pottery industry is one of the most extensive in Siam. Jars, jugs, pots, pans, furnaces and many other household articles are made in immense numbers and retailed by peddlers in boats, a large jar holding a barrel of water selling for fifty-five cents or ats. These large jars are used for catching rain water during the rainy season, in the place of a cistern, the water being used for drinking purposes, that in the river being too filthy for use, the refuse of the city being dumped into it.

Chinese artisans abound, workers in gold, silver, copper, brass or iron ; some of their work is artistic and novel, their gold and silver jewelry is very handsome and unique, especially that which is set with sapphires and rubies. The stones are found in the ruby fields that lie adjacent to Chantaboon, a populous city on the west side of the gulf, where the pepper plantations abound. The iron workers are also very skillful and manufacture everything needed out of that useful metal which is smelted in the hill country in the most primitive fashion, but it is of a superior quality, as can be seen from the swords and knives fashioned from it. Several gold mines have been worked in various parts of the country and considerable of the royal metal unearthed, both from quartz and placer washings, but at present only one is but partially operated; the expensive machinery imported for that purpose fast falling to decay, and the Europeans in charge understanding but little about mining, drawing large salaries and doing but little for it in return. The metal used in the fabrication of jewelry is pure gold leaf, brought from China, and is twenty-two karats fine, too soft for general wear, but a vast amount is annually converted into chains, bracelets, anklets, rings, ear and finger rings, charms, pendants, plate, tea-pots, belts, betel boxes, salvers, etc. The wealth of many of the people consists of jewelry, so that no matter what may happen they can hold on to their treasure. So far no silver has ever been found in Siam, but tin is being mined extensively in the Malay peninsula, and it is fast becoming an article of commerce, shipped to America and Europe

The main industry is the planting and rearing of rice, which is shipped to various parts of the world, and the rafting of teak timber down the Menam to be shipped abroad; it is also used in Bangkok for the erection of buildings, floating houses, bunding, vessels and boats, in fact, it is the only timber available for such purposes. Bamboo is also extensively used for light structures, and is cut in the interior and rafted down the streams. The teak forests are located about three hundred miles in the interior and are being rapidly cleared up, much of the work done by elephants; these sagacious animals dragging the logs to the river and piling them to await the annual rise of the water, when the rafts are formed and floated down the stream. At one place on the river a spirit tax is levied. The bonze and soothsayers charge a number of ticals to keep the spirits, or lorlei of the stream from harming the raftmen, and no native will pass that point till these guardians of the stream are paid and the raft blessed by a weird and solemn ceremony. At various points government officials levy and collect a custom tax as the raft passes, which frequently causes delay and litigation, the officials squeezing all that they can get out of the teak traders, and each one of them are required to have his private mark on file and properly registered. Dacoits, also, depredate along the river and rob the raftsmen and boats, so that at times it is hazardous to travel on the stream, and parties have to go well armed, as it is better to rely on self-defense than to appeal to the native officials, the umpers, who correspond with our justices of the peace, most of whom are corrupt and incompetent. It was the general belief among foreigners that many of these officials winked at the transactions of the dacoits and reaped part of the profits of their brigandage. This state of affairs is well considered one of the drawbacks of the country and tends to check its growth and progress; no native is safe from the greed of rapacious officials; hence they do not try to accumulate, and their taxes are excessive. The international court at Bangkok is a fraud that should be abolished, as it is almost impossible to get a case tried, and frequently when it is heard it takes months to get a decision, and you are never sure of justice. His Majesty is trying to remedy this evil, but it is hydra-headed, beyond the power of a Hercules to remedy. Bangkok is well policed and strangers are safer there than in any American or European city of metropolitan proportions. During my five years stay in that city and trips through the country I never heard of a white person being molested, and it is my belief that a foreigner could walk from one end of Bangkok to the other at midnight and not be interfered with. The police are neatly uniformed and numbered and the city laid off into three departments, each under the control of a superintendent, who reports directly to the mayor, one of the Princes

In the native courts native lawyers practice, but their idea of law and justice is very crude and their clients are generally badly plucked; when the lawyer is paid and the court officials are properly greased so that the wheels of justice may run smooth, there is but little left.

Peonage prevails throughout Siam in its worst form. A native once in debt can scarcely ever shake off the shackles, he is virtually a slave for life. Prior to the reign of King Chulalongkorn a man could sell his wife and children and they were subject to arrest for debt, but much of that has been done away with and no child can now be sold for a longer term than when it becomes of age, nor is a man allowed to gamble away his wife or children. It is the intention of the King to do away with the whole system as soon as his people are ripe for it. He has already done more in this direction than any other oriental sovereign, ranking him with other great reformers the Alexander of the East. He is kind and humane to a fault, and but seldom is the death penalty exacted for crime among his subjects.

The musical instruments of the Siamese are quite numerous and some of them very peculiar, gongs, drums, flutes, string instruments, harps, and a crescent-shaped instrument fitted up with glasses which, when hit with a small wand, makes excellent music, the performer sitting on the floor before it; but the most singular is the Lao reed or bamboo organ, which is made of fourteen pipes of reed or bamboo of various lengths, ranging from six to ten feet, placed in pairs and fastened with ribbons of bamboo; near the base is an oval piece of teak or some rare wood, into which the reeds

open, the mouthpiece, which is hollowed out with a
small aperture to blow in. Each pipe has a fingerhole
immediately above the block and another more or less
removed from the base, regulating the tone. When
used the organ is held by placing the hands around the
block, holding it in an upright position, blowing into
the aperture, requiring a strong pair of lungs to fill it.
Its music, when in the hands of a skillful performer, is
peculiarly sweet and spirit-stirring, its symphony like
the organs in our churches, but not so loud, the strains
being soft and melting. The young men serenade
their girls at night with these organs and they are
adepts at it, some of them very fine performers. The
Kawng Wong is another peculiar instrument, which
consists of from twenty to twenty-five small gongs or
bells, so regulated as to form a perfect scale of notes
of the same number, and is shaped so as to form three-
quarters of a circle three feet in diameter, suspended
by two cords within a neat frame of woodwork, ele-
vating the circle about a foot from the floor, the performer sitting cross-legged within the circle holding a
small mallet in each hand with which he taps the gong
and thus makes the most fascinating music, entirely
unlike the Chinese, which is anything else but pleasing
to the ear.

One of the characteristics of Siam is to be noted,
especially in the interior. When you call on a high
noble your approach will be announced by the servants
all squatting down before you, and when you reach his
anti-chamber and are ushered into his presence they
all fall on their hands and knees before him, with their
faces to the floor and do not dare to look upward.
When they approach him for the purpose of handing

betel or anything else, they crawl forward in a crouching manner and always throw their clasped hands up before their face, the usual form of salutation. When a Siamese desires to rest he squats down on his heels and will remain in that position for hours, never sitting on a chair or a bench, and when they eat they all squat around the rice pot and dip in promiscuously, eating with their fingers. In former times every one fell down with his face to the ground when the King or a prince passed by; but His Majesty has done away with much of this oriental subserviency. To him and his father this people are indebted for many reforms, religious as well as social.

In parts of the country exists a singular race of beings, known as Jungle people, who hold but little intercourse with the outside world, live in the densest jungles, build their habitations in the boughs of trees, are devil worshipers and have a language peculiarly their own, not using over fifty words. They average about five feet in stature, are dark copper-colored, have no fixed laws; generally reside in villages of from ten to fifteen families, which is controlled by an elder or head man, whom they obey. Persons who have penetrated the jungle and seen their dwellings could do nothing with them, they are very suspicious of strangers, have no use for or knowledge of the value of money, but would at times barter skins for cotton cloth and knives; the former they tear into strips about six inches in width, which they wear as a panung, all the clothing they use, men and women alike. They are but a slight remove from the orang-outang, the great Malayan ape, found in the same jungle, and it is thought that they are a remnant of the aborigines of the country, now nearly died out, pretty near the connecting link between man and beast. It is but seldom that they are seen, they live on fruit and nothing but the direst necessity will cause them to enter a village or solicit aid of any kind. Brutal, ignorant, decrepid, dirty and dwarfed, they are a type of humanity to be found in no other section and are sometimes called by the more advanced natives monkey men. At one time King Theebaw, of Burmah, had a family of them in his palace at Maulmain. It is said that the Malayan ape took its name from these jungle people.

In the country bordering between Siam proper and the Lao states are some very fine iron mines, especially in the mountainous country of Matabar, where can be found a growth of large pine trees, it being beyond the teak range. Ben Bor, the town in which the miners live, is two days travel from where the ore is mined. The ground surrounding it being very sterile, the miners imagine that the country is infested with evil spirits, and at stated periods they go there in bodies of from two to three hundred at a time and carry with them bullocks, pigs, fowls, and other things which they offer to the spirits as a conciliatory sacrifice, with solemn ceremonies; otherwise they think that misfortune would overtake them. The iron is abundant, but hard to mine, as everything is carried on in the most primitive manner. When smelted it is conveyed to the towns for sale in small pigs on elephants, each animal carrying from four to five hundred pounds. The process of working the ore, after it is smelted, is very crude. After the young men smelt it the old men work it up into articles for sale, the young women wielding the sledge hammers, which weigh from seven to ten pounds, according to the strength of the striker, while the old women and children prepare the fuel and blow the bellows. The forge is a simple apparatus, two bamboos about six inches in diameter, set upright a foot in the ground; a clay pipe leads from them into the fire-place and a stick, around which is wrapped a rag, is worked up and down the bamboo tubes, forcing the air through the clay pipe to a place just under the fire. Charcoal is the fuel used, and it frequently has to be brought a considerable distance. When going to work the blacksmith takes a piece of iron out of the fire with a pair of tongues and using a flat stone for an anvil proceeds to fashion it into shape, generally having three strikers, who continue to pound away till he bids them cease. Men and women smoke large black pipes made from the root of a tree, using the strongest tobacco. The women are well formed and robust, wear their hair long, and when at work are encumbered with but little clothing. They manufacture swords, elephant chains, manacles, mattocks, axes, scissors, knives, etc., which always find a ready sale in the bazaars ; some of their work evincing considerable skill, especially their swords, which are frequently encased in ivory scabbards elaborately carved and mounted with silver.

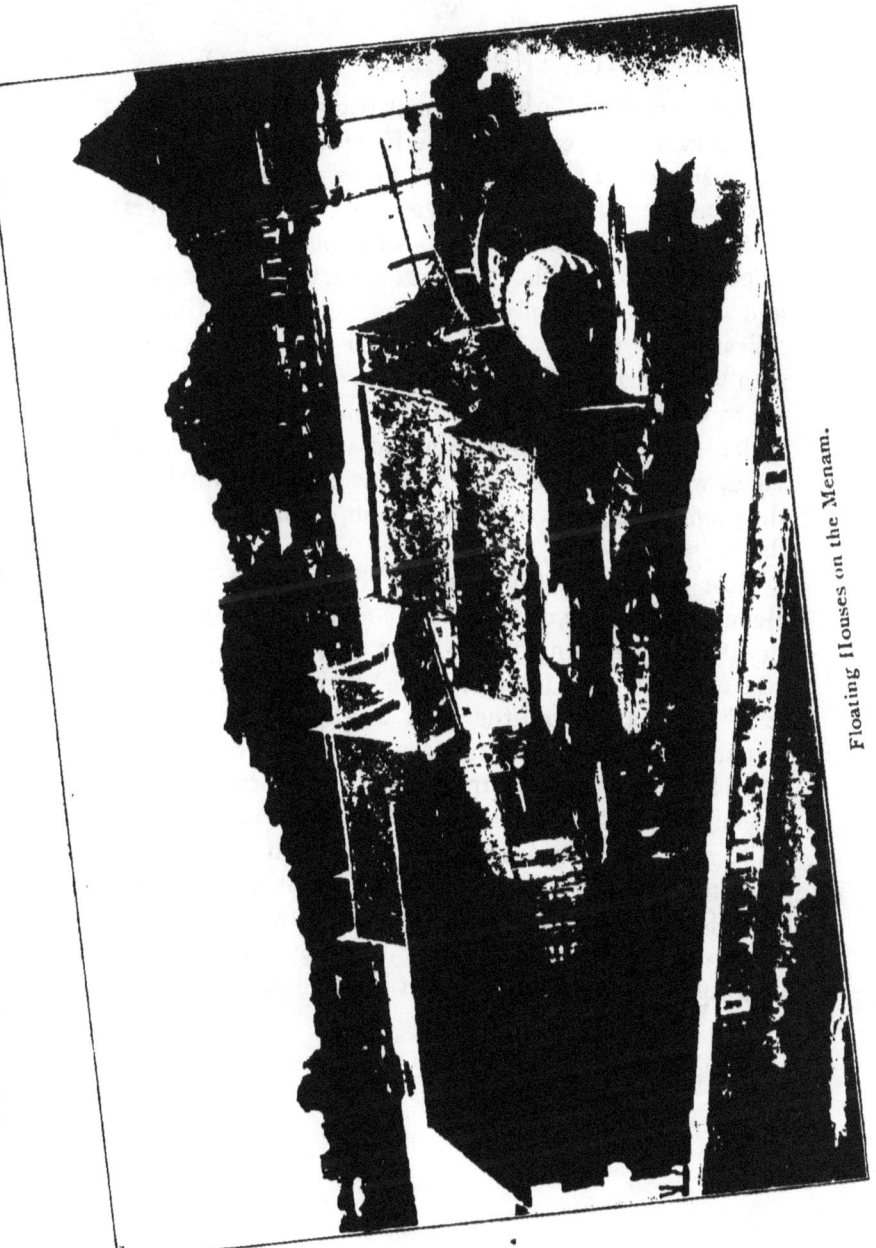
Floating Houses on the Menam.

V.
AYUTHIA, THE ANCIENT CAPITAL.

Gen. Grant and other eminent travelers have visited Ayuthia, the old capital of the Kingdom of Siam, once the residence of a long line of kings prior to the present dynasty. It was destroyed by Burmese invaders in 1767, since which it has been a place of but little importance, noted solely for its ruins, which are massive and wide-spread, amply worth the trouble and time it takes to visit them. Scattered over the plain can be seen the debris of over fifty temples and pagodas, their white walls, like sentinels, standing out from the jungle, while many others are trellised with a network of vines, whose bell-like blossoms toss back and forth as the monsoon swings the parent stem, lending beauty to the scene.

Most persons now take a steam launch and go up the Menam, a distance of only thirty-five miles, to the old city, thus saving time. The most pleasant way is to take a couple of boats, each rowed by eight men, "con ruas," who stand on the deck and push their oars through the water; the oars are fastened to row locks or posts with a whisp of dry grass; throwing the weight of their bodies on the handles of the chow or oar. They make good headway against the current, which at times is strong. The middle of the boat is covered with a house for travelers to set or lounge in, as the spirit moves one; when night comes on mosquito nets are hung up, mattresses are brought out, the boat moored to the bank, and one sleeps as calmly as if in Bangkok, no fear whatever. Under the deck of the boat is stowed provisions, clothing, rice for the boys, and other necessaries; just back of the house the cook makes his kitchen and he gets up a good meal in a short time, using canned goods or fowls; fruit and vegetables can be obtained *en route*. The trip is anything but monotonous to the seeker after strange sights. In company with a jolly party early one morning we unmoored our boats, gave an order to the con ruas to go ahead, and soon with steady strokes we went speedily up stream, on by the royal palace with its spires gleaming gloriously in the sun, on by wats embowered in greenest of foliage, flitting by miles of floating houses, passing numerous rafts of teak and bamboo, on by villages of common looking houses and bamboo shanties, many of them built on piles out over the river, dodging the many rice and provision boats descending the stream, and the small canoes rowed principally by women, the only class of Siamese that wear hats, which are made of bamboo and are about the size of a half bushel measure, fastened on their heads by strips of the same material, peddling all kinds of marketable stuff, who sing out the names of the articles they sell: fruit, cakes, bread, rice, samshoo (a villainous article of rice whisky), flowers, dry goods, water jars, lime and betel nuts, lamps, china ware, tin and iron ware, stacks of sugar cane cut in two-foot lengths, and you can hear the girls at all hours singing out "Oi Chen," sugar cane, as they paddle their canoes alongside, as do the venders of fruit and sweets. Frequently the boatmen chaff the girls and then a volley of the most horrible oaths follow, as rough language and indecent epithets come from these dwellers on the water as easily as breathing. At noon we land at a monastery, take possession of a sala, and soon the servants have a meal prepared, which is eaten with a keen relish under the observation of a score or so of half-clad natives, who look on and wonder how the white strangers can eat so many different things and much thereof, his fare being but a small measure of rice and condiments, with some fruit or a fish taken from the stream. At the close of the repast it is amusing to see the little fellows scramble for the empty cans and bottles that the servants throw away. Then we again take to our boats, soothed by the ripple of the waters as they flash by the prow.

Salas or rest houses are built as a means of merit making and are very numerous; they are simple structures consisting of a plank or tile floor, a tile roof supported by wooden columns, no walls, as the weather is always warm, but most of them have seats or benches around the sides for persons to lay on; the Siamese, when tired, squats on the ground and sits on his heels. Some, built of brick, are handsome and artistic, the roof handsomely decorated in true Siamese style with elaborate gilding and colored tiles. As night falls a cool breeze fans through the windows of the cabin, the soft susurrus of the water sounds like a lullaby, and from out the dark foliage on the banks come flashes of luminous light, whole trees ablaze, lighted up by fireflies, millions glowing at once; then all is dark till the flash comes again, making it seem the creation of fancy, lovely as a gleam from fairyland. For hours, in the gloom, I have watched the flashing of these luminous insects, trees fifty feet in height outlined with them, while all around was dense darkness, a truly tropical scene that I do not think can be seen elsewhere than in the realms of Chulalangkorn I.

At daybreak, having moored our boats near a monastery, we were awakened by the beating of a huge drum and the ringing of a large bell, rousing the monks from slumber so that they could start out in their boats to secure their rice for the day's food. Entering their boat they paddle up to a house, hand out their rice pot into which a ladle full of cooked rice and condiments is placed, together with some fruit; the donor, generally a woman, vyeing, *i. e.*, raising her joined hands to her forehead, as a mark of respect and gratitude to the priesthood—the "Khun," or benefactor, as he is designated, who thus gives her an opportunity to make merit—while the yellow-robed solicitor of alms looks on stolidly, taking it as a matter of right instead of accepting it as a favor. The priesthood in Siam is very peculiar. In Buddha's time it was the custom of the priests to reward the donors by preaching the law or reading extracts from the Pali version; now none but the higher order of the clergy, who reside in the leading monasteries, know the law, in fact, the majority scarcely knows a word of Pali, the written language of their church. But few have any idea of leading a monastic life, most of them remaining only a few months in a monastery, in compliance with their idea that during a portion of their life they should enter the priesthood. After receiving a sufficient quantity of food they return to the wat and satisfy the cravings of nature. In accordance with their law they eat but once a day, in the morning, after which they must be satisfied with tea and cigars until it is time for them to again go forth soliciting. The church of Siam is thus self-sustaining; it costs the government nothing, and a priest is prohibited from accepting money, no salary being attached to his office; all are on a common level, prince and peasant, all go bareheaded and barefoot, from the King's brother down.

If it was not for the various villages, wats and boats that one passes the trip might prove tedious, as the scenery along the banks is not very attractive, palms, bamboo, tamarinds, banyan and other trees fringing the water; but at every bend you can see nestled amid the green verdure a white temple with decorated roof and golden spire, or through a rent in the trees a vast stretch of paddy fields on which herds of water buffalo are pasturing, they being the Siamese beasts of burden; in the distant background can be seen some lofty hills that look blue in the ambient air, etherial as a cloud on the horizon. About noon our servants shout "Kroong Kao," and the ruins of the old city rise into view; with a spurt the boys rush the boats through the water and we are soon landed at the sala in front of the Governor's palace, a dilapidated building, and were made welcome by one of his retainers, the Governor being absent, who led us through the palace grounds, showed us the audience room used by His Majesty when he visits the ancient city, a dingy place, the throne covered with dust, thence to a watch-tower in the garden, about one hundred feet high, from the top of which we obtained a grand view of the old city and its surroundings, a vast mass of ruins, no effort having been made for over a century to stop the ravages of time or restore the desecrated temples, a wreck of buildings in "ruinous perfection;" walls, columns, images, spires and palaces covered with vines and tropical foliage, the home of venomous serpents, lizards, chamelions and small jungle animals. The groves were full of birds, some of rare plumage, and the chatter of paroquets was incessant, while ever and anon, by close watching, you could see a monkey glide from tree to tree, keeping his eye on the stranger who was trespassing on his domain. At one time tigers roamed through the ruins, but they have been scared off since the natives commenced using rifles, though at times large tiger-cats have been seen prowling through the jungle.

Since its destruction and abandonment by the present rulers, Ayuthia, "the unassailable," as it was termed, has never recovered its former prestige, but it is still quite a good-sized place, the modern city built mainly on the river and canals, several of which center there. It is a good business point for boats ascending and descending the river and canals, the traffic being mainly in the hands of Chinese. The attractions for strangers, outside the many ruins, are two temples, one a ruin, and the stockades where wild elephants are captured for the King, and at times His Majesty gives a grand elephant hunt to which distinguished strangers and the diplomatic corps are invited. He gave one last year in honor of the visit of the Grand Duke Alexis, of Russia, who was visiting Siam on his tour around the globe. The first object to attract the attention is the "Gold Mountain," the highest and best preserved of all the ruins, a typical pagoda, which differs somewhat from most of the Siamese towers in having three accessible terraces, the highest of which tops the tallest trees that surround it; from it a splendid view can be had of the whole country, taking in the rivers and network of canals whose waters sparkle in the sunshine like molten silver. We were told that the ruins of over fifty temples and pagodas could be counted from its summit, thus carrying out the statement that at one time, ere the Burmese came down like a wolf on the fold, over two hundred of these stately buildings reflected back the glory of the godhead from their gilded tapering prachedis. This temple is built of brick and is one of the earliest specimens of Buddhist architecture. As I could not obtain a photo of it I will give a brief description of this still beautiful building. It is built in the form called "Phra Chedi," which represents the primitive tope or relic mound; based upon an extensive square it rises a pyramidal tower in three parts, to represent the Buddhist trinity, the world, the Dewa heaven, and the Paradise of the formed Brahmis, the three tiers being separated by wide terraces; cornices of many forms, round and angular, encircle it in close succession, while flutings and re-entering angles reduce the squareness of the four corners. Two flights of steps lead to the terraces. From the highest terrace, sixty feet from the ground, rises a tower thirty feet in height, of pyramidal form, same as the lower part, in which are two niches containing gilt statues of the great teacher seven feet in height; above these niches the still tapering tower is without cornices and perfectly smooth for about fifteen feet, then changing from a square pyramid to a cone it rises to about forty feet to a point, the upper part ornamented with narrow beadings or rings, lying close one over the other. The tower is solid brick, except a small chamber, which at one time must have held relics or a statue of Buddha; it is now empty and the abode of bats.

Access to it is from the highest terrace. This is the only prachedi or large pagoda that has an accessible chamber, though they are frequently found in the smaller ones. Several small temples can be seen in the new town ornamented with a mosaic of bits of crockery set in cement representing flowers, animals, nondescripts and fanciful designs, interlarded with gay saucers and plates, bright china birds on the cornices, colored and glazed tiles for the roof, at each end of which can be seen the ox horn ornaments peculiar to Siamese architecture, presenting a gorgeous appearance at a distance, but, like most modern buildings thereabouts, the form and color being good, but the material is both common and perishable, hence it does not bear close inspection.

Turning from this monument of a past age we were taken to Wat Cheun, built by a Princess of that name. It is a conglomerate of buildings and seems to be controlled by Chinese monks. You enter by a door that opens into a Chinese joss house decorated with a fantastic roof; inside is the altar covered with tawdry articles and illuminated with lamps and candles that fill the room with smoke; everything is covered with it, a greasy-looking priest being in attendance. Passing hurriedly through we found a large monastery with a "wihan" or idol house and "bort," or holy building where the monks assemble for consecrations and other religious ceremonies are held; close by were a number of small white pagodas, from ten to twenty feet high, built for merit, as they are neither ornamental nor useful, all built alike, a waste of brick and mortar. These small pagodas can be found everywhere over the kingdom. In close vicinity to the "wihan" are the residences of the priests and the cremation grounds; the embers of a "burning," as the Siamese term a cremation, were still glowing as we passed to enter the idol house or hall, which is an uncouth-looking structure of Chinese architecture; but the interior is very effective, the room being about one hundred and twenty feet square and about seventy feet in height; the walls are pierced with a fretwork of niches, in each of which is a gilt idol about six inches in length, myriads of them. On all sides are hundreds of pedestals on which are placed statues of Buddha and his disciples in various attitudes, most of them life-size. In the center of the vast hall, between six huge pillars, plastered over with gilding, whose capitals can only be outlined in the gloom, on a throne is seated a collossal image of Buddha, heavily gilded, in the position of contemplation, such as the Buddhists delight to portray him, legs crossed, the right hand clasping the right knee, the left lying palm upward across the thighs, while the massive face, as seen in the dim light, appears as if he was steeped in meditation, placid and mild, as are all of the statues of this great man, and the effect is grand upon a stranger as well as on his followers. On the right and left of the Buddha are two standing figures, about twenty feet high, representing Sariputra and Maggalona, the disciples of the left hand and the right hand. The priests in attendance could not tell us the exact size of the Buddha, but we were assured that it was the largest sitting idol in Siam. To judge of its dimensions one of the attendants climbed up and stood in the palm of its hand, and he did not look as large as one of its fingers. I saw seven persons stand on the thumb of the reclining Buddha in the grotto at Petchaburee. This, like most of the large idols, is made of brick and cement, covered with lacquer and then gilt. All have the same look of supreme meditation and placid repose, as if all worldly thoughts had been banished from his mind.

Leaving the gloom of this abode of idols, one could almost realize, as he looked around him, ruin piled on ruin, that he stood in the Sparta of Siam; here are the vast relics of its former greatness, when its mailed warriors battled for this Pearl of Asia in all of its tropical grandeur. The history of Ayuthia reads like a romance; the crumbling walls and prostrate idols tell us the story with mute tongues as convincing as if outlined by a painter's pencil or recorded by historian's pen. In the shadow of its ruined fanes, with the silence of desolation around you, one can not help reflecting that he stands on a spot that was once the scene of one of the most sanguinary struggles in the East, almost the entire overthrow of a gallant people. Here the fairest of Asian flowers were crimsoned with the life-drops of brave men, and here a great city was literally wiped out, its people captured, a Kingdom prostrate at the feet of its captors. This occurred over a hundred years since; its ruins attest its greatness, and it is well that nature, kinder far than man, has hid the rents of ruin with a tapestry of flowers and clinging vines, making that more beautiful which was so, hiding the work of the iconoclast. With an eye to the situation, the early founder of this now desolated place saw that here in the clasp of a majestic river, and the center of an emerald plain, with mountains in the distance, a city could be built worthy to be the capital of this sun-kissed land. His name has perished amid the cycles of time that crumbled his capital to dust. At his command a city sprung into existence, for years it was the center of a vast civilization. It grew, flourished, was captured and recaptured, destroyed and rebuilt, its people made slaves and its holy places a desolation. Years filtered through the hour-glass of time, centuries left their impress on field and river, the city that had been battled for so long was then known as Loweck, the "city of plenty," but in 1350, then a mere mass of ruins, it was selected by one of the Siamese kings, who was pleased with its site, to rebuild it as his capital, and styled Ayuthia. Again it was restored to its past greatness; once more it became a royal city, and so continued till the Burmese invasion. Being almost surrounded by the Menam, it was still strengthened with massive walls and on the debris of ages, on the foundations of temples that had been reared for the worship of now forgotten gods majestic wats and palaces were built and along its highways and on its canals moved a half million people, its waterways being covered with boats bearing to it the wealth of gulf and land. For over four hundred years it bid defiance to foes, grew in grandeur and known as the "golden city" became an object of envy to the surrounding nations. At that time Burmah was at the zenith of its power, ruled by a grasping monarch who resolved to crush his neighbor and put a stop to the wars that had been waged between them for centuries. Collecting an immense army his generals swept onward, a resistless horde, marking their path with desolation. Reaching the environs of the doomed city, which refused to surrender, hurling back a haughty defiance to the invaders, a siege was commenced and for two years every assault was repulsed; but in March, 1767, the river being low, the Burmese forded the Menam, battered down the walls and entered the city sword in hand, a tidal wave of ruthless murderers. The provisions of the defenders were exhausted, they had suffered untold horrors; decimated by disease and starvation, they yielded without further struggle. Then followed a massacre, the place was given up to the sword and pillage. For days the heavens were lurid with the flames of burning palaces, temples and habitations, the air filled with the frenzied shrieks of its devoted people in the agonies of death. The Burmese had carried out his stern resolve, Ayuthia was no more. Desolation followed, silence replaced the hum of the busy multitude, its people made captives, but the heroism of its defenders lives in history, its site is considered hallowed ground, its ruined fanes held in reverence, and a mammoth statue of Buddha, slowly crumbling to dust, has its hosts of worshipers.

In the contemplation of the ruins of this once great capital one can realize how the plowshare of time overturns vast metropolises, how here on the confines of Asia a tragedy as gigantic as those that befell Carthage, Perseopolis and Thebes has been enacted.

Amid Ayuthia's crumbled grandeur one can read of the civilization and wealth of a people who had a well-written code of laws and followed the teachings of Buddha while Britain was under the sway of the Druids and Greece her Olympian gods obeyed, when the prophets of Israel preached Jehovah and gilded Jerusalem with glory, ere the gentle Nazarine gave us our code and the Roman legions had destroyed its temple and leveled its battlements. The shades of evening falling fast, we turned to our boats, leaving the dead behind us, to mingle once more among the living; we had had enough of ruins, as one of the party remarked, the whole place was terribly out of repair.

VI.

DINING WITH THE KING.

While lying in a chair on the veranda of the Legation building, indolently watching the ever-changing panorama on the swiftly-flowing Menam covered with boats, from the tiny canoe of the rua chong, ferry boatman, to the majestic ocean steamer, and contrasting the difference between the land of the prairie and the land of the palm, I was aroused by the approach of my kavass, a native who speaks English and is an attache of the Legation, who, after the usual salam, said: "Your Excellency, a messenger from His Majesty awaits an audience." "Admit him," and in a moment an attache of the Court appeared and bowing low presented me with a missive about twelve inches in length by eight in width, with the remark " from His Majesty;" he then again bowed to the ground and retired backward. Opening the envelope I found a handsomely embossed card upon which was printed the request that I would dine with His Majesty at the supreme palace on the following day at 7:30 P. M. I immediately sent a reply that it would give me great pleasure to do so.

At the hour mentioned I drove into the outer palace grounds and was received by a high Siamese official who, expressing himself in good English, informed me that he had been awaiting my arrival and was highly gratified to receive me. Under his charge I proceeded to the palace where Prince Devawongse and others in attendance on the King received me in true oriental style. After partaking of the usual cup of tea and refusing a cigar—the Siamese are inveterate smokers—I awaited the arrival of the other guests, the Duke De-Lucca, Italian Minister to Siam and China; the English Minister, Mr. Satow; the French Charge d' Affairs, Count DeKercaradeck, Commodore DeRichelieu and Dr. Gowan, physician to His Majesty. Most of the guests were resplendent in gorgeous uniforms and wore orders, while the representative of the great republic wore a plain evening dress. The guests having arrived, a blare of bugles was heard and we were ushered into the banquet hall, one of the handsomest rooms that it has ever been my good fortune to enter, the walls and ceiling a mass of fretted gold, the elaborate frescoing a work of art, the floor covered with a Persian carpet. Magnificent chandeliers with wax candles lighted up the place and it looked as if some genii had fashioned this superb room in a moment of inspiration. Running the full length of the room was a table covered with the whitest of damask, down the center of which ran a glass canal, made in sections about six inches wide and four deep, filled with perfumed water and flowers of the rarest kind. It was made so that it enclosed a number of solid silver stands, about two and a half feet in height, which held flowers and fruit; the stands represented palm trees and at their base were elephants, deer and gazelles enshrined in foliage, each stand a masterpiece of Asiatic art. The table furniture had on it the monogram of the King; the goblets were of the finest Bohemian ware, with gilt rims; the plates and dishes of the finest porcelain and the chairs, covered with leather, also bore the royal monogram carved on the top, all of which were made to order in Europe. Covers were laid for about forty, most of the guests being Siamese Princes, Governors and high officials. In the place of a punkah the air was kept in motion by eight pages, dressed as Scotch Highlanders, who gracefully waved large peacock fans above the table, which added no little to the comfort of the guests. The waiters were dressed in swallow-tail coats. At a signal, the King seated himself at the center of the table on the right side, with his foreign guests facing him. The menu was quite elaborate, embracing all of the delicacies of the season, prepared by a French cook, which were served cold with the exception of the fish and soup, as everything had to be tasted before being brought to the table so that there could be no opportunity to tamper with the food to the injury of His Majesty or any of his guests. Wine of all kinds was served, and after remaining at the table a couple of hours, closing with ices and liqueurs, the King rose and we were invited to accompany him to his private reception room where coffee was served and general conversation indulged in, His Majesty listening with considerable interest and frequently asking questions that kept the conversation from flagging. Though the King does not speak English, he understands it perfectly, and could do so fluently if he so desired, but prefers to express himself in his own tongue, which is then interpreted by one of the Princes or the court interpreter. Upon entering the reception room each one was presented with a sash of white flowers, woven in the shape of a rope, Indian mogaries, the tassel or pendant made of a salmon-colored flower, very fragrant. These sashes are worn over the shoulder and hang down on the left side and are as fragrant as they are beautiful.

While admiring the sashes His Majesty presented the Duke DeLucca with a magnificent crimson rose about eight inches in diameter, a marvelous flower, which astonished everyone at its mammoth proportions; it was the imperial rose of roses. Upon close examination it was discovered to be a manufactured article, each leaf was carefully sewed to a center and so deftly was it done that it required the closest scrutiny to discover that it was not one of nature's choicest productions. The natives are very skillful in the fashioning of flowers into hanging baskets, chandeliers, wreaths, ornaments and bouquets; they revel in their beauty and seem to become intoxicated with their perfume. Flowers are used upon every occasion, and they can be found ornamenting the lowliest hut as well as shedding their fragrance in the palaces of the nobles; the women wreathe them into coronets to decorate their children, and they are sold in the bazaars for that purpose, a large bunch of tuberoses being sold for a couple of pennies. I was particularly impressed with the skill shown by these people in the manufacture of flowers and blossoms, many artificial ones are as handsome as the dew-kissed buds that hang upon the parent stem.

Conversing with his guests for about an hour the king rose, shook hands and we retired much pleased with our reception, realizing the fact that we had been the partaker of a royal feast, having dined with royalty, and most agreeably entertained, an evening that would long be remembered as one of the most pleasant that I had spent in the Siamese capital. Our carriages were in waiting and we were soon driven homeward, the guards at the gates saluting us as we passed. It is only on special occasions that His Majesty invites foreigners to dine with him. At the table he partook of the various dishes as they were passed, enjoying the feast; partook sparingly of the wine, as did all of the nobles. The Siamese are an abstemious people, the priests inculcating sobriety, the Queen particularly so. When her brother, Prince Swatsi, returned from England, having graduated at Cambridge, she presented him with a palace; to commemorate the event he gave a house warming, and a number of leading citizens were invited to be present. After dancing the guests were asked to partake of a banquet prepared in the most lavish manner, and, as usual, the soft-spoken servant asked, "What will you drink?" "Champagne and soda," he replied, in mournful tones, "Your Excellency, there is nothing but Buddhist water: lemonade, ginger ale and soda." Her Majesty had issued her commands that nothing stronger than tea and coffee should be served upon the occasion, and her word was law. Most of the younger nobles are cultured gentlemen who understand the amenities of private life and polite society, but it goes hard with some of the older ones to handle a knife and fork properly, they having been accustomed to eat with their fingers, as is the usual mode in Siam. Children of foreign parents reared among the natives assured me that rice eaten in Siamese style tasted much better than in any other way. Custom is imperial the world over.

Ruins of Nagkon Wat.

VII.

WONDERFUL RUINS OF ANGKOR AND NAGKON WAT.

But seldom has a white traveler visited the marvelous and stupendous ruins of Angkor and Nagkon Wat, in the sylvan solitudes of Siam, but those who have been so fortunate speak with awe of its immensity and beauty, remarking that these relics of a past age "are as imposing as the ruins of Thebes or Memphis and more mysterious." While making a tour of the East, Frank Vincent, Jr., in company with Rev. S. I. McFarland, made a visit to Angkor, the first Americans that had penetrated the vast wilds of that section, and in his "Land of the White Elephant" gives an elaborate description of Nagkon Wat, which has also been described by M. Mouhut, whose work he drew liberally upon for information, in which he describes this temple as "one of those temples—a rival to that of Solomon, erected by some ancient Michael Angelo—that might take an honorable place beside our most beautiful buildings. It is grander than anything left us by Greece or Rome." These ruins are situated in the province of Siamrap, eastern Siam, and are described by M. Mouhut as of colossal size. The entrance to Nagkon Wat, the main temple, is described as a massive causeway 725 feet in length, paved with hewn stones four feet in length by two in breadth, flanked with six huge griffins, each carved from a single block of stone, leading directly to the main entrance, on each side of

which are two artificial lakes covering about five acres
of ground, the whole structure embowered in the midst
of a forest of cocoa, betel nut and toddy palms, no
other buildings in sight but some bamboo huts occupied
by a few cadaverous priests and slaves who have charge
of the place.

At the first glance one is struck dumb at its immensity, its grandeur and sublimity—the mind grows dizzy
with wonder at this marvel of the wilds, at the bold
conception of the genius which planned and the skill
and patience and labor which executed such a masterpiece of architecture. The outer wall of the Wat,
about a half mile square, is built of sandstone with
gateways upon each side handsomely carved and
as perfect as if did yesterday, with figures of gods and
dragons, arabesques and intricate scrolls. Upon the
western side of the main gateway, passing through this
and up a causeway, paved with slabs or stone, for a
thousand feet, you arrive at the central entrance of the
Wat. Its foundations are ten feet in height, massively
built of volcanic rock. The edifice is composed of
three terraces; the one about thirty feet above the
other, including the roof, is of a hard blue stone, but
without cement, and so closely fitting are the joints as
to be scarcely discernible. The quarries, where the
stone was hewn, is thirty miles distant from the building, and the immense boulders in the wall and building
could have been transported only by water, possibly a
canal having been dug for that purpose. The shape of
the building is oblong, 796 feet in length and 588 feet
in width; the central pagoda rises 250 feet above the
ground, and four others at the angles of the court are
each about 150 feet in height. The main entrance is

through a columned portico, the facade covered with mythological subjects. From this doorway, on either side, runs a corridor with double rows of columns, cut base and capital, from single blocks, with a double oval-shaped roof covered with carving and consecutive figures on the outer walls. Mr. Vincent says that this gallery of sculptures, which forms the exterior of the temple, consists of over half a mile of continuous pictures, cut in basso-relievo upon sandstone slabs six feet in width, representing subjects taken from Hindo mythology—from the Ramayana—the Sanscrit epic poem of India, with its 27,000 verses describing the exploits of the god Rama and the son of the King of Oudh. The contests of the King of Ceylon and Hanuman, the monkey god, are graphically represented. There is no keystone used in the arch of this corridor, and its ceiling is uncarved. On the walls are sculptured the immense number of 100,000 separate figures (or at least heads). Entire scenes from the Ramayana are pictured; one occupies 240 feet of the wall. Weeks might be spent in studying, identifying and classifying the varied subjects of this wonderful gallery. You see warriors riding upon elephants and in chariots, foot soldiers with shield and spear, boats, unshapely divinities, trees, monkeys, griffins, hippopotami, serpents, fishes, crocodiles, bullocks, tortoises, soldiers of immense physical development with helmets and some people with beards, probably Moors. The figures stand somewhat like those on the great Egyptian monuments, the side partly turned towards the front; in the case of the men one foot and leg are always placed in advance of the other, and I noticed, besides, five horsemen, armed with spear and sword, riding abreast, like those seen upon the Assyrian tablets in the British Museum. In the processions several of the kings are preceded by musicians playing upon shells and long bamboo flutes. Some of the kings carry a battle-axe, others a weapon which much resembles a gof-club, and others are represented as using the bow and arrow. In one place is a grotesque divinity who sits elegantly dressed upon a throne surmounted by umbrellas; this figure, of peculiar sanctity, evidently had been recently gilded, and before it upon a small table there were a dozen or more joss-sticks kept constantly burning by the faithful. But it is almost useless to particularize when the subjects and style of execution are so diverse. Each side of the long corridor seemed to display figures of distinct features, dress and character. The most interesting sculptures, says Dr. Adolf Bastian, who explored these wonderful ruins in 1864, are in two compartments, called by the natives respectively the procession and the three stages (heaven, earth and hell). What gives a peculiar interest to this section is the fact that the artist has represented the different nationalities in all their distinctive characteristic features, from the fat-nosed savage in the tasseled garb of the Phon and short-haired Lao to the straight-nosed Rajaput, with sword and shield and the bearded Moor, which gives a catalogue of nationalities, like another column of Trajan, in the predominant physical conformation of each race. On the whole, there is such a prevalence of Hellenic cast in the features and profiles, as well as in the elegant attitude of the horsemen, that one might suppose Xenocrates of old, after finishing his labors in Bombay, had made an excursion to the East. These are figures sculptured in high relief (nearly life-size) upon the lower parts of the wall about the entrance. All are females, and apparently of Hindoo origin. The interior of the quadrangle bounded by the long corridor just described is filled with galleries and halls, formed with huge columns, crossing one another at right angles. In the Nagkon Wat as many as 1,532 solid columns have been counted, and among the entire ruins of Ankor there are reported to be the immense number of 6,000, almost all of them hewn from single blocks and artistically carved. On the inner side of the corridor there are blank windows, each of which contains seven beautifully turned little columns. The ceilings of the galleries were hung with tens of thousands of bats and pigeons and other birds have made themselves comfortable nests in the out-of-way corners. We pass on up steep staircases, with steps no more than four inches in width, to the center of the galleries, which here bisect one another. There are two detached buildings in this square, probably used formerly as image-houses, and they now contain wooden Buddhas, though of recent date. In one of the galleries, we saw two or three hundred images, made of stone, wood, brass and clay, of all shapes and sizes and ages (some of the large stone idols are said to be 1,400 years old), a Buddha's sacred foot, etc. Joss-sticks were burning before the largest images, which were besides daubed with red paint and partly gilded. We walk on across another causeway, with small image-houses on either hand, and up a steep flight of steps, fully thirty feet in height, the other galleries crossing each other, in the center above which rises the grand central pagoda—250 feet in height—and at the four corners of the court four smaller spires. These latter are much dilapidated and do not display their full height; the porticoes also bear evidence of the "heavy hand of time." Upon the four sides of the base of the highest spire are collossal images of Buddha, made of plaster, and other smaller divinities in various positions. These figures of Buddha are grandly placed, for, when the doors of the enclosing rooms are opened, from their high position they overlook the surrounding country; and the priests of Nagkon Wat worship here at the present day. There is one more gallery and then we come to the outer corridor and pass through a magnificent doorway to the rear of the temple and walk round to our sala, not knowing which to admire the most, the vastness of the plan or the propriety and grace of the performance.

Speculation has been rife as to who built Nagkon Wat and at what period of time its majestic towers were first gilded by a tropic sun. So far no one has reached a definite conclusion. Native Cambodians date back the time 2400 years, others 1300 years and state that it was built by a number of Kings and completed by a Buddhist. It is all a matter of conjecture. Dr. Bastian says that this temple was built by the Cambodians for the reception of the learned patriarch Buddhaghosa, who brought the sacred books of the Trai-Pidok from Langka (Ceylon). Bishop Pallegoix, who wrote a valuable work on Siam, dates the erection of this edifice to the reign of Phra Pathum Suriving, at the time the holy books of Buddha were brought from Ceylon and Buddhism became the religion of that section. M. Henri Mahout, who gave the first account of these now celebrated ruins, was of the opinion that they were built by some of the lost tribes of Israel. In his travels through Indo-China he made many efforts to discover Jewish traces in Siam or Cambodia, but met with nothing to confirm his belief but a record of the Judgment of Solomon, attributed to one of their Kings who had become a god after having been, according to their ideas of metempsychosis, an ape, an elephant, etc., which was found preserved in one of the Cambodian sacred books verbatim. It was M. Mahout's belief that the older parts of Angkor was over 2,000 years old and the more recent parts not much later, and it is his belief that the people who erected it have passed away, be they who they may. There is no trace of any such people now existing among the surrounding nations, and the Abbe Jaquenet, a missionary in Cochin-China, writes that after the dispersion of the ten tribes, instead of returning from captivity, they set out from the banks of the Euphrates and reached the shores of the ocean, and this may be the result of their labor, and, as he says, "the shining of the light of revelations in the far east is not the less incontestible." Native historians credit the foundation of Ankor to a Prince of Roma or Ruma; Roma is familiar to all the Cambodians, who place it at the western end of the world. That it is of very ancient origin is indisputable; its crumbling columns and towers, deeply worn stone stairs, absence of keystones in the arches and the undecipherable inscriptions all denote that the waves of centuries have passed over its moss-covered and fallen roofs, and it would require the lapse of ages for a race to thus pass away and leave no vestige of its existence behind save these artistic ruins, positive evidence of another people and another civilization. The style of architecture is peculiar to itself, somewhat resembling the temples of India and Java; there is but little to denote it of Egyptian origin, as that is massive and ponderous, this is light, airy and graceful. There are no tablets eulogizing the founder of the Wat or commemorating its establishment; no inscriptions concerning its building on its walls, that so far have been translated, though there are some that are undecipherable, others that give a description of offerings at different times with allusions to religious ceremonies and mythological objects; among them one of black marble, about five feet square, let into the wall of the rear corridor, and from this this information has been gained. The inscriptions which can not be read resemble the ancient Cambodian or the Pali character, but in a more antiquated form. It may be possible that same learned savant who has made the lore of the East a study will be able to unfold the annals of this lost people, if they have ever been written or carved on tablet or monument. Christoval de Jaque, a Portugese adventurer, took refuge in Cambodia in 1570 and describes these ruins, stating that at that time the inscriptions were unintelligible to the natives. To the labors of M. Mauhut, Dr. Bastian and Mr. Thompson, an English photographer, are we mainly indebted for a description of these wonderful ruins, unrivaled as forgotten works of an unknown people.

About three miles from Ankor are the ruins of the citadel of Taphrom, and near it a wat styled Prakeoh, or the Gem tower, a royal and priestly residence. Four miles east of Nagkon Wat are two other remains of antiquity: Bakong and Lailan. At the latter are several images of Buddha, built of bricks which are exceedingly hard and made in a manner not now understood by the people of the country. They are polished and laid upon each other so neatly that no trace of mortar can be discovered. The whole valley of the Makong river, to the very borders of China, is spread with majestic ruins. Near the monastery of Prakeoh is an artificial lake built by the kings of Patentaphrohm, and surrounded with the ruins of pleasure houses for their recreation. It is a work of stupendous labor, and Dr. Bastian asserts that it would now require the whole population of Cambodia to raise such a gigantic structure. He describes the lake Sasong as being "of oblong shape, about 2,000 feet broad and 4,000 feet long, surrounded by a high embankment of solid masonry. Some of the blocks are fourteen and sixteen feet long and highly finished. In convenient places square platforms were built overhanging the water, with broad flights of steps leading down to it, and, in such places the huge masses of stone laid on each other are embellished by delicate chiselings, bearing the figures of serpents, eagles, lions (in their fabulous shapes as Naga, Kruth, Sinto), on the ends. In the middle of the lake is a small island with the remains of a palace on it. Of all the figures used for ornaments that which occurs most frequently is that of the Naga, and a Chinese officer who visited Cambodia in 1295 describes the pillars of the stone bridges as adorned with serpents, each of which had nine heads."

Realizing the importance of these ruins to the world and recognizing the hardship and danger that attends one in venturing so far into the interior of the country,

His Majesty, King Chulalongkorn, has had a model made, the reproduction in miniature of Nagkon Wat, that at once attracts the attention of beholders when they visit the palace grounds. The model is about twenty-five feet in length by about twenty in breadth and shows the lofty domes, high porticos, majestic columns, high flights of stairs and the innumerable alcoves and entrances. With the exception of the leading towers the model shows the building in a remarkable state of preservation, just as it was when Mr. Vincent was there. It is hard to realize that that was once the capitol of a section of country that teemed with an active and energetic people, now nothing remains but a crumbling monument of the vast power and wealth of a nation apparently now forgotten. Aside from its immensity it is a marvel of architectural skill, and this model has caused these stupendous ruins to be known by many who would otherwise have regarded them as a myth or the vaporing of some fanciful traveler; he has thus rescued them from oblivion. It was with feelings of awe that I contemplated the outlines of this massive building now buried in the forest, unknown its builder, its legends and history written on its walls in forgotten characters and dedicated to a mysticism by a host of yellow-robed priests whose religion is a species of forgetfulness of which this temple is a true type, crumbling slowly to decay. Nature is slowly spreading a network of vines and shrubbery over it, bushes are springing up where once knelt worshipers and Buddha sits enthroned on a gigantic pedestal alone amidst the desolation, ignored and almost unworshiped, as there are but few to do him reverence save a few cadaverous priests and slaves, living in miserable thatched bamboo huts. And this was once the temple of the East, the capitol of a mighty people, now the forest trees hide all its grandeur from the world and it is only seen by the lone traveler who braves the danger of the jungle to feast his eyes on a scene that has no parallel on our planet, a mighty monument of man's skill, a wonder to all, now a " wreck in ruinous perfection." Absorbed in thought one's memory runs back over the gamut of centuries; from the misty legends of the ages fled was evolved the mighty edifices told of by historians: of Babel's towers, of Baelbec and Palmyra, Troy and Carthage, of Ephesus' proud temple, the Parthenon pride of the Peleopenesus, all dust, each kingly column shattered, while here another Palenque, amid palms and tangled vine and banyan tree, rears its stupendous piles toward heaven, unknown its architect or kingly builder, silent as the sphinx, but massive as the pyramids. The sun of centuries has gilded its spires, the winds have sung requiems through its corridors and for cycles to come it will stand unrivaled as one of the grandest monuments conceived by genius and reared by man, before which the Colosseum shrinks as a work of art and will rank in majestic proportions with the pyramids

VIII.
THE SUPREME PALACE AND ROYAL TEMPLES.

Nowhere can be seen a more unique collection of buildings than those closely grouped together within the palace walls of Siam's capital city, the most important of which is the supreme palace, the residence of His Majesty and his many queens, where he grants audiences to the diplomatic corps and receives distinguished guests, also, the Princes and officials of his realms. The building (as can be seen from the engraving) is very handsome, pure white, built in the French style with a magnificant facade and portico, the roof strictly Siamese, covered with green and gold tiles, so that when the sun shines on them they glow like a mass of gold and emerald, dazzling to the beholder. Leading to the portico, with its tall columns, are massive marble steps, at the base of which are two elephants heavily gilded, about five feet in height, while along the front large windows, heavily draped with yellow damask curtains, look out on the courtyard. The main entrance to the building is through large two leaved teak wood doors, elaborately carved and ornamented, into a spacious anti-chamber, the floor of which is covered with square blocks of white and black marble; the walls of highly polished teak are ornamented with all kinds of weapons, from ancient spears and battle-axes to the most improved repeating rifles. To the left as you enter, up a flight of four marble

The Supreme Palace of the King.

steps, is the reception room of His Majesty, one side of which is supported with massive columns and filled with statuary, bronzes, vases, one pair from Bavaria of massive size; also, a chair manufactured from elephant's tusks carved most artistically, the ceiling magnificently frescoed and the walls decorated with life-sized portraits of the kings of Siam and leading 'men of the Kingdom. Passing through this room you enter a smaller one, the private reception chamber of the King, which is most royally furnished, as is the entire palace, with furniture made expressly for this building in Paris. This room seems to be the receptacle of the many works of art and objects of interest presented to the reigning dynasty, also portraits of the late Queen, the Crown Prince, the Emperor Frederick of Germany and other distinguished personages, an alabaster bust of the present Queen of Italy and a number of magnificently bound albums filled with photographs of notables, one filled exclusively with Americans, embracing General and Mrs. Grant, President Cleveland and wife, Mr. Bayard and others. On the right of the anti-chamber is a corridor leading to the private apartments of the building, while nearly facing the entrance is the door of the grand audience hall or throne room (Pra-ma-ha-pra-sot), a magnificent apartment, containing no furniture, as no one is supposed to sit in the presence of the King while he is standing, the floor covered with a lovely Persian carpet; an immense chandelier is suspended from the ceiling, the walls ornamented with pictures and arms of all kinds. Facing the entrance at the extreme end is a dais surrounded with four steps surmounted with the pagoda-shaped umbrella (sa-wekra-chat), an insignia of royalty, under which the King stands when he gives audience to the Princes and nobles or the diplomatic body when they call upon him. The structure is large and is a perfect poem in stone; it was erected at vast expense by King Chulalongkorn, the palace of his predecessors, adjacent, now being used for state ceremonials and religious purposes. But few persons save those in immediate attendance on His Majesty have the entree of the palace, and his servitors are jealous of the approach of foreigners, the guards at the door scrutinizing every one most closely, and it is only upon special or important business that foreigners are allowed to cross its portals, one or more of the Princes or leading nobles always being in attendance. As a specimen of superb architecture the supreme palace at Bangkok stands unrivaled.

The next building of importance is Wat Phza Keau, the temple of the Emerald idol, or Royal wat, which is the finest in the kingdom, costing an immense sum and nearly fifty years in its erection. It is built similar to other wats, but the workmanship, both interior and exterior, is of a much higher order, evincing great skill on the part of the native artisans. The floor is laid with brass brick, six inches square, and the walls are covered with well executed paintings, illustrative of the life and adventures of Buddha; the ceiling is a mass of fretted gold, from which hang a number of magnificent chandeliers, sparkling like diamonds when the light falls upon them, and casting a glory on the high altar that is situated near one end of the room. This altar is about sixty feet in height, pyramidal in shape and surmounted by the Emerald idol, from which the wat takes its name, an image of Buddha twelve inches

Wat Pheree Keo, or Temple of the Emerald Idol.

high and eight in width, in a sitting position. It has the appearance of having been carved out of an emerald, but close observers assure me that it is of jade stone; its collar and hair is of the purest gold, and while the metal was in a molten state rare jewels were poured into it, diamonds, sapphires, rubies, topazes, amethysts, onyxes, crystals, and emeralds, which were blended in such proportions as to enhance its value to the greatest extent and thus render it an object of adoration, akin to the well-known lines,

> "A cross she wore
> That Jews might kiss or infidels adore."

On each side of the altar is a statue of Buddha over six feet in height, heavily plated, with raised hands, palms turned out, and in the palm of each hand and on the fingers are diamonds and other jewels of rare value while, as may be seen from the engraving, are smaller statues of the great teacher, many of them of solid gold and silver, presents from Kings and Princes; also silver and gold trees, royal umbrellas, rare vases filled with golden flowers, and a myriad of other things that have been presented by votaries as offerings to the representative of the founder of their religion valued at about $5,000,000. The origin of the emerald idol is legendary and partakes somewhat of the miraculous. Many years since the lightning struck a Burmese temple and completely demolished it. In searching among the ruins a priest was startled by a gleam of light beneath a mass of rubbish, and on clearing it away the image was unearthed and shone with undimmed glory. It was immediately placed in another temple and since then regarded with great reverence. During one of the many wars that have occurred between the Burmese and Siamese the idol fell into the hands of its present owners and this magnificent wat was erected as a fit place for its final abode. The large square pillars of this gorgeous temple are ornamented in an arabesque of mother of pearl and the balusters that lead to the portico are large carved serpents with three heads, the windows and doors are massive and elaborately carved. In this wat the King worships and it is here that his nobles assemble and drink the water of allegiance and subscribe to a most blood-curdling oath that they will ever prove faithful to His Majesty under the severest penalties here and hereafter. In the court surrounding the wat are a number of marble statues of persons and nondescripts, among them one supposed to be Peter, one of the Apostles; another of Ceres, the Grecian goddess of agriculture.

There are quite a cluster of buildings around the royal wat, near it a temple that is considered one of the handsomest buildings in the world, which was commenced by the founder of the present dynasty and completed by the present king, requiring nearly one hundred years to build. It is a mass of mother of pearl inlaid with precious metals in arabesque, while the inside walls are studded over with small mirrors and precious stones inserted in the plaster which glitter like so many gems, the doors, walls and ceiling a marvelous mosaic, in the center a magnificent altar, over which hangs a most elaborate chandelier. The history of Siam and the travels of Buddha are painted on the walls of the corridor leading to the wat in grotesque but brilliant coloring, not obscene like many paintings in India, while surrounding it are a number of heavily gilt images, large as life, with roosters' tails and feet, peacocks, eagles, monkeys, etc., and on each side of the four black marble steps that lead to this temple is the representation of a dragon with three women's heads, the heads forming the ornament at the base of the steps, while around the court, which is paved with black and white marble tiles, is about fifty marble statues of the various nationalities and grotesque figures, some of them uncouth. Adjacent to this wat is a small pagoda in which is a massive pyramidal cabinet, a mosaic of mother of pearl and ebony, the receptacle of the sacred books of Buddha. The floor of this room is covered with a carpet of woven silver, but the attendants, with the indolence that seems to belong to this people, have allowed it to become so filthy that one has to rub his foot over it to see that it is made of silver. Immediately opposite is the golden pagoda, bell-shaped, about sixty feet in height, covered from base to summit with small tiles, one inch square, heavily plated with gold, which causes the building to glow like a mass of burnished metal. It is entered by three doors, and in the center is a smaller pagoda, similar to the large one, heavily gilt, in which is deposited some of the relics of Buddha, supposed relics, as the captain of the guard assured me; the walls are covered with angels, well painted, and the whole is as unique as it is beautiful. Near this is a pagoda, built of porcelain, the receptacle of the gold urns that contain the ashes of the royal family of Siam. It is the most elaborate building in the palace grounds, built of tiles of various colors, representing birds, animals, flowers and foliage, the whole surmounted with a handsome bouquet of lotus blossoms. This building is sealed from the prying eye of the public. In a square close by is a model of the great temple of Angkor, the most collossal ruins in Asia, which I have spoken of elsewhere.

Surrounding these wats is a high wall with several portals, the inside of which is converted into a corridor, and on its walls are depicted quite artistically many of the superstitions and legends of this land of the lotus. The courts are all paved with black and white marble, and on the inside of each entrance are two large wooden statues, about twelve feet high, hideous old fellows, ostensibly the Gog and Magog of Siam. Foreigners have but little trouble in visiting these temples as a tical (sixty cents) is the open sesame, and there is always some one at the gate to show strangers around. In the royal wat, in the large show cases, can be seen rare treasures, dishes full of uncut stones, robes in which are woven rubies, emeralds, sapphires and diamonds, cloth of woven gold and other articles of rare value, computed by some to be worth millions of dollars. Salas and other small buildings are scattered over the ground, and with their brilliant tiles and ornaments make this spot a scene of oriental enchantment unlike any other place on the globe. I have spent many hours there, and each time I left it more and more impressed with its beauty and grandeur; words are inadequate to do it justice. On some of the wats are hung small bells, brass lotus leaves, which, as the wind blows them back and forth, make weird music that lend additional enchantment to the scene. But few priests are found about these buildings, and what seemed strange was to notice many of the servitors lounging on the porticos and playing Siamese games for money; playing with dice as well as with cards; but the most popular game seems to be to pile up a lot of ats, similar to our pennies, in a small ring and then by throwing another knock as many as possible out of the ring. Men, women and children gamble, from playing marbles to chicken fighting, and there is no village too small not to have its cockpit.

The other portion of the palace grounds is filled with various buildings, the Mint, Foreign Minister's palace, Courts of Justice (?), Royal Library, which contains some very valuable books of the western nations, with a large collection of Indian works and manuscripts and Siamese literature; residences of nobles and servitors of the King and Queens, numbering about five thousand persons; barracks for the guards, and the stables for the white, elephants, a place that always attracts the attention of foreigners, and once seen, all the romance that travelers have woven around these peculiar animals fade away and one realizes the truth of Falstaff's assertion, "Lord, how this world is given to lying."

The animals are kept in a large building, each having a room for itself, and are attended by a keeper. The rooms have no ornaments, are filthy, and the animals are not white, but a dirty coffee color, and no one seems to hold them in special reverence. For an at, the keeper will make the royal beast throw up his trunk and salute you. There were four elephants in the stable, and they are undoubtedly albinos, the word white being a misnomer. The assertion that the Siamese adore them and that they are fed off of gold salvers by Princes on bended knee is a traveler's tale, which no doubt grew out of the fact that they are held in reverence from the supposition that Buddha, in one of his many metamorphoses, through millions of years, must necessarily delight to abide for some time in the grand incarnation of purity which is represented by the white elephant. The priests teach that there is no spot throughout the universe that is not at some time visited by the great teacher in his peregrinations, whose every step is toward purity, and as the elephant is the largest of created animals and white being the emblem of purity the chances are that, should he dwell for a time in one of God's creatures, he would remain longer in one of that color than any other, hence in the possession of this sacred creature they may secure the presence of Buddha himself. Sometimes the elephant is regarded as an oracle, as he is one of the most intelligent of beasts, and the Siamese whisper their secrets in his ear and request an answer by some movement or sign; as wise a plan as appealing to the oracles of old. The last elephant admitted to the royal stables was caught about ten years since and brought to Bangkok in regal style, where he was received by the King and Court as if he had been some potentate on a visit to royalty. He was carefully groomed and around his body was placed a broad belt flashing with jewels. After much ceremony he was conducted in grand procession with music, flags and a body-guard to his stable, where he is now well cared for and only makes his appearance with the other white elephants on state occasions. From time immemorial the elephant has been the oriflamme of Siam, everything pertaining to the kingdom is stamped with his portraiture; it is the badge of distinction and shows grandly on the Siamese flag, the white elephant on a crimson ground, it is a part of the coat of arms of royalty. Like our eagle, it is an important appendage of state, nothing less, nothing more. When the father of the present King ascended the throne he did much to disabuse the minds of his people of many of their superstitions; in fact he founded a new school of Buddhism which is being followed out by King Chulalongkorn, and the reverence formerly paid to the white elephant has faded away before the blaze of enlightenment of the present age. Much of this is due to the fact that the deceased King was a fair English scholar and a good astronomer; he encouraged the missionaries and others that came to Siam in an early day, not fearing that they would make any inroads on the religious beliefs of his people, and his intercourse with the consuls and merchants from other lands made him liberal in his views and progressive. Fifty years since Siam was a sealed book, to-day it is open to be seen by all, and its fertile valleys and emerald plains yield ample crops to the husbandman, and its rice and other products are eagerly sought for and give employment to a vast fleet of vessels that daily fret the waters of the Menam. All of the modern inventions have been introduced into the Kingdom, and each year marks a new departure over the highway of nations that must redound to the glory of the King and the prosperity of his people. American and European doctors have charge of his hospitals, an American is at the head of his University, an American ran his lines of telegraph through jungles that no other white man had ever penetrated, and in the American mission schools are now being educated the sons and daughters of the leading Princes and Governors, while the missionaries are received and treated with a cordiality that must be pleasing to those soldiers of the cross who have thus gone into exile for the purpose of the carrying out of the great work of Christianity.

Imperial Altar and Emerald Idol.

IX.
PECULIAR MANNER OF SCARING AWAY THE DRAGON.

While lying on the river at Petchaburee, an inland city, about seventy-five miles from Bangkok, I was awakened by the most hideous noise; the firing of guns, shooting of crackers, beating of drums and tom-toms and the shouting of a vast multitude. Looking out of the window of my boat a weird spectacle presented itself to my vision. The whole place was lighted up by huge bonfires on the banks of the stream and the air full of glittering rockets. Calling my kavass I inquired what was the occasion of the hubbub? With his usual vye, touching the points of his fingers together and raising them up on a level with his breast, he replied, "Your Excellency, the great dragon has the moon swallowed up." Having heard that the natives thus celebrated the approach of an eclipse, I stepped ashore and mingled with the crowd which was made up of all classes, old and young, with a large sprinkling of yellow-robed priests who were as active as the others in keeping up the unearthly din. It was a lovely morn, the southern cross hung like a gleaming jewel in the upper deep, gentle zephyrs perfumed by myriads of flowers fanned the brow and waved the feathery bamboo as gently as the coquette her fan, the round orbed moon, a bright silver disk, was suspended in the western heavens, burnished like the shield of Achilles, while all around burned the many fires which shed a glare on the crowd of half-clad adults and naked children. A shadow had just fallen upon the surface of the queen of night, slowly it spread over it until the face of the great luminary was covered, and it hung in the cloudless heavens an orb of roseate hue, its radiance all gone. Then the noise became terrific, the reports of guns and crackers were almost deafening, which increased as a gleam of silver tinged the outer rim of the dimmed goddess. Slowly the shadow passed away, the light growing brighter and brighter, the great dragon Asura Rahu, that had attempted to swallow the moon, had been driven away and it again shone in all of its brilliancy, but soon faded away before the corruscations of the coming dawn. It was a scene photographed on the memory worthy the pen of an Arnold or the pencil of a Titian: the ruddy glow of the flowing water, the multitude upon the river banks with its white houses embowered in dense foliage, the frantic efforts of the people as the shadow drifted across the disk of the moon and fell across the landscape and the glare of the fires that lighted up the immediate surroundings, a spectacle that could be witnessed nowhere else save in the interior of Siam, where no white man dwells and the native clings to his superstitions as religiously as did his forefathers ere the present dynasty ascended the throne of this kingdom. It was early morn ere peace reigned once more, and when the sun rose amid the pearliest of skies its beams lit up a lovely scene, gilding the spires of the wats and roofs of the palaces; business had resumed its sway, the fisherman was hawking fish, the fruitier his fruit, the merchant had displayed his goods on the counter, the priests were gathering their food into their rice pots for the day's provender and the moon and the dragon seemed to have passed into oblivion, the only evidence of the nocturnal saturnalia being the smoking pyres that had been lighted and the exploded red and white crackers that strewed the ground.

Upon inquiry I learned that it has been the custom of the people of Siam from time immemorial to thus drive off the dragon Rahu and the legend runs thus: According to Buddhistic belief, in a former state of transmigration the sun (Athil), the moon (Chen), and the Asura Rahu were brothers. They gave alms to the priests, the first on a golden salver, the second in a silver vase and the latter in a black pot, which led to their all being born as angels; the first as angel of the sun, second as angel of the moon and the third as the angel Rahu. The latter, who had been on bad terms with his brethren, sinned and became one of the Asuras, or fallen angels, who were expelled from heaven by Indra, king of the lower heavens, in a drunken state and driven to a region underneath Meru, the central mountain, from which they make continual sallies, vainly attempting to regain their former abode, the most powerful of which is Asura Rahu, who is always known to be abroad by his attempting to swallow the sun and moon, his brothers, which occasions the eclipses; but the rapid motion of these bodies make it impossible for him to hold them for any length of time. At some great Siamese ceremonies one may see an enormous serpent or dragon, made of lamps, ingeniously joined together, and borne about by a number of men, intended to represent Rahu chasing the moon. Conversing with some of the leading Princes in regard to this legend, they smilingly remarked that the ceremonies now attending the eclipse was but the mere keeping up of an ancient custom, like the western nations hanging up stockings for St. Nicholas to fill with sweets; that the belief in the dragon Rahu of Siam was but a myth, as was that of St. George and the dragon of Britain.

X.
THE WATER RITE.

Among the many religious ceremonies of the Siamese none is more peculiar or more closely observed than the water (nom) rite, which takes place during the month of April, about the time the mangoes are ripe. Then the natives assemble at the nearest wat close to the shore of the gulf or by the banks of a river and build myriads of sand piles about eighteen inches high, shaped like a bee-hive, which they decorate with flowers and small paper flags of various colors, then sprinkle them with water highly perfumed. I have frequently seen hundreds of men, women and children, with a number of priests mingled with the crowd, making these mounds. After the sprinkling is over each person fills a cocoanut shell with water which they throw over one another amid shouts of laughter; the half-clad lithe-limbed maids enjoying the fun immensely as the young men chase them backward and forward over the beach, when, to escape, they frequently plunge into the tide and swim out into the water, diving like mermaids, the sport ending in a ducking match. When tired out they swim back to the beach, amid the laughter of the spectators.

Water rites enter largely into the ceremonies of the Siamese, and ablution is encouraged as one of the essentials of health. While rowing or sailing on the Menam, numbers of persons of both sexes, can be seen swimming in the river or bathing in the canals scantily clad, with nothing on but a cloth wrapped about the loins, about the size of a Turkish towel, while the children are as nature fashioned them and their merry laugh rings out merrily as a boat glides by. The Siamese seem to be as much at home in the water as on land, many live in boats or floating houses and learn to swim at an early age. It seems strange to them that any one can not swim; this, together with their belief that it is unlucky to save a person from drowning, the rescued ones' sins being unloaded on the rescuer and his future peccadilloes, also, credited against him, has led to the loss of several foreigners who could have been saved had the natives gone to their assistance, paying no heed to their cries for help. The current of the Menam at Bangkok is swift and full of eddies, and a person that is so unfortunate as to be overturned out of a boat or fall overboard from a vessel and can not swim is soon drawn under the surface, and several days elapses ere the body is found, miles away from where the treacherous stream swallowed it up, a victim, as the natives assert, to the genii of the waters.

Many of the Buddhist ceremonies consist in the pouring of water, and are frequently mentioned in Buddhistic literature. In the life of Buddha, when the village maiden Suchada is about to present him, whom she believes to be an angel, an offering that she had prepared especially for him, she, as a preliminary, poured water perfumed by the mogra, sweetest of India's blossoms, and other flowers on his hands, and when the King of Magodho tendered Weloowon, his pleasure garden, to the great teacher as a site for a monastery, he ratified the gift by pouring water from a jeweled shell on the earth, and as the glittering drops fell Buddah blessed the ground which rendered it sacred. Among the Hindoos, from whom the Siamese have derived many of their customs, the ceremonies for sacrifices, marriages, hair cutting, cremations, etc., consists in part of sprinkling and pouring of water. The priests pour water, that has been blessed, over the persons of the sick that are brought to the wats to be cared for, and frequently fill their mouths full of water and blow it in the face of the invalid and on the part of the body that is affected.

When the present King of Siam, Chulalongkorn I., was crowned, the pouring of water was one of the essentials of the coronation and not neglected in the elaborate ceremonies. Henry Alabaster, interpreter at the English Legation and afterwards councellor to His Majesty, briefly records the ceremonials upon that occasion, from which I condense the following:

The King, robed in white, placed himself in a gold bath, under a canopy from which a shower of water (collected, I was told, from all parts of the kingdom) fell upon him, and for about fifteen minutes afterwards His Majesty sat shivering, whilst the chief Brahmin and the highest princes and ladies poured over him each a bowl of water. This ceremony was conducted in an inner court of the palace, in presence of a very small and selected audience, and no foreigner had been allowed to witness it until this occasion, when the courtesy of His Grace the Regent, breaking through customary prejudice, procured the honor for a few. After the bath, the King changed his dress for one more gorgeous, and proceeded to a hall, where, in presence of a larger but still select audience, he sat on an octagonal throne, and changing his seat eight times, to face the eight points of the compass, repeated each time the formula called the coronation oath. He then marched along the center of the hall, and, taking his seat at the end opposite to that where the octagonal throne was placed, he was invested with the crown, sword, and other insignia of royalty. A variety of war-like weapons were then presented to His Majesty, each one of which, having been touched by him, was returned to its place.

His Majesty then received a bowl full of small gold and silver flowers to distribute as a token of his royal desire to rain prosperity on the recipients.

His Majesty first handed some of these flowers to the leading princes and ministers, and then turned to give some to the foreigners present, and what remained were scattered among the audience.

After this ceremony the King rested for a short while, and then, in one of the great audience halls of the palace, gave audience to the whole body of nobles. Then each leading chief, each head of a department, in turn or order of rank resigned into the new King's hands the rank and power conferred on him by the King who had passed away, and the new King in a few, short, graceful words re-conferred all upon him.

To this audience the Siamese admitted many foreigners, who, for want of space, had been debarred from the honor and pleasure of participating in the preceding ceremonies.

When the Crown Prince was declared heir apparent to the throne a large pavilion was built out into the Menam (see engraving), at a vast expense, in the center of which was a pool, about twelve feet square, lined with marble and having silver rails to lead to the water, into which the Prince descended and was received by H. R. H. Prince Ong Noi, brother of the King, who poured the water of the majestic river over the Prince from a cup flashing with jewels, after he had immersed him, the leading astrologers having fixed the time for the ceremony, the bishops, abbots and priests meanwhile chanting their litany and quoting passages from the works of the great teacher, in the Pali language. As the water fell upon the bowed head of the Prince the ordinance from the forts and shipping thundered forth salute after salute and ten thousand soldiers and mariners, who were stationed in and around the pavilion and palace, discharged their muskets and rifles, making the welkin ring with their reverberations, and the immense crowd that lined the river banks and filled to suffocation the avenues that led to the palace knew that the Prince had undergone the ordinance of baptism. This grand oriental ceremony lasted three days, and in commemoration thereof the King caused medals to be struck of gold, silver and bronze, which he presented to the Ministers and Consular body and the Princes and nobles as souvenirs of this great event, the most important in the annals of the Kingdom of Siam. While the ceremonies were progressing, tea, coffee, ices, cakes, candied fruits, ginger ale and soda water were handed round to the guests by uniformed servants on silver salvers, many of the cups and plates used being of the rarest porcelain.

XI.

CEREMONIES OF HAIR CUTTING.

When a Siamese child, boy or girl, has reached a suitable age, the time for which is fixed by the soothsayer, or astrologer who casts its horoscope, ranging from nine, eleven, thirteen or fifteen years; the even numbers being avoided as unlucky—no more superstitious people exist than the Siamese—the coming of age, as it is termed, is celebrated with the most elaborate ceremonies called So-kan or "hair cutting." Prior to this time the head of the child is shaved with the exception of a tuft or top-knot, which is allowed to grow on the crown of the head until the time comes when the child, if a boy, is to be emancipated from female control in the harem, or, if a girl, as soon as she reaches the years of puberty. This custom is observed by the nobles or well-to-do Siamese and by most of the people. When the time has been designated for shaving off the top-knot the palace or residence of the parents is placed in perfect order, festooned with flags of every color, garlanded with flowers, priests engaged to chant their litany, bands of music employed who day and night keep up a hideous din, a splendid repast spread for the family and guests and rare presents made to the child for his or her future benefit; fire-works of all kinds are let off and the air is filled with bombs and rockets, golden showers and silver trees dazzle the eye and a bamboo torpedo, called the "howling elephant," which, while burning, makes a most mournful noise like one of those huge beasts in pain. At times, during the ceremony, one can imagine himself in pandemonium; on most occasions the ceremony lasts three days; but when a "Chow Fa," the Crown Prince and heir apparent to the throne, born of royal parents on both sides, his mother being half-sister to the King, which makes him a celestial Prince, has his hair cut, as was the case with the present son of the King, the rites are more elaborate and splendid, lasting one week. For months before the day set by the astrologers preparations had been going on on a grand scale for the coming ceremony; a sacred mountain, over one hundred feet high, was erected in the outer palace yard and from its summit the Prince descended and was received by the King and the priests, typical of a passage in the life of Buddha, who, after fasting on a mountain, descended and was received by his followers who had patiently awaited his coming. Vast expenditures of the resources of the Kingdom were exhausted to do honor to the occasion, which was of the greatest solemnity.

The date of the hair cutting, or "Bai si," as the Siamese term it, was set for the 19th of January, 1891, and the morning, one of unrivaled brilliancy, was ushered in by a royal salute from the vessels in the stream lying in front of the palace and by the various batteries in the forts and on the esplanade. Soon masses of gaily-dressed natives were seen wending their way toward the palace and all that could pressed forward to the entrance and surged through the iron portals of its white walls, then squatting down patiently awaited the commencement of the gorgeous ceremonies that were to convert the young Prince into a full-fledged nobleman, one of the highest grandees, and to eliminate him from his mother's control and to see him shorn of his top-knot. For hours procession after procession passed and repassed along the wide avenues of the palace grounds, each section headed by a leading noble, representing the various tribes that are ruled by Chulalongkorn I., Laos, Mauns, Peguins, Annomites, Cochin Chinese, Malays, etc., each in their peculiar costumes, while at intervals lacon girls, clad in glittering vestments, went through their dances and posturing, which is unlike any other performance of the kind and always attracts the attention of foreigners as well as being pleasing to the natives, the girls being lithe of limb and dressed to represent "nats," or angels, also the Siamese word for a handsome woman. The religious ceremony when the hair was removed was witnessed only by the King, the Princes and the royal family and the higher order of priests, the brother of the King, a leading bishop, officiating. As usual there was the pouring of holy water from a crystal chalice sparkling with gems, the clothing of the Prince in vestments prepared for the occasion, blessing by the bishops and chanting of priests. After the hair was cut the King and all those in attendance were sumptuously feasted and then two standards, called Bai see, were placed in the center of a circle and had the appearance of the Siamese Sawekrachet, or royal umbrella, one of the five insignia of royalty peculiar to the reigning dynasty. These standards are about eight feet high, having from three to five stories, the staff fixed on a wooden pedestal, light and portable. The different stories of the Bai see are made of plantain leaves interspersed with gilt and silvered paper. Each story is circular in form with a flaring and deeply serrated brim and has a flat bottom; within these receptacles are placed a little cooked rice, called khao khwan, a small quantity of cakes, some sweet scented oil, a handful of fragrant flowers, young cocoanuts and plantains; other edibles, also, are arranged around the Bai see and a tastefully arranged bouquet adorns the topmost story of each. A procession is then formed of the princes, noblemen and others, who march around the standards nine times. There are also three golden candlesticks, holding each a large wax candle, which, being lighted, are carried by different princes and other dignitaries in the procession and handed from one to the other as they move around the standards; meanwhile the royal son or daughter, for whom the festival is held, is seated on a kind of throne between the two standards, arrayed in splendid costume. The persons holding the candles wave them when passing in front of the Prince, and fan the smoke of them into his face, as the influence of this has much to do in conferring the desired blessing upon him. This moving of the procession around the Bai sees is denomiated Weean t'eean, literally marching round with candles. There are nine of these evolutions for a child of a king, and five for a child, of a subject.

This being finished, one of the old and most respectable Brahmins then takes a little of the rice from the Bai see, and sprinkling upon it a small quantity of cocoa-nut water gave the Prince a spoonful of it. Then dipping his finger into the sweet-scented oil, and this again into the fragrant flour, he applies it from the point of his finger to the right foot of the Prince in three places. To the children of the people, this mixture is always applied to the head; but to a child of a king it would be improper, because his head is accounted too sacred to be touched in that way. This ceremony having been completed a revered doctor of divinity addresses the child, in words said to be suited to invite the k'won of the prince—that is his courage and pluck, —to a permanent abode in his bosom, so that he shall spend his days without agitation or fear, as it becometh a man whom the fates have determined shall pass through this world of conflict.

Siamese of the middle classes nearly all follow essentially the same custom for their children in regard to the puberal hair-cutting as the King does for his. Their festivals are of course much less imposing, and are continued only a part of two days, and sometimes only one. The presents made to their children on these occasions would not often exceed eighty ticals from a single person, and very rarely be as small as four. A millionaire might ape the King very nearly by sending out invitations to hundreds of his wealthy friends, to attend the hair-cutting of a son. Few of them would be absent, and such not without some valuable silver substitute, and few if any of those wealthy attendants would be likely to think of giving less than one catty, that is, eighty ticals each. But this custom of making presents is but a system of exchange, in its operation among the subjects of Siam; because every man favored with the gift of children has the privilege of making a hair-cutting festival for each one of them, and will probably receive as much in presents for his children on such occasions as he ever gave away to others for the same purposes.

The children of the lower classes who are not able

Wat Sa-Ket, or Gold Mountain.

to bear the expense of a public hair-cutting for their children take them to a Buddhist temple at the proper time in life, and have the priest shave off the tuft with some little accompanying religious exercises ; and this is accounted far better for the child than to have it cut in any common way.

During the ceremony the Crown Prince was the recipient of costly presents which he received with the stoicism of a noble-born Asiatic whose forefathers had ruled Siam for over one hundred years, and he looked, as he is, the worthy son of one of the most liberal as well as brainiest men that now sits upon a throne, the virtual head of the Buddhist church. All of the feudatory nobles of His Majesty were assembled in Bangkok with their retainers, among them the Rajah of Kedah, the Sultans of Patani, Kelanton and Tringanu, the governors of Singora, Renong and Kroh, as well as those of other provinces with their retainers, all of whom bore gifts consisting of silver and gold trees, ornaments, jewelry, boxes, rare fabrics, jeweled swords and in some instances large rolls of dollars and sacks of ticals the coin of the realm. At the conclusion of the ceremonies the King, now that the Prince was removed from the influence of the women of the palace, set apart a palace for his residence which will be occupied by him and his retainers and Mr. Morant, his English tutor. It is the intention of His Majesty to make his heir realize the duties of the position. Though but thirteen year of age the Prince shows marked ability; he is a good English scholar, highly advanced in mathematics, thoroughly conversant with the literature of Siam and India and bids fair, should nothing intervene, to make a monarch as wise and just as his father, who is worshiped by his people for the liberal measures that he has carried out for their amelioration and the progressive spirit manifested in his efforts to encourage education, establish hospitals and railroads. Since he ascended the throne prosperity has smiled upon the emerald plains and verdant valleys of this sun-kissed land which can well be called the Pearl of Asia, and he has linked his Kingdom to the outside world by telegraphic lines, while his postal system is the equal of any of the Western nations. All that the Siamese ask is to be let alone, they can care for themselves, and the baneful shadow of British greed and French spoliation once removed Siam would step rapidly to the front as one of the most progressive nations of the far East, a benefit not only to its people, but the world at large.

XII.
WAT-SA-KET AND THE SIAMESE GOLGOTHA.

One of the first places visited by tourists while in Bangkok is Wat-Sa-Ket, a temple erected on a vast mound of brick at the intersection of two of the large klangs or canals that permeate the city. It is about two hundred and fifty feet in height, built about sixty years ago, in the form of a bell with a circumference of one thousand feet, and is surmounted by a temple that can be seen from any part of the city, access to which is by a flight of stone steps in front, or by a circular roadway that winds round it from base to summit. This mound was raised at great expense so much so as to give it the name of the gold mountain and is the only elevation in the city, Bangkok being laid out on a level plain, the delta of the Menam, and from its lofty summit the city, embowered in foliage, stretches away for miles; the river, in the distance, like a ribbon of silver, flowing on to the gulf, and the spires and roofs of the wats and palaces shining like burnished gold in the sun, as most of them are covered with a gold tile that reflects the beams of the day god most brilliantly. The eye never grows weary looking over this lovely landscape dotted with feathery bamboo, the deep emerald banyan tree and palms and foliage of all kinds, a scene of oriental beauty unique and worthy a visit to the orient to witness. Within the boundaries of Wat-Sa-Ket are a number of other temples and the residences of priests. A portion of the temple grounds is set off for purposes of cremation and a large court-yard adjacent is used by the custodian of the temple as a receptacle for the bodies of criminals and paupers, which are taken thither and exposed to the dogs and vultures, who soon dispose of the remains, and bird and beast fight over their horrid feast while the stench is intolerable. Looking on at this cannibalistic repast one can realize the truth of Byron's description of the desecration of the dead in his poem of "The Siege of Corinth."

In company with some friends, who had heard of this modern Golgotha, we proceeded in a boat to the temple and were ushered through the dark and heavy gateway of the building by a yellow-robed priest who regretted that he had no bodies that day to feed to the vultures, which were roosting on the roofs and trees waiting for their daily feast. As we did not feel like returning without looking at the spot where common humanity was thus primitively disposed of, we requested to be shown the place, and were soon ushered into the yard which was about seventy-five feet wide and one hundred feet in length, with a bamboo building at one end. While examining the place we noticed an old woman neatly dressed lying upon the ground, apparently asleep, and while we were wondering what she could be doing a vulture tripped up and pecked out one of her eyes which it swallowed with great gusto, then a mangy, dun-colored pariah dog crept up and bit a piece out of the cheek of the corpse and soon the air was full of the foul birds as was the ground with dogs, all eager to partake of the hideous feast, literally covering the body, fighting for the flesh and the bones, and in forty-five minutes nothing was left but a few of the largest bones and the soles of the feet, the whole body having disappeared within the maws of these hideous ghouls. When the repast was ended the vultures lazily flew up to their perch and sleepily awaited another human feast. It was with feelings of loathing that the party left the foul enclosure wondering why so progressive a monarch as King Chulalongkorn did not put a stop to this beastly way of disposing of the pauper dead of his capital city, notwithstanding it has been the custom of the country for untold years. In a lot adjacent to this Golgotha were large piles of human remains in boxes in all stages of decomposition awaiting to be cremated, their relatives not having raised a sufficient amount to pay the expense of the ceremony, about five dollars; but having paid some on account the bodies were kept waiting for the remainder and then were converted into ashes. To say that the air was rank with the odors of putrefaction would be drawing it mild; camphor was lavishly used and for hours ones nostrils seemed to be affected by the villainous smell. One visit to this place is satisfactory and lasting, and it would take the weird penciling of a Doré to portray its horrors: the old gray-haired woman, the sable birds and dun-colored curs fighting over what had once been a mother, with yellow-robed priests standing by, while in the bamboo house were some of her children listening to the teaching of Buddha as they were drawled out by one of the many priests who loiter around this place of horrors. These exposures of the remains are of frequent occurrence, but most of the Siamese are properly cremated; frequently large sums are expended on these ceremonies and are conducted with great pomp and ceremony, the solemnities being kept up for three days.

It is the custom of the country to keep the remains encased in coffins after they are embalmed for six months and then have the cremations. Prior to the burning and while the body lies in state all kinds of amusements are held at the residence of the deceased, fire-works are shot off at night, feasting of the family and slaves, presents are made to the priests and the spirit of the departed and kindred spirits are cared for by a sumptuous repast being daily spread for them, as it is the belief of the relatives and friends that his or her spirit is hovering round and mindful of what is being done in its behalf; hence lacons are held, musicians are employed and as long as the body is not consumed a perfect saturnalia is kept up and large sums are thus expended which are encouraged by the priests who are not forgotten. Immediately opposite the Legation grounds is the palace of a high noble who had passed his allotted time on earth and passed over the invisible river; his remains were encased in a large rosewood coffin, after which it was filled with spices and oils, covered with costly silks, then encased in a teak wood box and the whole carefully sealed up. After being painted and gilded it was placed on a stand and for six months it was watched daily by a number of priests, and each night lacons were held and fireworks let off while bands of music kept up a din till midnight; then it was removed in a handsome barge and taken to one of the leading wats for cremation and placed on an altar built for the occasion, covered with a small temple made of palms and ornamented with flags and colored cloths, draped around with handsome curtains which were drawn back so that the coffin could be seen. When everything was ready a high nobleman stepped forward with a small lantern which he brought with him from the king's palace and lighted the pyre; the lantern contained the holy fire that is never allowed to go out and is only used upon occasions of this kind and then by the special favor of His Majesty. While the body was burning all kinds of lacons and Chinese performances were going on, tea and sweets were passed around among the invited guests and a large banquet spread so that all who desired could go and partake thereof; fireworks were let off, and the bursting of bombs was almost deafening. This was kept up till midnight, and then the immense crowd commenced to drift homeward; the body had been consumed, and when morning came the ashes that were left were carefully collected and placed in a small gold urn and carefully stowed away among the valuables of the family. At intervals while the burning was going on men stationed in various portions of the ground flung handfuls of small limes, in which were inserted a fuang or salung, small silver coins, among the crowd, who scrambled for them in the liveliest manner. The scene was weird in the extreme, and the lower order of the Siamese always welcome the cremation ceremonies of a noble with exceeding joy, an evening of unrestrained enjoyment. Death to them seemingly has no terror, as they look upon their passing away as the translation into some other sphere, and they accept the inevitable as calmly as if unrobing for their nightly slumber; it is a part of their religion, a belief that is hoary with age. That is one thing that the missionaries have to contend with, the indifference manifested by these people in regard to the hereafter; they regard the to come beyond the grave as merely a state of transition that covers millions of years before they can pass through the seven heavens, as is taught by the priests before they can enter Nirvana. They believe that the spirits of the dead are always about them, and they are thus induced to perform meritorious acts to appease or please them, such as furnishing robes for the priests, giving food to the needy, building wats and making donations for charitable purposes. This is called merit making. Buddhists believe that every act, word or thought has its consequence which will appear sooner or later in the present or in some future state. Evil acts will produce evil consequences, that is, may cause misfortune in this world, or an evil birth in hell, or as an animal in some future existence. Good acts will produce good effects; prosperity in this world or birth in heaven, or a higher position in the world in some future state. There is no God who judges the acts and doings of mortals in regard to the awards of recompense and punishment; it is simply the inevitable effect of Kam (consequence) which works out its own results. Kam literally means that which is not foreseen as is illustrated in Buddhistic writings by the story of Phra Maha Chanok, who escaping from a shipwreck fell asleep in the woods and on awaking was received with royal honors and made king of the country. This happening without any foreknowledge on his part is classed with the Kam of the meritorious kind. The demeritorious is when an innocent one is punished for another's crime, for instance where when two men were in bathing and a crocodile devoured the one and left the other; also, when two men were equally liable to execution the judge condemned one and set the other free. Merit or demerit will cause a tendency of the spirit or soul in one direction some times to as many as seven births and deaths, which will be followed by a relapse in the opposite direction for six, five or less times in accordance with the demerits which sometimes result from the slaughter of a single ant. The writings of Kam are voluminous and like most of the literature of the East tedious and frequently irrelevant, made up of legends and fables. To students of Buddhist mythology it may be interesting, but it would tire the general reader who doubtless cares very little concerning the mysticisms of these people.

XIII.

A SIAMESE EXECUTION.

It is seldom that the Siamese resort to capital punishment, most violations of law being punished by imprisonment, the major crimes by incarceration for life, such as murder and treason. As soon as sentenced the prisoner is manacled and turned over to some Prince or noble, whose slave he becomes, and he is then placed under a task master who proceeds to get all the work out of him possible. Under his control the doomed one has a foretaste of hades ere he shuffles off his mortal coil. The life prisoner has a chain fastened to a steel ring riveted around his neck, and this is never taken off till death claims him; the chain from his neck is also riveted around his ankles, and the clanking of these fetters can be heard in every part of Bangkok, as long lines of prisoners are daily driven through the streets to their work. The other prisoners are chained around the ankles with a chain about eighteen inches in length. Any one owning slaves has a right to put them in chains on the most frivolous pretext, and I was assured by a gentleman who had traveled through the interior of the country that he saw large numbers thus manacled, male and female. The prisoners in Bangkok are put to work in the gardens of the nobles, sawing teak wood logs into boards, working on the streets and cleaning out canals, in fact all kind of hard work, and at night men and women are locked up together in close rooms and treated

Courtyard of Bangkok's Golgotha.

as if they had lost all the rights of humanity. Should they desire any favor they can only obtain it through the greed of the guards who extort from them all the money that their relatives can give for this purpose, frequently holding back the small amount of rice doled out for their food till they are on the verge of starvation so as to induce their friends to come to their assistance. The prisons, I have been informed by those who have entered them, are filthy in the extreme; the stench intolerable. Within the past year His Majesty has attempted to alleviate the suffering of the prisoners and has had erected a large prison house in accordance with modern methods, but so long as a prisoner is looked upon as a mere beast and brutal jailors have him in charge but little can be done to benefit his wretched condition. Persons are arrested on the frailest pretexts and knowing the horrors that are in store for them if convicted "see" some one in power who "sees" some one else and if he can raise the requisite number of ticals escapes with a lightened pouch; in fact this state of affairs was so prevalent a couple of years since that a band of dacoits operated openly in Bangkok until their crimes became so bold and flagrant that the attention of the King was called to it and then fourteen of the leaders, whose money had hitherto shielded them, were arrested and tried; the evidence against them was conclusive and they were sentenced to be executed. Every effort was made to save them by their friends, but it availed not, in this instance money was powerless, the King had moved in the matter. That settled it, no one daring to set aside the edict of royalty.

A Siamese execution is a peculiar affair After

sentence of death is pronounced on a prisoner he is confined in jail till the morning of execution and then a bamboo yoke, about a yard in length, is placed around his neck and fastened to a round piece of wood that encloses his wrists, thus keeping the arms stretched out in front of him and with chains on his neck and ankles he is led to a wat in the neighborhood of the execution ground where he is bambooed by the executioner and after prayers by the priests is taken to the spot selected for the purpose where a small bamboo cross is stuck in the ground; the yoke and chain around the neck is then taken off and the prisoner ordered to squat down in front of the cross to which his arms are fastened, he is then made to bend forward with his face toward the ground, in front of him are placed some flowers and a few lighted joss sticks, then one of the attendants takes some mud and plugs up his ears and makes a mark across the back of his neck. All being ready at a signal the executioner enters and as soon as he gets immediately behind the prisoner gives his sword a whirl and bringing it down with full force severs the head from the body, except a small piece of skin which connects it with the torso.

Having a curiosity to witness an execution I attended that of three dacoits, three of the fourteen that had been sentenced, His Majesty having commuted the sentence of eleven to imprisonment for life, a worse punishment than death. After the prisoners had been bambooed they were escorted to the ground by a squad of soldiers and police. Then their chains were stricken off and they were made to seat themselves before the crosses to which they were fastened, mud was then placed in their ears and marks drawn across their

necks. The feeling of the crowd now became intense
and all eagerly awaited the appearance of the executioners. The victims seemed more composed than the
spectators; the head dacoit, a man about fifty years
old, asked for a bogee, a Siamese cigar, which one of the
attendants lighted for him and he smoked it as coolly
as if he felt no terror of the fate that hung over him,
that his stay on this earth was encompassed but by a
few minutes; another, a magnificent young half-
cast Chinaman, smiled placidly and leaned over
and inhaled the perfume of the flowers placed
in front of him, the other evinced some feeling. It was
a strange spectacle to see those men squatting on the
ground with bowed heads inside a cordon of soldiers
and immediately behind them a mass of people eagerly
awaiting the coming of the executioners. In about ten
minutes after the prisoners were brought on the
ground I observed a slight commotion among the crowd
and upon looking up noticed three men enter the circle
dressed in scarlet with gold fringe trimmings on their
coats, each bearing a heavy shining sword; they
advanced dancing and saluting with their weapons
until they were immediately behind the prisoners
when with a sudden whirl they struck, you heard a
simultaneous thud and then saw the blood spurt upward
as three bodies rose upright and fell forward, being
held in place by the crosses. It seems as if death was
instantaneous. As soon as the blows were struck the
executioners disappeared and then a man came forward
with a large knife and severed the small piece of skin
that held the heads to the bodies and stuck them on
small bamboo poles about six feet high. The eyes
opened repeatedly and the jaws closed and opened

as the blood ran out, the faces bleaching nearly white. It was a horrible sight. After impaling the heads the man in charge proceeded to cut off the heels of the dead bodies so as to secure the chains around the ankles, and then the torsos were left on the ground for the dogs and vultures to feast on, but generally the friends of the doomed men wait till night and bear the bodies off, assisted in this by some of the priests, and convey them away for the purpose of cremation. Executions are rare in Bangkok, as the prisoners can be put to better use than executing them; it is only resorted to in such cases as I have mentioned to act as a check on the outlawry that would otherwise exist in a community where money can be used to evade justice and brigandage thus go unpunished. The curse of gambling is the cause of most of the crimes in Siam, which is mainly confined to petty stealing in the cities. In the country the outlaws frequently band together and then they bid defiance to the authorities, and when they are arrested the officials fail to punish them, if the necessary inducements are offered for their release. A reign of terror sometimes exists in and around the small towns in the interior. While at Ratburee a Chinaman told me that he had been for over three years endeavoring to bring to trial some scoundrels who had entered his house and assaulted him, killed his wife and gutted his place. He had them arrested, they were in chains and working for the governor, and that was the end of it. They will thus remain slaves till they die, if they have no one wealthy enough to buy them off, and thus escape the extreme penalty for their crime. Chapters could be written on prison life in this kingdom, of its untold horrors, and still the half would not be told. It is so all over the East, in fact much worse in China, where prisoners are subjected to all kind of torture by their jailers till the last tael is extracted from them, starvation and thirst being the mildest means used. The power of the jailer is absolute and there is no one to stand between him and the code that he lays down for the management of those who are so unfortunate as to fall into his power. In Bangkok the subject of prison reform has been agitated to some purpose by the missionaries and others, and prisoners are now better cared for, and treated with more leniency than in the past; much of this is owing to the fact that His Majesty is looking into matters of this kind, having had his attention called to it.

XIV.

PADDY (RICE) AND ITS CULTIVATION.

Paddy or rice fields are seldom sown in Siam, the plant is raised in beds and then transplanted. They prepare the beds or nurseries, as they term them, by breaking the ground and harrowing it until it is soft, and then irrigating it so that when they sow the seed the bed is in a semi-fluid state. The seed, which has been sprouted, is then sown so that it will come up as thick as possible. This part of the work is always done by the women, during the latter part of May or early in June. Being sprouted and sown in the mud the seed does not need to be covered and is called kla, the sowing of it they term tok kla, sowing the sprouted seed. If the water is muddy on the bed, and the seed is covered by it, it will rot, but if it is clear so that the sun can shine on it it will grow. When there is too much water on the bed the women and children bail it out by means of the common well sweep and bucket, and sometimes by a scoop or basket spread over with pitch and attached to a pole; when the patch needs irrigation they resort to the same means to throw the water back from the canal or pond near by. The plants are thus kept flourishing so as to be transplanted at the first favorable moment, which is generally during the heavy rains of June, August or September. When the plants are between twelve and twenty inches in length they are ready for use, if less than twelve inches they would be liable to be covered with water, if more than twenty inches they would be top heavy and fall down. The fields for planting are prepared the same as the nursery beds, plowed and harrowed. When the wet season has flooded the fields and the water is standing from six to ten inches deep, then the whole population turn out and commence transplanting, called dam na, to dive into the rice fields, for they plunge the roots and three-fourths of the stalk in the soft mud. Each transplanter takes a handful of plants and wades into the water, then separating three or four stalks from the bunch he takes them with the toes of his right foot and crowds the roots down in the mud, then he takes another bunch of four stalks and plants it about ten or twelve inches from the other, measuring the distance by his eye so as to have the plants about a foot apart each way. It is said that a good transplanter can complete a lot of about one third of an acre in a day. It is indispensable, after planting, to keep the fields thoroughly drenched, as the best crops are harvested from fields where the water has covered the half of the stalk until nearly the time when the rice is in ear. Even from that time till harvest, though the field should continue to be inundated, the crop will not necessarily suffer unless the wind should blow the straw over, which seldom occurs. Much of the rice is cut while standing a foot or two in the water. The crops are precarious and liable to be cut off by either too much or too little water; also, by worms and a kind of land crab that attacks the roots of the plant and frequently make sad havoc in the fields. Hands are employed for planting rice at the rate of from eight to ten ticals per month, at times when help is scarce the farmer has to pay an advance on this price.

If employed by the season, commencing at the beginning of the wet season in May till threshing time in December or January, a good hand receives one koyan of paddy, worth about sixty ticals or about $33. A rie of good soil will yield fifty buckets of paddy, poorer land less. The fields are all taxed by the rie, one-third of an acre, each field paying twenty-eight cents per annum.

Rice is the great staple of Siam. It has been an article of export since 1856, when the treaty with Siam, then ratified, opened up the kingdom to foreign trade. Prior to that the laws of Siam required that a three-years' supply of rice should remain in the country before any was allowed to be shipped abroad. When this law was abolished a demand for rice sprung up, and the natives, learning that it was a cash commodity, commenced planting for export, and yearly the acreage has steadily increased, thousands of Chinamen engaging in the business. The demand for land has caused canals to be opened through sections which have lain fallow for centuries, and thousands of acres which were useless and breeders of malaria, now stretch out for miles with fields of grain, billows of emerald blades greeting the eye until lost in airy undulations on the rim of the horizon. The natives use the most primitive appliances in the cultivation of their fields—breaking up the ground with buffaloes and oxen attached to a wooden plow—but the soil is so prolific that the grain grows almost spontaneously. At times the fields require irrigation, the water for which is easily obtained from the rivers and canals which cross the country in every direction. As the land is level the water rises and falls with the tide, hence the canals require no locks, and are navigable for boats, which do all the carrying, since there are but few wagon roads which are traversed with buffalo carts—huge, unwieldy two-wheeled vehicles.

The rice fields are laid off in lots of about one-third of an acre each—surrounded by an embankment of earth, from eighteen inches to two feet in height, for the purpose of holding water when the land is being prepared for planting or irrigation.

To encourage the natives to open up new fields no tax is levied on the land the first five years. When matured the grain is cut with sickles and stacked similar to American wheat, and when needed is tramped out by buffaloes and oxen, six or eight animals being attached to a post, around which the straw is strewn, and over which the cattle tramp round and round until the grain is separated from the straw. Then the straw is piled up for the cattle to eat, and the grain is winnowed from the chaff and dirt in a machine, a Chinese invention of a thousand years ago. The rice for export—Kow Moong and Kow Soon—is brought to the mills at Bangkok to be hulled, and then sacked for shipping. The natives hull their rice for home consumption in wooden mortars with wooden pestles; the latter they work with their feet, though many pound it out by hand. The first steam rice-mill at Bangkok was established by an American firm, but not finding it profitable they disposed of their plant. Now the preparation of rice for market has grown into a prosperous business. The large crop last year and the increased demand has induced Messrs. Markwald & Co. and others to put electric lights into their mills, so that they can run night and day. There are now twenty-five steam rice-mills in Bangkok, one in course of construction, and three at Patriew, a city 30 miles west of the capital. Most of the mills are in charge of foreign engineers. The only fuel used in these mills is the husk of the rice. Having traveled over a considerable portion of central Siam, I am satisfied that it has no superior as a rice-producing and fruit-growing country, and when it is opened up with railroads, and modern appliances are used to cultivate the soil, the crops will be quadrupled.

VARIETIES OF RICE.

1. Na Moong, which is sown broadcast over the fields and allowed to mature without further care, and in a few years yields its annual crop in the form of wild rice.

2. Na Soon, or garden rice, is allowed to grow to a certain height and is then transplanted. This is the rice of commerce, and is the best and highest priced of all grades.

The unit of land measure is the rie, almost identical with the English land unit. The average yield per rie is one (1) coyan, which contains 20 to 22 piculs, according to the quality of the rice.

The freight by steamer to Europe ranges from 33 to 55 shillings per ton. The bulk of the Siamese rice crop is exported to China. The present rate is 32 cents per picul.

Good judges estimate the daily consumption of rice by the average Siamese family to be from 1 to $1\frac{3}{4}$ cocoa-nut shells, or from 1 to $1\frac{3}{4}$ English quarts.

XV.

EXCESSIVE TAXATION OF THE PEOPLE.

The King is the collector and disburser of the revenue of his kingdom and it is impossible for any one not conversant with the internal affairs of Siam to know what the amount of the revenue is, as it is derived from various sources: First, imports and exports; second, direct taxation, which is annexed; third, donations to His Majesty and the corvee. This latter is unlimited, as hundreds of thousands have to pay a personal tax ranging from ten to twenty ticals, and then the King, through his officials, has simply to notify one of his Governors that he is in need of something and it is forthcoming; such, for instance, a notification to the Governor of Chantaboon that he wanted two hundred and forty logs of timber, fifty feet in length, for the purpose of erecting a premaine, cremation building, which it was expected that he would do at his own expense or see that his subordinates did so. Outside of this it is generally supposed that the revenue annually collected will amount to about $10,000,000, all of which is unloaded into the King's treasury by the various farmers who have charge of the various taxes, they having purchased the right of collection, it being sold to the highest bidder, thus giving them and their subordinates an ample chance to squeeze the people indiscriminately. Annexed is the statement of the annual levy and source of revenue of the Siamese government:

STATEMENT OF TAXES AND SOURCES OF REVENUE OF THE SIAMESE GOVERNMENT.

(1) Taxes on exports:
   Principal article of export, rice, on which the duty is from 10 to 12 cents per picul.
(2) Taxes on imports:
   Uniform rate of 3 per cent. on the market value of the goods.
(3) Taxes on cultivated lands:
   About 60 cents an acre.
(4) Taxes on fruit trees, etc.·
   A list of the duties is given in the treaty. These taxes are in lieu of land tax.
(5) The revenue derived from certain monopolies which are either in the hands of Government or farmed out by them, viz.:
   Preparation and sale of opium.
   Manufacture and sale of spirits.
   Tax on gambling-houses.
   The collection and sale of edible birds' nests.
   The collection of turtles' eggs.
   The manufacture and sale of cakes and confectionery.
   The manufacture of iron pans.
   The manufacture of iron.
   Taxes on prostitutes.
(6) Taxes on houses, floating houses, shops, godowns, etc.; and on boats employed in a certain manner, viz.:

	Ticals.
Boats engaged in carrying bricks...per fathom...	1
Boats engaged in carrying sand........do........	1
Boats engaged in carrying tiles........do........	1
Boats hawking miscellaneous hardware.do........	1
North country boats bringing goods to Bangkok for sale..........................per fathom..	¼
Boats moored with goods for sale, for more than two months, but under twelve months..per fathom..	¼
Boats moored with goods for sale, over twelve months........................per fathom..	1
Floating houses:	
With goods for sale..................per room..	1½ to 3
Used as brothels......................do......	3
Used as lottery stations................do......	3

	Ticals.
Used as gambling-houses............per room...	8
Used as liquor shops.....................do......	3
Those rented out.......................do......	3

Houses godowns, shops, etc., on shore, with goods for sale, used as brothels, lottery stations, gambling houses, or liquor shops; also those rented out; if within the district guarded by the police, must pay 12½ per cent. of their annual rental; if not in the district of the police, must pay 8⅓ per cent. of the rental.

There is also a tax on fresh provision markets.

(7) Inland taxes:

	Ticals.
White sugar................................per picul..	½
Red sugar..do....	¼
Peper...do....	1

	Per cent.
Fish (pla thoo)...	8⅓
Teel seed........	8⅓
Beans..	8⅓
Petchaboon tobacco.................................	10
Silk.................	8⅓
Beeswax...	6⅔
Raw cotton..	10
Paw (vegetable fiber)................................	10
Indigo...	10
Salt sea-fish...	8½
Smoked fish...	8½
Fresh fish..	8½
Shrimp paste...	10
Charcoal...	10
Posts (wood)..	10
Cocoanut oil...	10
Red and white lime..................................	10
Palm sugar..	10
Molasses..................................	8⅓
Tin...	10
Fire wood..	20
Attap..	10
Kacheng..	10
Torches...	10
Resin..	10

	Per cent.
Oil of fang tree	10
Rattans	10
Bamboos	10
Redwood	10

		Ticals.
Onions and chilils	per picul	10
Hemp (for sails)	do	10
Vegetables	do	5
Pork	do	8⅓
Fowls	do	8⅓
Ducks	do	8⅓
Eggs of fowls or ducks	do	8⅓

	Per cent.
Blackwood	10
Mai Takean wood	10
Wood called Mai Phya Loi	10

	Ticals.
Salt ....(per coyan, or $\tfrac{1}{10}$ per cent. per picul.)..	6

	per cent.
Teakwood	10
Tobacco	10

(8) Taxes on implements used for catching fish in salt or fresh water:

	Ticals.
Rafts, in line, to which nets are attached, for each aperture	4
Boats with large net........per annum	10
Boats with smaller net........do	6
Boats with small net........do	1
Boats with dragging net........do	10
Large round net streched on crossed bamboos with handle attached, per fathom	1½
Spoon-net, with wider mouth than 10 cubits..per annum	2
A boat with big spoon net........do	½
A boat with small spoon net........do	⅝
Basket used for catching fish in shallow water....do	¼
Net for the fish "Ta phien"........per annum	1
Harpoon or spear........do	⅛
"Laup" a long trap or basket........do	1½
A string of hooks........do	½
Each line for chawn or kado-fish........do	⅛

THE PEARL OF ASIA. 151

	Ticals.
Small net stretched on two sticks............per annum	⅛
Scoop made of split bamboo....................do....	½
Other snares, from...........................do....¼ to ½	
Beds of water-plants in front of houses for attracting fishes, per fathom.................................	⅛
Fish pools..............................per fathom..	½
The following are used in salt water:	
Fishing stakes, disposed in a circle.........per annum..	6
Fishing stakes, disposed in a circle..............do....	12
Fishing stakes, in triangular form, with net at apex.................................per annum..	3
One boat with hooks for dragging...............do....	2½
Fence for confining shrimps....................do....	1½
Casting net......................................do....	1
Spoon net for shrimps and prawns..............do....	⅝
Fishing stakes..................................do....	10
A large fishing boat............................do....	6
A very large net used by very many men........do....	12
Boat for catching "pla kuraw"..................do....	4
"Lamoo" a large inclosure of bamboo...........do.:..	6
"Lamoo" for deeper water.......................do....	20
Close bamboo fence............................do....	12
Close bamboo fence for deeper water...........do....	16
A kind of fishing net...........................do....	16
Net for shrimps.................................do....	20
Net for beche de mer............................do....	24
Spears for beche de mer........................do....	4
Harpoon for turtle..............................do....	8
Plank for sliding over the mud..................do....	½
Hook and line............................do....¼ to ½	

(9) The revenue derived from money paid in commutation of Government service, to which all adult males are liable, to which may be added the services performed by cowee.

(10) The revenue derived from a poll-tax of 4½ ticals on Chinese every third year.

(11) Taxes are also levied on theatrical representations and plays of various kinds.

	Ticals.
Drama of "Rama Kien"....................per diem..	28
Drama of "Anirut"...........................do....	12

	Ticals
Theatrical representation "Nang"..........each night..	½
Chinese theater............................per diem..	2
Chinese puppet show..........................do....	1
Drama "Ih Henao"............................do....	20
Dramas, various kinds........................do....	2
Singing......................................do....	½
Chinese theater (special)....................do....	4

NOTE.—A picul, 133⅓ pounds avoirdupois; a Siamese tical, 60 cents.

XVI.

THE KING'S INSTRUCTIONS TO HIS SON.

Several years since His Majesty concluded to send several of his sons to England, for the purpose of having them educated at Cambridge and Oxford, but before doing so prepared a series of instructions for their guidance while in that far-off land, which are worthy of perpetuation as coming not only from a monarch, but a father who felt a deep interest in the welfare of his children. The following is a correct translation:

"I desire to put my wishes in a form of written instructions for the guidance of my children who are being sent to receive their education in Europe, and I beg to enjoin upon them that they shall follow the instructions herein given.

"First. My object in sending you is that you may obtain an education, and I have no desire to obtain renown and honor for you while pursuing your studies; and for this reason you may not assume the rank and title of Princes, but must assume the position of the son of persons of rank in Siam, namely, you may not use the title of 'His Royal Highness' prefixed to your names, but shall employ only your own personal names. If others shall prefix to your names the title of Mr. or add Esquire, according to English custom, let them do so without objection, but you must not use the Siamese prefix Nai, which is often used as a prefix to their names when pronounced in English by sons of noblemen, as corresponding to the title of Mr., as this has a disagreeable sound. To explain my wishes in regard to this matter plainly, the reason why I do not wish you to assume the title and rank of Princes as your uncles did who have preceded you are as follows: My wish does not arise from want of affection towards you or from a wish to prevent its being known that you are my children. Your father will certainly recognize you as his children, and will cherish his affection for you as it is natural for a father always to love his children, but I consider that it will not be of any benefit for you to assume the title of Princes because there are few Princes in their country, and in our country there are many; and because they have but few Princes, they laud and honor them much more than we do, and if on our own part we should put ourselves on an equal footing with them, whereas we have not wealth and dignity equal to theirs, we should suffer in comparison and should make Siamese Princes appear inferior. Also, if we assume the rank of Princes we must keep up a dignity in all things that we do for the sake of appearance, and to make others admire us, and we must therefore be constantly on our guard. Even in purchasing anything a higher price must be paid than common people pay, because they consider us wealthy, and thus a useless expense is occasioned. Whether princes or common people, when in a foreign country, one has no power to make one more illustrious than the common people, and the only advantage Princes have is that they can enter assemblies of distinguished persons, but the sons of the people of rank will likewise be admitted to the same privileges enjoyed by Princes as regards society. For these reasons, I direct that you will not boast or allow any of your attendants to boast that you are Royal Princes, and I desire you to follow out these instructions.

"2d. All the expenses of your education, including board and clothing, will be paid out of my privy purse, viz., the funds which are your father's private property and not funds used for defraying the ordinary expenses of the State. This fund will be deposited in the banks, and instructions will be sent to my minister to defray the expenses of your education out of this fund, namely: For the first five years' education each of you will receive £320 a year or £1,600 for the five years, and for the succeeding five years you will be allowed £400 a year, or £2,000 for the five years, making your complete education £3,600 each. As this fund will be deposited in the banks bearing interest, there will be a surplus over and above your educational expenses, which will be yours and can be used in whatever manner you please. The portion of each will be deposited in his own name, but before attaining the age of twenty-one years you will not be allowed to draw money on your own account and a person must be appointed to attend to this business for you. The amount deposited and the name of the persons managing your business are given in separate instructions, which you will have to use in obtaining the money when needed.

"I have considered it best to use my private funds and not the funds of the State, as has been done in the case of Princes and sons of the nobility heretofore. This opportunity and appropriation of funds for your education is a rich legacy of more value than money, for an education is of lasting and personal value and nothing can harm it or take it away from you. It is my intention to send all my sons to receive the advantages of an education whether they are of quick intellect or dull, so far as opportunity shall offer, deeming it as an inheritance which I am giving to each of my children.

"If I should use funds belonging to the State for this purpose, and it should turn out that this money was spent upon a person devoid of wisdom and who upon his return would do nothing to repay the State for the money expended upon him, it would give occasion to a certain class of people to find fault, and they might say that I had too many children and was obliged to draw large sums of money from the funds of the State for their educational expenses, and that I did not even make a selection of such as had ability and would prove of benefit to the State, but sent even the stupid and ignorant simply because they were my children and wasted money on them. I desire that there shall not be any derogatory remarks made in connection with my purpose to give my children these educational advantages, and have not, therefore, used any of the funds belonging to the State for this purpose. But even the funds in my privy purse are in a certain sense the property of the State and they are simply a portion which is set apart for your father's private use, and the purposes to which these funds are applied are charity and the maintenance and support of the family. I consider that the advantages of an education are of more value than other things and this use of money will be indirectly a benefit to the State, for the funds of the treasury of the State are not drawn upon for this purpose, and by this is avoided the various derogatory remarks which might be made, for the reason that your father uses his private funds for this purpose and no one can say that the money should be used for this or that purpose.

"3d. You will ever remember that although you are born princes and have dignity and honor thereby, yet it is not necessary that any person who may be the sovereign of this country will require your services for the State, and thus offer an opportunity for you to obtain honor and wealth for yourselves.

"If the past be considered it will be found that there are less opportunities for princes to receive positions of trust and influence than for the sons of the nobility; for the reason that they having rank and honor by birth, can not accept inferior positions as stepping stones to something greater, for example, they can not become Nai Rong or Hum Preh or Royal Pages and they can not be appointed to such positions as would be in keeping with their rank without first having obtained experience and wisdom fitting them for such positions. For this reason a prince who shall become noted and receive an elevated appointment can do so only when he is possessed of superior abilities. Therefore you are urged to pursue your studies with the greatest possible earnestness and faithfulness so that you may have an opportunity to do something which will be a benefit to your country and to the world in which you live. To consider that being born princes it is better to remain quiet and enjoy yourselves through life is not very different from the lower animals which are born, eat, sleep and die. But some animals have hides, and horns and bones, which remain and are of benefit after they die, but people who conduct themselves like animals are not of as much use as certain animals even. For this reason make an effort to gain an education, which will enable you to make yourselves better than the lower animals and thus you will be considered as having repaid your father's affection and efforts for your benefit and the care which has been expended upon you from your birth.

"4th. Do not consider that, because you are the sons of a king and your father is all powerful in his country, that you can therefore be unruly and obstinate, and need to fear no one and can misuse and abuse others and they will make no complaint or resistance. This is entirely wrong. Your father's desire is that his sons shall not have any such power to be unruly, as he feels certain that a misapplied affection to one's children, which allows them to fear no one, will be injurious to them in the present and future. For this reason you must remember that whenever you do wrong, you must suffer the consequent punishment, and the fact that your father is a king will not save you from such punishment. Again, the life of a man is of short duration and is not as enduring as iron or stone, and although now you have a father living, the time will certainly come when you will be without him. If you do wrong while your father is living, even if you are able to cover it up for a time, after your father is gone, your faults will appear to your disadvantage and will follow you as a shadow. Therefore you must be teachable and not headstrong, you must always endeavor to do right and avoid that which you know yourself to be wrong, or which you are taught is wrong by others.

"5th. The funds provided for your expenses, you must economize, and you must not be prodigal and extravagant, believing yourselves to be rice princes, or that your father is a king and has plenty of money. I warn you from the beginning, that if any one of you shall return in debt, such debts shall not be paid for you, or if it shall be necessary to pay them, you will not escape punishment, you may know that whenever your debts have to be paid, you must receive punishment. Do not believe anything said to the contrary or fancy that you can be extravagant as some who have preceded you whose fathers were noblemen and who have paid their debts without objection. If you have this idea you are entirely wrong. Your father does indeed love his children, but he does not love such conduct in his children, for he certainly knows that if he should allow you to do so, it would be of no possible benefit to the children who receive his love, as you would not in that case receive the education, which I desire you to obtain, but would gain only practices which would disgrace you and give continual annoyance to others. You must always remember that this money which seems a large amount to you now, is not as easily obtained as as it is expended. The yearly portion which you always receive comes to you through your father, and the money which your father receives is that which comes to him as being the ruler and sovereign of the country, and is the contribution of the people for the support of their sovereign, that he may enjoy it with happiness, as a recompense for his labors in this exalted position, namely that of the guardian of their welfare. This money should not be spent for useless and injurious purposes and should only be employed for objects which will be of real benefit to one's self and to others. Is it fitting to pay it away for the debts of one's children who have squandered money in evil practices ? For this reason I must declare that I will not pay your debts, and if I am compelled to do so there must be a penalty which will serve as a guarantee that I shall not be obliged to do so again; the penalty must be sufficient to cause such a one to avoid a repetition of such actions, then only will the debt be paid, and it will only be done for the sake of preventing loss to the creditor, and not out of love for the child or pleasure in his conduct, therefore you will remember and consider that you are poor and have only sufficient means to support yourselves comfortably and are not rich as the wealthy in Europe. Persons of wealth in Europe have inherited it from generation to generation and receive rent and interest from various sources, but you receive a certain sum from the people sufficient for your support and keeping up your dignity. Do not be ostentatious and try to imitate them, and to make a vain display.

"When you have contracted debts and you fear your father will not pay them, or in case he does, he will impose a penalty, do not think you can use the annual allowance which is laid by for you and accumulating while you are abroad, to pay such debts. If you should think so and therefore contract debts while abroad it will be likewise wrong for all the advantages which you enjoy while your father lives, or which may continue after he has passed away, you can not say that they will remain always the same, and as you grow older you will have families to provide for and will need money for your support, and possibly your income may not be sufficient for your expenditures. You can not be sure that your education will give you positions of influence and remuneration equal to your wants, for the reason that the fact of your being princes may possibly at some future time, be a barrier to your holding office, and if you should turn to business pursuits such as receiving employment as clerks, etc., there will still be difficulties in consequence of your being princes. If your capital is all spent in the payment of debts where will you then find your support? Therefore I say if you think of spending such funds as these so as not to annoy your father it will still be the cause of future difficulties and embarrassments which you ought not to bring upon yourselves.

"6th. The education which you are to receive will consist of the acquiring the fluent and accurate use of three languages, English, German and French, so that you will be able to compose in at least two of these languages. Also that you must acquire a practical knowledge of mathematics. These two branches you must acquire with proficiency, for they are the foundation of all other studies. Next to these you must acquire a knowledge of the sciences and arts, but I can not now decide upon the exact course of study which you are to pursue. This will be decided upon after you have acquired a knowledge of the primary branches. I wish, however, to impress it upon your minds that in sending you to acquire a European education, I do not wish that you shall possess only a knowledge of European languages and sciences. The Siamese, which is your own native language, you will have occasion to make use of always, and you must consider that the European languages are to be the foundation of your knowledge, because Siamese books are few and old, for the reason that there has been little intercourse with foreign countries, which is different from what has been the case in Europe, where by the constant intercourse and interchange of ideas, great advance has been made in knowledge. For this reason, there can not be sufficient knowledge obtained from Siamese books, and therefore it is necessary to study foreign languages so as to obtain a larger field of knowledge and then this knowledge can be introduced into the Siamese language. Therefore it is not at all wise or suitable for you to forget your own language so that you can not express yourselves properly, or forget how to write the Siamese language. If you acquire a knowledge of foreign languages only, and cannot read and write and translate into the Siamese language correctly, it will be of no practical advantage, because in this case we can employ as many foreigners as we wish.

"What is wanted is that you shall be able to translate from the Siamese language into a European language, and from one or more European languages into Siamese; thus only will your education be complete. Do not consider that having studied foreign languages and forgotten your own it will make you appear highly fashionable, as some students have wrongly supposed. While you are pursuing your studies I wish each of you to write a letter to your father at least once a month in Siamese, until you can write English or some other European language, after which you must write in English, or some other language besides Siamese, and send also a translation in Siamese, because you are still young and your knowledge of Siamese is not yet permanently fixed. You will therefore consult your Siamese teachers who accompany you or search in your Siamese text books with which you are provided, and you will thus find suitable language in which to express yourselves in translating from a foreign language into Siamese. The Siamese books which can be of help to you are still very few, it is true. Whatever mistakes are made in these letters will be corrected, and these corrections be sent to you and you must remember these mistakes and avoid them in future. Do not be afraid or ashamed, but do the best you can, and if you make such mistakes they will be corrected, and you will not lose or suffer anything by it.

"7th. You must remember that the education of all my children is entrusted to your uncle, Krom Mun Devawongse Varoprakann, who has solemnly promised me to do his best during the present and future to attain the best possible results, and I have confidence in him and have given him full authority to manage all matters here in connection with your education.

"If you have any difficulties or business of any kind, you must write to him, and your father will know of it through him.

"Krom Mun Devawongse will manage everything and bring it to a successful accomplishment. In Europe, if you are in a country where I have a minister, this minister will arrange your affairs for you, and whatever difficulties you may experience you must tell them to the minister and he will help you.

"When you enter school you must follow the rules, and must not be headstrong or obstinate. Be industrious and studious, that you may return and be a help and a blessing to your father, and thus repay him for his love."

XVII.

FUNERAL OF A CHINESE MANDARIN.

A novel sight is frequently witnessed in Bangkok, conveying the remains of a mandarin from his residence to one of the Hong Kong steamers, so that it can be transported to the home of his nativity and buried beside his parents. The boat that contains the coffin is filled with friends and relatives, all dressed in white, that being the color of their mourning garments, this is accompanied by other boats decorated and containing musicians, priests and others making quite a display. The beating of gongs and blowing of horns announce that the flotilla is coming, generally five or six boats, that containing the corpse in the lead. The body is encased in a handsome coffin covered with gilding and elaborately carved, more like an ornamented chest than a coffin, and on it is fastened a beautiful white bantam rooster; over the casket is suspended a pavilion and above it two blue banners and two large blue lanterns with other decorations. As soon as the steamer is reached the casket is placed in the hold with the rooster still on it, and by the time the vessel reaches its destination the doomed bird has also gone out into the unknown with the spirit of the son of the celestial. I failed to learn why a rooster was thus sacrificed, though it is supposed that the purity of the white bird might aid in blotting out some of the sins of the deceased or possibly his spirit would seek it as a tabernacle to dwell in during his transmigrations. It is a curious custom of this curious people.

At times the passing of a funeral flotilla is quite a gorgeous pageant; the weird music, loud sounding gongs, the beating of tom toms and shrill notes of the flute, the measured dip of oars and fluttering of flags of various colors, fringed with gold and silver, furnish the spectator with a panorama of oriental splendor that remains indellibly photographed on the margent of memory. The remains of a Chinese mandarin lies in state about one hundred days, during which time bonzes, or priests, pray for the soul of the departed singers chaunt their native hymns and songs, theatrical performances are held and clowns perform all kinds of antics to drive away the gloom and sorrow of the family, to make them forget their loss, they also think this pleases the spirit of the dead who is supposed to be hovering around to see what disposition is being made of his earthly casket. During this time lamps are constantly burning to drive away evil spirits and a feast spread for their entertainment while the priests in attendance and the family are regaled with choice viands and feasted sumptuously.

As their religion makes them fatalists they do not seem to grieve much on account of the death of a relative, but they leave nothing undone for the care and sepulcher of the dead; they see that his debts are paid, his family properly cared for and his grave located in a pleasant place where the sunshine can fall upon it and face a running stream of water, or the wide expanse of gulf or ocean. Their tombs or vaults are built in the shape of a horse shoe and present quite a curious appearance, as they are arranged in rows. Frequently the graveyard is located on the side of a hill, which is terraced for the purpose. That at Hong Kong is one of the curiosities of the place while the cemetery at Canton covers many acres and is closely filled with their tombs.

Modern skeptics could learn much from these stoical Asiatics who thus care for the bodies of their deceased relatives, which proves conclusively that their belief in the beatitude of the life to come is serious and well founded, that they will live again in the hereafter and meet beyond the invisible river in the celestial Nirvana, a reunion that shall be eternal, where the heavenly savannahs undulating far away shall yield the choicest rice, the waters that flow through emerald vales be plethoric with fish, umbrageous trees that furnish shade bend to the earth with choicest fruit, birds of rarest plumage fill the groves with melody and demoselles, fairer than the blush of morn, welcome them to joys supernal, a land of dreamy wantonness that they have caught glimpses of after inhaling the poppies languorous power, the curse of the mongolian.

XVIII.

ROYAL PALACES AT BANG-PA-IN AND RATBUREE.

Siam is a land of legends that run back into the storied past, when an almost unknown civilization flourished ere its present religion, from a faint spark was blown into a blaze by the saintly Gautama, the Buddha of the East, whose myriads of followers have reared their temples on mount and in emerald vales and beside flowing rivers, whose white walls and gilt spires dot the landscape far and wide and from their cloistered halls can be heard at early morn the beat of drums and the clangor of bells summoning the faithful to prayer, or to listen to the reading of the sacred works of the great teacher, whose statues are held in special reverence by the Buddhist, as do many of our people the cross, merely symbols of their belief, no one regarding Buddha as a divinity, solely a great teacher who incull cated charity, morality and benevolence to the fullest extent, the genesis of Buddhist belief to-day as it was for centuries before the son of Mary proclaimed his divine truths on Olivet, and gave us his universal prayer that has been a solace to the seeker after truth for nineteen centuries. Such was my thoughts as I sped past many beautiful wats on my way up the Menam to Bang-Pa-In, the king's summer palace, which is considered the handsomest place in the kingdom. The palace is built in semi-oriental style and surrounded with spacious grounds laid out in the most elaborate

Ruins in Ayuthia.

manner and skill, under the charge of an experienced Swiss landscape gardner, filled with all the flowers the orient can boast of, a wealth of floral beauty, paths winding in serpentine sinuosity in every direction, skirting miniature lakes on whose placid waters float mammoth Victoria reginas and the fragrant lotus, mirroring a number of buildings nestled on their margins, set apart as the habitations of favorite Queens, the main building being reserved for his Majesty, through which we were shown by his retainers, he being absent, and it was well worth the visit. It is such a spot as Bulwer describes, when he pictures a palace by the lake of Como, "lifting to eternal summer its marble walls from out a grove of greenest foliage musical with birds." The palace is built in the modern style, by an Italian architect, of brick and stuccoed white, its interior panneled with padoo, ebony and other rare woods of the kingdom, the hard wood polished like a mirror bringing out the fine grain, the ceilings are lofty and laid off in handsome designs and elaborately gilded, the floors a mosaic of many kinds of wood and highly polished, each room different and furnished according to the finish. The broad flight of stairs that lead to the upper story, the King's sleeping apartments, were the most elaborate and handsomest that I have ever seen, the carving being most artistically executed, in keeping with the entire building, large mirrors, tapestry, and handsome pictures graced the walls on every side.

The King's chamber, bath and toilet rooms were magnificent and his couch a thing of beauty. It was made of ebony and carved with the most exquisite designs, draped with rare lace curtains trimmed with gold, a gold embroidered quilt covering the mattress, the pillows and bolster trimmed with gold lace and it looked more like a work of art, to please the eye, than the resting place of one who wears a crown and sways the destiny of ten million people. Each room was furnished in the richest manner many containing rare padoo tables, handsome cabinets, crystal and alabaster vases, etc. It was just such a place as one tired with pomp and power could spend a month most pleasantly in, in oriental ease, waited on by jewelled Queens and servile servitors, lulled to slumber by the fragrant breath of the lotus and the carrolling of birds amid the hush of the golden afternoon. In the center of several of the lakes pavilions have been erected where a band discourses music and on their rippling surface float barges to bear the wives and children of the King from sylvan spot to marble steps as fancy dictates. In various parts of the garden are large cages containing monkeys, birds and animals that add no little to the picturesqueness of the scene. In the palace is preserved a rare collection of serpents found in the dank vegetation of this country, some unknown in other sections.

For a couple of hours we strolled through the well-kept grounds and gardens, fifty persons being constantly employed in beautifying and keeping them in order. On an island in the river, amid a grove of emerald verdure, has been erected a memorial chapel to the memory of the late Queen, a handsome gothic structure with stained glass windows, more like a Christian church than a Buddhist temple. The Queen was drowned by the overturning of a yacht and in the palace grounds a handsome marble monument has also been erected, detailing the circumstances of that sad event. As our time was limited we had to take a hurried view of this lovely place, with its various palaces scattered over its floral grounds, the tall oriental watch tower that stands like a sentinel looking down on all its sylvan lakes mirroring the bluest of skies, but the shrill whistle of the boat reminded us that time was up and with a sigh of regret we left Bang-Pa-In, its world of flowers, towering trees, fragrant atmosphere and paradisacal beauty, an elysium where one could dream life away without a pang or wish for wordly honors, the Nirvana of a poet.

While on the wing, in company with several others, after a couple of days travel in our boats we reached the city of Ratburee and after spending some time in the palace of the late Regent, were furnished with a conveyance to visit a royal palace that had been erected a number of years since by the King on a small mountain about four miles from the city. The carriage was a dilapidated affair, the best of over a dozen rotting down in the carriage house, paint and grease having been strangers to them for years, but it bore our party over the broad and smooth avenue safely to the foot of the mount where a handsome stone walk and steps led up to the palace, a massive pile of stone and brick, beautiful in architectural design and romantically situated. From its broad verandas and columned porticos a lovely view of the country for miles can be seen, in the far distance, the blue mountains of Burmah; a palace seemingly worthy of any monarch. Slowly mounting upwards a hundred feet we were ushered through its portals by an attendant who was in charge of the place and were surprised to note the ruin and desolation that prevailed throughout the whole establishment, magnificient in its decay; the ceilings of rare wood, handsomely ornamented, were falling off and littered the marble floor of the reception room and a massive chandelier, hanging by a frail support, was ready to fall, many of its prisms already broken off. Most of the furniture of the place had been stolen and what was left evinced good taste; the kamoys or thieves having had good pickings, carrying off everything portable. This palace had been erected at considerable expense by the present monarch and to expedite the work a railroad was built from the river to the foot of the mountain, for the purpose of conveying the heavy material of which it was constructed, the rails are now turning to rust and the cars falling to pieces, no longer of any use, and the dwelling of the King is tenantless, its foundations crumbling and its walls toppling to a fall. It was heart rending to see this magnificent edifice thus deserted while thousands of the natives had but flimsy bamboo huts to reside in, a type of the stagnation of the East. After its completion His Majesty spent but one week within its walls and as it is possible that he will never occupy it again it will slowly yield to the ravages of time, crumble into a shapeless mound and thus add another pile to this land of many ruins, the very air of which is freighted with lethargy and indolence. The custodian of the place informed us that since the death of the late Regent, Ratburee had almost ceased to be a royal city and that bands of dacoits and kamoys roamed through the country at pleasure, bidding defiance to the officials who, being too far away from Bangkok, were powerless to check their ravages.

Extensive rice fields surround the city for many miles, groves of palm and bamboo enliven the view and thus break the monotony of an almost prairie country. Dr. Thompson and wife are the only white persons in the place, leading a lonesome life, they are connected with the Presbyterian misson and are doing much good among the natives, the King having kindly granted them a palace to reside in and for hospital purposes. The missionary doctors are fast superceeding the native practitioners, and as far as getting into the confidence of the native, one doctor can do more real good in advancing western ideas than a brigade of missionaries— the lancet being a more potent weapon than the bible among the followers of Buddha. On the outskirts of the city are the foundations of two immense buildings, that had been started by some Prince, but he dying, the work was stopped and the buildings abandoned, that being the usual course pursued by the Siamese as they believe that the originator would get the merit of the work if it was completed. Some of the stones in these foundations were of immense size and it is marvellous how they were placed in position by manual labor, as they have no other means of working, a derick seemingly unknown. The Regent's palace, a magnificent building and the best in the city, is handsomely furnished and was occupied by one of his grandsons, who was very proud of his collection of knives, manufactured by the natives, hundreds of them, which were displayed on the walls, and an unique collection of tea pots, from the gold one presented by the King down to the tiniest one of the mandarin china, worth ten times its weight in gold. The grounds around this palace were handsomely laid out with fountains and reservoirs for irrigation, at times the heat there being intense. On the façade of the main entrance mottoes in English were carved: "Charity," "Virtue," "Benevolence," which seemed strangely out of place in that far away Eastern city, whose highways and bazars were thronged with the followers of Gautama. We had a call from the Governor who invited us to his palace, which is situated on the opposite side of the river, surrounded by massive walls with retainers at the gates, and he received us royally in a large sala, which was covered with a bamboo carpet woven in one piece. Tea and other refreshments were handed around and he wondered why I should bring my wife so far when women were a drug in the market, while the natives were much impressed with her dress and carriage, as she was taller than the average women and many had never seen an American lady. While there we had a chance to note how justice was dispensed. A policeman led in a trembling native and vyeing before the Governor proceeded to relate the offence that the crouching culprit was charged with. The Governor asked the policeman a few questions and then told him to take the fellow out and hit him ten strokes with the bamboo. The prisoner had pilfered some fruit. He got off easily, most of the time the Governor sentences them to the stockades for a month or more, and once there the jailer gets him in his debt and the chains once on they rarely come off till his body is cremated or given to the vultures. While a prisoner he is made to work for the Governor or some other noble, without pay or emolument, and his friends, if he has any, have to furnish him with rice and clothes. Truly the way of the transgressor in this country is hard and the jailers make it harder, so as to induce the relatives of the prisoner to buy them out by paying the extortionate charges they run up to the account of the unfortunate that may fall into their clutches. A visit to the stockade was sufficient to convince anyone that Dante's inscription of Inferno would not be out of place here. The prisoners were confined in a place about an acre in extent, closed in with a double row of bamboo posts about twelve feet high, with a row of open sheds on one side in which the manacled occupants slept on the ground. Filth of all kind abounded and the stench was akin to that of a durian. The inmates, about forty in number, were squatting around and perfectly callous, they had apparently cast hope behind and were waiting to be translated to some other sphere. They were in for numerous crimes; a few for murder, the latter had been in the stockade over three years and had had no trial, virtually the Governor's slaves. Leaving there and wandering out under the trees that were clothed in the loveliest of blossoms, the air freighted with their perfume, I could scarcely realize that so much suffering existed in this land of sunshine where man alone seemed vile. Just beyond the Governor's palace flowed the majestic river bearing on its pellucid bosom many boats, some from where the glittering fountains lave the flowery meads of Burmah, others from the sparkling waters of the gulf, and beyond the white walls of the temples and palaces of the city, while far away, fringed with fern and palm and tamarind tree, the stream shrank to a slender thread and was lost in the dip of the horizon. This was our first visit to the interior and we were astonished at the fertility of the soil and the resources of this favored section. It requires but little labor to raise a crop and the native does not care to make any more than enough to pay his rent, taxes and to subsist on, fearful of being squeezed, and well he may be, if one-half the tales told of grasping officials are correct. In the interior justice is a misnomer and no one expects it. The man that has the first say or is a favorite or relative of the powers that be, generally wins and it is useless to appeal to the King; their petitions will be suppressed and never reach him. The Governors of provinces are supreme and accumulate large fortunes out of the miseries of their subjects. When the shades of evening fell we turned the prows of our boats down stream and after winding through numerous canals and floating down a couple of rivers we found ourselves again at Bangkok.

XIX.

THE LEGAL OATH ADMINISTERED TO WITNESSES.

The Siamese have regularly appointed judges and various courts are held for the purpose of trying criminals and the settlement of disputes. Among the oaths administered to witnesses, after they are taken to a Buddhist temple by an officer of the court, is the annexed. It has been partially amended by the judges in Bangkok, but is still used in the interior towns and villages and would seem to be binding enough for all practical purposes. This oath was translated and published in the Siam Advertiser a number of years since and pronounced correct by Siamese scholars. Something similar is taken by the officers and officials of the palace when they drink the water of allegiance. Such oaths should stick if there is anything in tall swearing:

"I, who have been brought here as a witness in this matter, do now in the presence of the sacred image of Buddha, declare that I am wholly unprejudiced against either party and uninfluenced in any way by the opinions or advice of others; that no prospects of pecuniary advantage or advancement to office have been held out to me. I also declare that I have not received any bribe on this occasion. If what I have now to say be false, or if in my further averments I shall color or pervert the truth so as to lead the judgment of others astray, may the **Three Holy Existences** before whom I now stand together with the nine glorious *Thewedas* of the twenty-two firmaments punish me. If I have not seen and yet shall say I have seen; if I shall say I know that which I do not know, then may I be thus punished. Should innumerable descendants of Deity happen for the regeneration and salvation of mankind, may my erring and migratory soul be found beyond the pale of their mercy. Wherever I go may I be compassed with dangers and not escape from them, whether murderers, robbers, spirits of the earth, woods, or water or air, or all the divinities who adore Buddha; or from the gods of the four elements and all other spirits. May the blood pour out of every pore of my skin, that my crime may be made manifest to the world. May all or any of these evils overtake me within three days or may I never stir from the spot on which I now stand; or may the lightning cut me in two so that I may be exposed to the derision of the people; or if I should be walking abroad, may I be torn in pieces by either of the supernaturally endowed lions or destroyed by poisonous serpents. If on the water of the river or ocean may supernatural crocodiles or great fish devour me; or may the winds and waves overwhelm me, or may the dread of such evils keep me a prisoner during life, at home, estranged from every pleasure. May I be inflicted with intolerable oppression of my superiors, or may a plague cause my death. After which may I be precipitated into hell, there to go through innumerable stages of torture, amongst which may I be condemned to carry water over the flaming regions in wicker baskets to assuage the heat of *Than Tretonwan*, when he enters the infernal hell of justice, and thereafter may I fall into the lowest pit of hell; or if these miseries should not ensue may I after death migrate into the body of a slave and suffer all the pain and hardship attending the worst state of such a being during the period measured by the sand of the sea, or may I animate the body of an animal, or be a beast during five hundred generations, or be born a hermaprodite five hundred times, or endure in the body of a deaf, dumb and houseless beggar every species of disease, during the same number of generations and then may I be hurried to narok and there be tortured by Phya Yam."

XX.

INSTALLATION OF THE CROWN PRINCE.

One of the grandest pageants ever witnessed in Bangkok was the occasion of declaring the Crown Prince heir to the throne of Siam. The ceremonies lasted four days and commenced with a grand procession within the palace walls to which the consular body and foreign residents were invited. A large pavilion had been erected for the nobles and consular body immediately opposite the royal pavilion to which the guests were escorted along the broad avenue, which was covered with matting, through long lines of soldiers standing at a present, their burnished rifles flashing brightly in the dazzling sun. At intervals were stationed five bands, modern music, while old Siam was represented by horns, tom toms, and drums of an oblong shape which the performers struck with their hands making a mournful sound. Waiting about an hour, at 5 P. M. the bugles blared, the loud reverberation of cannon was borne to our ears on the sultry air, the bands struck up the national air of Siam, the troops became alert and over 50,000 persons stood up to witness the coming of the King. He was preceded by a body guard of nobles carrying fasces and over their state dress they wore lace mantles, immediately in front was borne his sword with jeweled hilt and his palanquin, of gold and silver, borne on the shoulders of eight of the highest nobles, over him the royal canopy, surrounded by six attendants, who carried miniature

The Crown Prince, Heir Apparent to the Throne.

pagodas on gilded staffs. The King was clad in
a robe of yellow silk encrusted with gold embroidery,
purple silk panung, violet colored silk stockings, slippers embroidered with gold and jewels, and a flexible
gold belt, the buckle of which was studded with diamonds, rubies, emeralds and sapphires, across his breast
he wore a broad silk scarf from which was suspended
a number of medallions and orders flashing with
rare gems, carrying in his hand a white helmet.
Reaching the pavilion he stepped gracefully
from his chair, bowed twice to the diplomats
and nobles and then seated himself on his throne, a
massive affair, heavily gilded. The pavilion was
draped with silk curtains of gold and scarlet, the steps
that led to it were covered with crimson velvet carpet
as was the floor. By the side of the throne, on a gilt
table, stood a large betel box, cigar case and cuspidor,
of solid gold, handsomely chased with Siamese figures,
typical of the legends of the days when Buddha walked
the earth and taught the nations of the East a doctrine
that has outlived a score of dynasties and has still millions of followers. As soon as the King was seated a
dozen lacon girls came sweeping down the avenue,
dressed in their peculiar costume, with flowers in their
hands, intended to represent angels bearing gifts. A
procession then formed, made up of nobles, women and
girls, men and boys, representatives dressed in the
costumes of the various provinces of Siam, in the center of which was borne the Crown Prince, a bright
eyed youth of ten summers, who was escorted by
twelve nobles, prominent among them the King of
Changmai and the ex-Kramata, late Foreign Minister,
his sponsers. He was carried on a gold chair, preceded

by five girls, dressed like angels, bearing his gold betel box, tea pot and other utensils, canopied with a royal umbrella and surrounded by servitors carrying fasces and other paraphernalia. Reaching the throne he stepped off his chair and was seated at the feet of his father. The procession having passed the King and Prince retired and soon reappeared, the King with his royal robe on, a cloak of gold that reached nearly to his ankles and on his head a crown made in the shape of a pagoda, fourteen inches in height, of the purest gold, studded with jewels, surmounted with a diamond of fabulous value, weighing a number of pounds. He was forced to fasten it on to keep it from toppling to one side, a very uncomfortable headgear for the wearer, a literal carrying out of the assertion " uneasy is the head that wears a crown." The Crown Prince, also, wore a crown of similar shape, a mass of jewels; he was dressed in white silk and before he put on his crown his topet or tuft of hair, that each Siamese youth wears, was encircled with a coronet of diamonds set in silver, his collar, at least eight inches deep, was elaborately embroidered with diamonds as was the breast and cuffs of his coat, around his neck was swung a medallion of his father encased with brilliants, his fingers were hooped with gems and around each ankle were six anklets of gold encrusted with precious stones, the fastenings of his coat were five buttons as large as a filbert, diamonds set in a filigree of gold, his belt and slippers were also a mass of priceless gems, making up a costume regally beautiful, the value of which could not be computed under a half million of dollars. Other of the King's children were present in the pavilion and they also were covered with jewels, diamonds being the favorite. One of them wore a chain of emeralds and diamonds that crossed over the shoulder like a sash and fastened in front with a lovely sapphire clasp; another a sapphire chain worn similarly, each sapphire being surrounded with small diamonds and clasped with a royal ruby, others wore pendants and medallions, family heir looms. It would be impossible to compute the value of the jewels worn by the royal children alone, it being reported that the King had presented the Crown Prince with jewels to the value of $400,000 and the presents from Princes and nobles exceeded that sum. Those worn by the leading Siamese, who were in attendance, were also of inestimable value, most of whom were decorated with orders and medallions and wore heavy gold chains and gold belts, the clasps of which were works of art, scintillating with rare gems, while the buttons on some of their coats were costly solitaires, literally gems of Golconda. It was indeed a royal sight to look over the vast array of noblemen dressed in coats of gold and silver damascene cloth, silk panungs and stockings, with broad yellow, green and red sashes thrown across their breasts, their jewels sparkling, while among them were seated a number of officers of the army and navy in showy uniforms.

After the procession had filed by the King, Prince and attendant nobles repaired to the royal wat adjacent where the Prince Arch Bishop, assisted by ten Bishops, offered up prayers for the welfare of His Majesty and the Crown Prince, during which time the guests were regaled with ices, tea, cigars, etc. In about an hour the drums beat, the King returned, the procession reformed and marched before him, he then took off his royal robe and crown, the palanquins were brought up and the King and Prince stepping into them were borne back to the palace, His Majesty bowing repeatedly, returning his thanks to the diplomats and others for their attendance and requesting that they be present on the morrow. The bands then struck up, the soldiers marched off at a double quick, the crowd poured forth through the gates and seeking our carriage we were swiftly borne home. At night the palace and grounds were handsomely illuminated with electric lights, gas and colored lanterns while lacon performances and feasting were kept up till midnight. This was repeated on the two days following and on the fourth day at 10 A. M. the grand ceremony of the water rite was commenced. At an early hour a steady stream of humanity, old and young, dressed in holiday attire, flowed toward the palace, that being the main day, and by the hour named there could not have been less than 500,000 persons in and around the palace grounds. On the water front, extending into the river, had been erected a handsome temple (see engraving), a large pagoda in the center with four smaller ones at each corner, all heavily gilded and around them an enclosure elaborately paneled with pictures, Buddhistic mythological subjects, the platform and steps leading to the temple being covered with white cloth. In the center of the building had been sunk a marble pool, about twelve feet square, into which the river flowed and leading down to the water were marble stairs protected with silver rods, down which the Prince was conducted by the King and received by his uncle, Chowfa Bhanurengsi, Prince Ong Noi, who proceeded to perform the solemn ceremony of the sacred bath.

Golden Temple and Flotilla on the Menam.

At 10 A. M. the King accompanied by the Crown Prince, who had been attending religious exercises at one of the wats, surrounded by a number of bishops in their yellow robes, proceeded to a handsome pavilion where a number of tapers had been placed on a circular pedestal, when the King, after lighting several with the sacred fire that had been blessed by the Bramins, handed the torch to the Prince who lit the remainder. The priests then offered up a prayer after which the King, Prince and attendant nobles repaired to the Golden Temple which was soon filled, none but nobles and priests of the highest rank being allowed entrance. Around it on a wide platform were stationed courtiers in old Siam uniforms, armed with flint lock muskets, in the water a number of men swam around the temple to keep the water spirits from entering, while up and down the river were stationed gun boats and steamers, with a flotilla of barges decorated with flags and bunting. The astrologers had cast the horoscope of the young Prince and announced that the auspicious moment was 11:26 A. M., at which time a signal was fired, then the cannon on the vessels and a battery on shore thundered, thousands of muskets were discharged, the bands played and the thousands in attendance knew that the solemn rites had commenced that was to make the Crown Prince heir apparent to the throne. Handsome pavilions draped with white and red canvas richly carpeted and ornamented with silk curtains had been prepared for the diplomatic body and nobles, and while the water rite was being observed refreshments were handed around by palace servitors.

The sacred water rites over in the Golden Temple, which occupied about an hour, the King and Prince returned, His Majesty bowing most graciously as he passed apparently well pleased and no nobler specimen of his nation was present among the many nobles of his realm.

At 4 P. M. same day the diplomatic body and high officials assembled at the palace Abheren Pamehepard, a salute of twenty-one guns was fired when the Crown Prince was seated on a handsome throne, dressed in royal robes of gold encrusted with jewels, surmounted with a silk canopy, the King standing by his side a few feet to his left, back of him the Queen mother and other female residents of the palace with several children all handsomely dressed. To the right of the King was arranged the Princes and high officials, in front the diplomatic body and to the left the lesser nobles. The large audience room was ablaze with light from crystal chandeliers filled with perfumed oil that threw a mellow glow over silken curtains, burnished arms, and rich tapestry, falling with most pleasing effect on the vast number present, their gorgeous uniforms lending additional brilliancy to the scene, while the myriad jewels on their belts, scarfs and breasts flashed and scintillated like glow worms in a parterre of flowers. As soon as the various bodies had arranged themselves addresses of congratulation were delivered by Prince Ong Noi on the part of the royal family, Hon. Ernst Satow, H. B. M. Minister, in behalf of the diplomatic body, and Chow Fa Mahah Mahlah, Minister of the Interior, for the lesser nobles, to which His Majesty replied at some length and with considerable feeling. Upon his conclusion the Crown Prince arose, stepped off of his throne and without a tremor spoke a memorized speech which pleased all present.

The King then announced that the audience was over and stepping forward shook hands with the British and American Ministers, the French Charge d'Affairs and the Admiral of the French fleet, then in Tonquin waters. Bowing gracefully the King and Prince retired, and as the cannon thundered, the drums beat and bugles blared, the royal son was declared and recognized as the heir apparent and future King of Siam. Amid salvos of artillery the immense flood of humanity that overflowed the palace grounds slowly ebbed away, and as the upper deep became studded with the orbs of night, less numerous than the jewels of Ind that had for hours dazzled us, a practical realization of the wealth of the orient, for on the brow of the Queen blazed a coronet of purest stones that far outrivalled the paler beauties of the Empress of Night that hung like a silver sickel in the western skies, I drove rapidly homeward, having had a repletion of Asiatic grandeur and oriental splendor, pomp and power. The ceremony in the Golden Temple, the water rite, I have alluded to elsewhere.

His title is now Somdetch Phra Borom Orotsaterat Chow Fa Maha Chaeron Tit Aditoasa Chulalongkorn Bodintara Tetwaraugoon Baromagnduarensoon Bottesa Devawong OoKretepong Warosutochat Tanzarark Weratreeboon Serepepat Narwesoot, Crown Prince of Siam. Translation from the medal struck in commemoration of the event.

XXI.
PROMINENT TEMPLES AND PAGODAS.

Of the fifty-eight leading wats or temples in the city of Bangkok wat P'hya, or temple of the Emerald Idol, situate in the palace grounds, excells all others not only in the city but kingdom, for the beauty of its exterior and interior. Its style of architecture is similar to most of the wats but its main beauty is the finish of its exterior; the floor laid with German silver bricks, its altar surmounted by the sacred emerald idol, the walls elaborately covered with paintings representing Nirvana and from the ceiling is suspended innumerable chandeliers that sparkle like brilliants as the sun streams through the windows. This grand temple is the admiration of every one that is so fortunate as to visit it.

As regards architectural beauty wat Chang has not its equal in the East and as it rises up from the bank of the river it looks, with all of its spires and domes sharply defined, as if it was the creation of fancy rather than the work of man, perfect in its proportions, a vision of loveliness. It is a bell shaped pagoda with a lofty pracheda or sacred spire, about two hundred and fifty feet in height, with four smaller pagodas at each corner, all built solidly of brick and ornamented with a peculiar mosaic, grotesque and fantastic, made of porcelain cups, plates, dishes, etc. of all sizes and colors, whole and broken, set into a cement to form figures of elephants, monkeys, birds, demons, griffins, flowers, fruit, vines, and arabesque, unique and original. Nearly

half way up are four large niches in which are images of Buddha riding on three elephants, facing the cardinal points of the compass, which gives this pagoda its name, Chang being the Siamese for elephant. Other niches, near the base, are filled with statues of gods and nondescripts. About twenty acres of ground is attached to this wat, which is handsomely laid off, containing residences for priests, temples for preaching, halls and library, salas, flower and fruit gardens, ponds, grottos, statues of Buddha, giants, warriors, nondescripts, etc. The walks to and from the temple are laid with heavy stone slabs worn smooth by the bare feet of the numerous devotees that seek the cool retreat of the cloistered halls and the shade of the sacred trees that clasp the pagoda in a vast emerald frame. At the entrance of the main gate way are two immense wooden statues, Naks or demi-gods, holding huge maces in their hand, grotesque objects, and similar statues are to be found in the palace grounds and at nearly all the wats.

On the opposite side of the river is the much visited temple wat Poh, which contains the idol known as the Sleeping Buddha, the largest in the world, it being one hundred and forty-eight feet in length, and at its shoulders sixty-five feet in height. It represents Buddha as lying with his head on one arm in the act of meditation and is most admirably proportioned, its large mild looking eyes ornament a pleasant looking face that has upon it a look of supreme content, as if it was a sentient being, with its gaze fixed on the to come and impervious to the passions that rule men, such as Raphael gave his saints; its arms, head and neck are perfectly moulded notwithstanding its colossal size, as is also the body, which is built of brick covered with a thick coat of laquer, heavily plated with gold leaf. The greatest curiosity is its feet, the toes all equal, and the soles, sixteen feet in length, are perfectly flat, covered with the mystic symbols pertaining to a Buddha, inlaid with gold and mother of pearl, each of which is typical of something connected with the teaching of Gautama. The building in which it reclines was built expressly for it and is lighted by a large number of windows and doors which fly open at the request of sight seers, who always hand the keepers of the temple a tical or two as a recompense for their trouble. In the extensive grounds that belong to this favorite wat are a number of handsome buildings and five massive topes or pagodas, one by each King of the present dynasty. Along the broad paved walks are rows of trees that cast a cooling shade, and near the center of the gardens is a large pond in which a number of aligators are kept, and for a small sum are exhibited to visitors. The grounds are surrounded by high walls whitewashed, and the gates guarded by Naks. It is one of the best wats to visit if a person wishes to see all kinds of Siamese architecture, and the attendants are polite and accommodating. The wats and grounds throughout Siam are always open to strangers as well as to the natives.

The Chinese have several wats in the city, the largest of which is wat Conlayer Nemit, which occupies a square of ground and is noted for the number of its grotesque idols and statues scattered through its grounds. It is one of the largest temples in the city, its immense roof is at least one hundred feet in height and at one end of the mammoth chamber or hall is a gigantic brass Buddha sitting cross-legged, fifty feet in height and forty feet across its knees, one of the handsomest images in Bangkok, other idols are scattered through the building of various sizes. Two smaller wats are located in this compound, one containing a gilded Buddha sitting on a rock, supported by a copper elephant on one side and on the other by a large lead monkey in attitudes of adoration. In the other wat is located a large statue of Buddha standing, with about one hundred smaller statues, in different positions, grouped around it, made of various metals, many of them gilded, and a few of wood. It is said that some of the smaller ones were made of silver and gold, but the priests seemed ignorant of the matter and if there were any such refused to point them out. As is usual in most wats the walls were covered with highly colored paintings of Siamese traditions somewhat discolored with smoke and dirt, in fact, as a general thing, the wats are all filthy, smell of coal oil, and as the priests seldom preach in them they are not swept out or ventilated. After visiting one or two wats you get an idea of the whole, they are all built in the same style of architecture and have similar altars and surroundings, some more elaborate and costly than the others, the roof usually made of various colored tiles and at the ridge poles extend wooden ornaments very much in the shape of a bullock's horn which gives an artistic finish to the building. The doors are large and artistically carved and gilded, some very elaborate, the window shutters, as they use no glass, are massive and handsomely carved, many of them works of art, denoting great skill on the part of the designer and workmen.

The wat Pra Prat'om Chedee, is the oldest as well as the most magnificent and largest of the Buddhist temples. It is situated in the center of a vast wilderness of jungle grass on a canal leading into Tacheen river, about eight hours distant by boat from Bangkok and is erected on a spot where it is supposed that Buddha passed the night during a storm while on his peregrinations through Siam, its name meaning the pagoda of a god that slept, its height being 414 feet; this mighty edifice, from the ground up, being the work of man, as it is built on a level plain. Its origin is shrouded in mystery but tradition has it that it was originally built by Phya Kong, a powerful Rajah, who slew his father in battle. Having suffered the bitterest remorse a Buddhist oracle extended to him the idea that if he wished to have the sin of parricide removed that he erect on the spot where his father was slain and where Buddha slept a pagoda reaching above the highest flight of doves and enshrine in it a sacred relic of Buddha. In obedience to the oracle he did so, expending untold sums on the work. It is reported that a miracle was effected through the efficacy of a prayer offered here by the Chief Priest of Siam, who invoked the angel in charge of the temple that if any of the sacred relics of the Buddha had been enshrined there, that he would divide them so that he could deposit them in the royal wat at Bangkok, as the ancient pagoda was too far off in the wilderness for the people to visit for worship. A month or so after this, while the priests were worshipping in wat Ma-ha-t'at, where there is a very precious image of Buddha, of great antiquity, they beheld a red smoke ascending from this idol, having the fragrance of incense, while it glowed

Brass Idol in Temple, Bangkok.

as if red hot. Somewhat frightened they examined it, there was no heat, but the smoke hung about it like incense and filled the temple with its fragrance, seemingly a profound mystery. The Chief Priest was notified of the phenomena and he repaired to the temple with a number of his followers and while pursuing his investigations he discovered in the golden urn used for preserving sacred relics two more pieces than there had been before. He inquired of the resident priests and the keepers of the door if they knew how they came in the urn, no one knew, and all were convinced that they could not have been placed there by mortal hand, that the Chief Priests' prayer had been answered, that the angel that watched over Pra Prat'om Chedee had responded to the appeal and placed them in the urn. The relics were each about the size of a mustard seed, white like the flower of the P'eekoon and had each two white dots in a straight line on them. They are now deposited in a pagoda of precious stone in the Pra-rata-na Satradarom. Pra Prat'om was a mass of ruins up till 1855, when King Monkut and some of his chief nobles resolved to restore it and the result of their labor is that it is now the wonder and admiration of that section. Owing to its isolation but few Europeans have visited this magnificent specimen of Siamese architecture.

After a weary pull through the canals you step out of your boat and looking upward are struck with wonder at the magnitude of the structure and the vast amount of treasure and labor that had been expended in rearing this supreme monument to Buddha, having but seen its upper tower at a distance sharply outlined against the bluest of skies. It is surrounded on all four sides by a row of massive buildings, each fronting 750 feet by fifteen in width and thirty in height, covered with bright red tiles, the walls stuccoed yellow. On the corners, where the buildings connect, are towers finely proportioned and the gateways are surmounted with arched roofs. Inside these buildings form a verandah encircling the whole enclosure. Passing through one of the gateways you ascend three steps to a neatly paved plateau twenty feet or more in width, then up a flight of marble steps through a handsome porch to the second plateau, also about twenty feet wide, richly finished and filled with artificial lakes, mountains, caverns, miniature pagodas and temples, statues, etc., a portico surrounding a circular row of buildings. From thence you ascend to the third plateau paved with marble and shaded by trees and rare shrubs and scattered all around it granite circular tables, benches, flower pots, couches, &c. The circle of this floor cannot be less than two thousand feet by thirty in width. The fourth plateau is reached by a flight of four steps through another row of buildings, the door opening into a narrow hall also circling the pagoda which is lighted by scores of oval windows on the outside and on the inside a series of handsome arches open on the next plateau. The floor is laid with artificial marble and from the ceiling, the entire circuit, chandaliers of Siamese workmanship are suspended about ten feet apart. This hall is divided into four parts, temples, enshrined in them statues of Buddha from life size up to those of gigantic stature, most of them handsomely gilded. On the outer wall, in the spaces between the windows, are texts written in Pali, occupying about four foot space, the characters neatly executed in putty

Grand Temple at Phra Pratom.

and embossed on the wall by some process that makes
them hard as stone. This hall is about one thousand
feet in the circuit and on the same level is an open
court fifteen feet wide surrounding another structure
with embrasures in which are fitted large panes of
different colored glass for the purpose of holding lamps,
tastefully arched, and placed about three feet apart,
numbering two hundred and thirty. In the rear of
this wall of lamps is another open space handsomely
paved, about ten feet higher up, eight feet wide,
making the fifth plateau, nine hundred feet round,
forming the base of the pagoda at a distance of thirty
feet from the ground, three hundred feet in circumference, and from thence upward to the spire three hundred
and eighty-four feet. Above this plateau there are no
more places for walking and it then takes the usual
form of the largest pagodas, belted with seven zones,
which gradually diminish as they ascend about sixty
feet where the smooth face of the pagoda, its dome,
commences, running up one hundred feet, then the
pagoda proper takes the form of a pracheda and is
crowned with a frame work of royal metals having projections and a lance-like spire. On the projections are
suspended golden bells that ring out melodiously as
they are swayed by the breeze, sounding like the
whispering of angels in the ether as their soft tintinabulation fills the air and falls from above like a benison, ever sounding the praises of the liberal spirits that
have reared this vast poem of enduring brick and stone
in the wilds where Buddha slept and a King died, a
monument of merit, so that the sin of parricide should
pass away from a son stricken down by remorse. The
golden bells, of immense value, are hung so high heaven-

ward that no one has ever attempted to loot them. Surrounding this temple are a large number of brick and bamboo houses, erected by the King and others, now occupied by the priests, making quite a city. This whole structure, solidly built of brick and stone, from the ground up, was raised by manual labor and its cost, even in this land of forced labor, must have been enormous.

In its restoration Choo Phya Thepakin, the author of the "Kitchanukit," alone, spent a fabulous sum to carry out the Siamese idea of *tumboon*—merit making. A volume of many pages could be written on the temples of Siam, that would be read with interest if some "Old Mortality" would arise and devote his time to it. They are everywhere and like the monasteries of the dark ages occupy the finest places in the land, and I have been assured that at least one-third of the available sites for villages and farms are now occupied by the priests as wat grounds.

Far in the interior, two days journey from Bangkok, is an old wat fast going to ruin, in its wide court yard is one of the most singular productions of this artistic people, a procession headed by an elephant, made up of priests and people, as large as life, the elephant being over twelve feet high, all carved out of a solid rock. No one can tell who carved the stone nor why it was done, it stands there to-day amid flowering vines and sheltering Bo-tree as it did when fresh from the chisel of the designer, a singular work of art. There is nothing like it elsewhere in the kingdom and but few are aware of its existence, as it has but lately been rescued from oblivion by the ubiquitous photographer who has portrayed it on his plates for the admiration of man. The wat, in whose court this stone procession is found, is a ruin of vast proportions but the figures remain so perfect that the folds of their dress can be seen and the trappings of the elephant seem as if carved but yesterday. It must have required years to have thus hewn these numerous figures out of the rock, as they all have been carved from a single stone.

XXII.

BUDDHISM IN SIAM.

A number of learned oriental scholars have spent years in reading the vast mass of fact and fiction that has come down to us from the writers of the East concerning the Lord Buddha, whose followers now number at least one-third of the human race, but none have given it a closer attention than the late Henry Alabaster, who spent many years in Bangkok as interpreter to the British Legation and councillor of the King, a ripe Pali scholar, and from his work, "The Wheel of the Law," collated from Siamese manuscripts, the "Kitchanukit," and the Patamma Samphathiyan or First Festival of Omniscience, I have derived much information and annex his introduction to the Life of Buddha; as translated from the Siamese:

"The Great, the Holy Lord, the being who was about to become a Buddha, passed the first twenty-nine years of his life as a layman by the name of Prince Sidharta. He then became a religious mendicant, and for six years subjected himself to self-denials of a nature that other men could not endure. Thereafter he became the Lord Buddha and gave to men and angels the draught of immortality, which is the savour of the True Law. Forty-five years after this the Lord, the Teacher, entered the Holy Nirvana, passing thereto as he lay between two lofty trees in the State Gardens of the Malla Princes, near the Royal City of Kusinagara."

Mr. Alabaster was fortunate in his labors to have

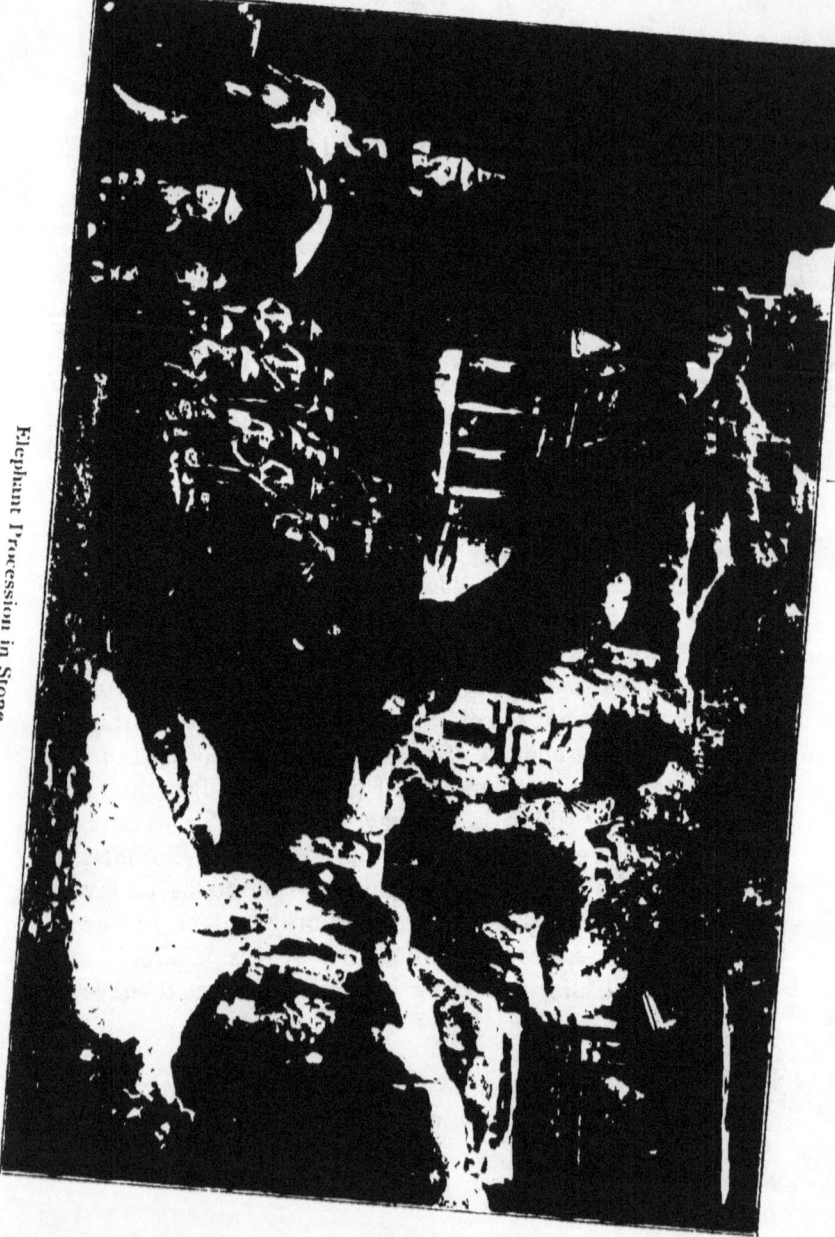

Elephant Procession in Stone.

the assistance of His Majesty King Monkut and Chow Phya Thipaken, both learned in Pali lore, in the preparation of the "Wheel of the Law," thus giving to the general reader a knowledge of the teachings of Buddha and his life which must prove invaluable to the searcher after knowledge in that direction, from which I have condensed a brief account of the Buddha of many nations, and his peculiar doctrines.

It would seem from his researches that the Siamese have derived their religion, most of their ceremonies and the better part of their language from the ancient Aryans, "the respectable race" of Central India. Buddhism, in its primitive form, consisted of four great truths conveying the idea that as all states of existence which we can conceive of are states of vanity, sorrow and change, the object of the wisely pious must be to escape from them, and that it is only possible to escape from them by eradicating all delight in worldly pleasure and raising the mind to that intellectual state in which there is no longer any cleaving to existence, but a tranquil readiness to pass into the perfect rest of Nirvana. In the course of time monasticism crept in, the result of the unnatural lives led by the monks, which combined the doctrines of the founder of the faith with their unauthorized dogmas and absurdities, the result of warped, fantastic and prurient minds. The Buddhist speaks of heaven rather than hell, thinks it uncharitable to damn everlastingly those who may differ with him, but with the degeneracy of his race he has accepted many false ideas and fables and thus invented a system of meditation which instead of expanding the mind tends to contract it almost to idiocy. Notwithstanding the Brahmins drove the

Buddhists from India their rites are observed in all State ceremonials and they live harmoniously in Siam where the Brahmin soothsayers and astrologers are regarded as prominent personages and consulted upon every important occasion, worship in their own temples, full of grotesque and obscene gods, Indra, Vishnu, Brahma and other Hindu divinities. The Siamese have a mixed mythology, mainly derived from the Hindu; their gods are regarded but as mortals in a superior state of transmigration. Among other things is found the Trinitarian idea represented by Buddha, the Law and the Church, also superstitions regarding Naga, (the snake,) powerful as a god; angels of the gate and trees, relic worship in the building of topes or parachedis, the worship of the Pipul or sacred Bo-tree, delineated in their ancient sculpture, seemingly one of the earliest species of adoration, such as the intelligent Buddhist of to-day tenders to the images of the great teacher: the worship of an idea through a symbol. To the uneducated mind there seems nothing nobler than the monarch of the forest. In its branches he finds shelter from an enemy or shade from the heat of the sun, its foliage inspires him with the idea of beauty, while its size and majestic proportions strike him with awe and he venerates it as a symbol of Deity. Picking up a blossom that had fallen from its sheltering bough and placing it on a stone, to preserve its beauty, apparently originated a worship, an altar and a sacrifice. This probably was the origin of tree worship and upon every festal occasion the Bo-tree is decorated with the yellow mantle of Buddha, wreaths of flowers and lacon images.

It has been held by some writers that the tenets of Buddhism are the same as the Sankhya and other schools

of philosophy in India, which is incorrect. While both
teach that the great object of man is to destroy the misery inseparable from ordinary existence, "neither I am,
nor is ought mine," and those systems are grounded on
transmigration, the belief that prevailed in India three
thousand years ago; the former recognized the existence of a personal God, actively interested in the
world and making his law known by revelation, and
that man was imbued with a soul, which is incompatible
with Buddha's teachings. The oldest Buddhist classics
deal but little in metaphysical niceties, but many of
them have since the days of Buddha been corrupted.
Those that have the most bearing and are regarded as
the true text of the teacher are the stone edicts of
King Asaka, in the third century before Christ. Desiring to extend the Buddhist religion he had edicts
cut in stone and disseminated throughout his realms,
which have been deciphered by Princep and other
oriental scholars, and they are very simple. He enjoins his subjects "Not to slay animals; to plant trees
and dig wells by the roadside for the comfort of man
and beast; the appointment of teachers to superintend
morals, encourage the charitable and those addicted to
virtue;" orders his subjects to "hold assemblies for
the enforcement of moral obligations — duty to parents,
friends, children, relatives, Brahmins and Sramanas
(Buddhist monks)." "Liberality is good, abstinence
from prodigality and slander is good, non-injury
of living creatures is good." "The beloved of the
gods (himself) does not esteem glory and fame as of
great value; for it may be acquired by crafty and unworthy persons." "To me there is not satisfaction in
the pursuit of wordly affairs; the most worthy pursuit

is the prosperity of the whole world. My endeavor is to be blameless to all creatures, to make them happy here below, and to enable them to attain Swarga (heaven)."

This last edict has been much commented on as he did not mention Nirvana only Swarga, the place to be sought, heaven.

The chief point and belief of the modern Buddhist is that of transmigration, not only into other human states, but into all forms, active and passive, in fact that all gods and animals, men and brutes, have no intrinsic difference between them. They all change places according to their merit and demerit. They exist because of the disturbance caused by their demerits. How they began to exist is not even asked; it is a question pertaining to the Infinite, of which no explanation is attempted. Even in dealing with the illustrious being who afterwards became Buddha no attempt is made to picture a beginning of his existence, and we are only told of the beginning of his aspirations to become a Buddha and the countless existences that he subsequently passed through ere he achieved his object. The teaching on this point is the equality of all beings, that the relative positions of all beings are perfectly just, being self caused by the good and evil conduct in previous existences; that if a good man is poor and wretched, he is so because he has lived evilly in previous generations; if a bad man is prosperous, he is so because he had lived well in previous generations. Having declared the fact of transmigration and the principle which causes its various states, Buddhism teaches that there is no real or permanent satisfaction in any state of transmigration; that neither the painless luxuries of the lower heavens, nor the tranquility of the highest angels can be considered as happiness, for they will have an end followed by a recurrence of varied and frequently sorrowful existences, thus Buddhists, rich or poor, acknowledge no providence and see more reason to lament existence than to be grateful for a future life. Nirvana, the extinction of all existence, they claim, must be the object of the truly wise man, but what that annihilation is has not been clearly defined and has been the subject of endless contention. The choicest epithets have been lavished on it by the Siamese, such as "Nirvana is a place of comfort, where there is no care ; lovely is the glorious realm of Nirvana;" also, "Jewelled realm of happiness, the immortal Nirvana."

One of the pertinent questions propounded by the seeker after knowledge is "how to attain Nirvana?" and the closest reasoners have reached the conclusion that the only solution is that as our every thought and word and act is voluntary, or the result of desire, and must be followed by its effect, we must annihilate our existence by removing all cause for future action, eradicate all desire, and then Nirvana may be attained. It is claimed that ignorance is the first cause of which worldly desire is but the effect, but Buddha had nothing to do with anything that pertained to the Infinite, hence it is argued had it not been for ignorance of the future, all beings having perceived that Nirvana was the only object desirable would have destroyed all that prevented its attainment, in fact would have destroyed existence.

The four emnient truths of Buddhism are termed the "Four Paths and the Four Fruits," or the four highest degrees of saintship, viz: First, Srota apatti— "the state of entering into the stream of wisdom."

The saint who has attained this cannot have more than seven births among men and angels before he enters Nirvana.

Second, Sakridagamin—"he who must come back once." After attaining this degree there will be only one birth among men or angels before reaching Nirvana.

Third, Anagamin—"he will not come back." There will be another birth, but not in the worlds of sensuality. From the heavens of the Brahmins Nirvana will be attained.

Fourth, Arhat "the venerable." This is the perfect saint who will pass to Nirvana without further birth.

These four "truths" only assert that purity is essential to the entering into the paths of the saints and that men by countless births can become a Buddha, a teacher of the paths, but the majority of those who enter the paths are only led into them by the personal influence of a Buddha, then by the inherent power of their accumulated merit they will be born to meet a Buddha and by his teachings be led into the paths of the saints; the object of men must therefore be the accumulation of merit and repression of demerit, thus Buddha inculcates a virtuous and self-sacrificing life, the practice of charity and the exercise of meditation, and all writers award the highest praise to the moral teaching of this great religion, of which the following are the five principal commandments, viz.:

First: Not to destroy life.

Second: Not to obtain another's property by unjust means.

Third: Not to indulge the passions so as to invade the legal or natural rights of other men.

Fourth: Not to tell lies.

Fifth: Not to partake of anything intoxicating.

Other commandments relate to the repression of personal vanity, greed, fondness for luxury, etc., and among evil tendencies, especially singled out for reprobation, is covetousness, anger, folly, sensuality, arrogance, want of veneration, scepticism and ingratitude. These bad qualities are personified as leaders of the army of Mara, the evil one, who, with a curious parallelism to our legend of Satan, is made out to be an archangel of a heaven even higher than that of the beneficent Indra. Charity seems to be the main pillar in the Buddhistic edifice, the whole character of Buddha is full of charity, insomuch that although his perfection was such that at almost an infinite period before he became Buddha he might, during the teaching of an earlier Buddha, have escaped from the current of existence, which he regarded as misery, he remained in that current and passed through countless painful transmigrations in order that he might ultimately benefit not himself but all other beings by becoming a Buddha and helping all those whose ripe merits could only be perfected by the teachings of a Buddha. The number of former Buddhas is countless, but they are all supposed to have lived and taught in the same manner. There is a history of the last twenty-four Buddhas preceeding Gotama Buddha, supposed to have been related by him. Twenty-one of the number appeared in eleven previous conditions of the world, which, they claim, is periodically destroyed and recreated by the influence of merit and demerit. In some of these eleven creations only one Buddha appeared; in others two, three or four. The present creation is highly fortunate, as it will number five. Of these three: Kakusandha, Konagamma and Kasyappa, preceeded Buddha, and Maitra Buddha will follow him after his doctrine will have been forgotten.

Meditation is regarded as the highest means of self improvement and is represented in three classes: Kammathan, Bhavanah and Dhyana. The first, by meditation on the nature of elementary substances, leading to the thorough appreciation of the unsatisfactoriness; the second, to the characteristics of charity, pity, joy, sorrow and equanimity, leading the mind to a pure state of intellectuality; the third, that each step, accompanied by a state of ecstacy or trance, is supposed, during its continuance to remove man from the subjugation of the ordinary laws of nature, so much so that he would become a master of magical arts, such as flying, becoming invisible, changing his form, etc. King Monkut laughed at such fables and remarked that "there are no such saints nowadays," that there were none that could achieve the state of Dhyana. With meditation was devised by its founders the system that facilitated its practice, monastic asceticism, but the monastic vow is not binding for life.

Prayer is not necessarily a Buddhist practice, as they have no divine being to pray to. What has been termed prayer by Bishop Pallegoi, and others are merely sentences from the Pali for repetition, a list of the thirty-two elements into which their philosophers resolve the human body, the repetition of which is supposed to assist meditation on the vanity and misery of existence; a list of the epithets of Buddha designed to help meditation on the excellence of his teachings, and the creed or profession of belief in Buddha, his law and his church. It is customary for the monks to recite formulas of this kind, but it cannot properly be called prayer. Invocations to a Buddha are frequently mentioned, for instance Maia's desire, the mother of Buddha, expressed to the former Buddha, Wipassi:* "May I be, in some after generation, the mother of a Buddha like thyself;" or the incident of Buddha throwing into the air his locks that he had just cut off, crying, "If, indeed, I am about to attain the Buddhahood, let these locks remain suspended in the air," and they remained suspended by his excessive merit. It seems that a species of prayer has sprung up from the superstitions that have been engrafted on Buddhism, as is recorded the appeal of the girl Suchada, to the angels of the tree, to grant her "a happy marriage and a male child." The Siamese are angel worshippers, many of them ignorant of the tenets of their own religion, pray not only to angels but to Buddha and worship him with offerings, as they do the spirits of the air that they suppose is always hovering about them, but the monks only recite the montras, that is verses and other formulas, which are mainly written in the Pali, and many of them do not understand their meaning.

The sermons of Buddha have been carefully preserved and handed down, denoting a powerful intellect. He was undoubtedly one of the greatest and most original thinkers that the world has cognizance of, and his scheme of salvation, if it can be so called, was promulgated at a time when superstition, sophistry and priestcraft held supreme sway. He laid down his scep-

* In Turnour's "Pali Annals," Wipassi is mentioned as the nineteenth of the twenty-one Buddhas, Dipongkara having been the earliest. Since Wipassi's time the world has been twice destroyed and re-created.

ter and went among the people clad as a mendicant
and without the charm, rites or priestly fancies then in
vogue; in fact without any of the gods that men loved
and trusted; enunciated a creed based solely on the
cardinal principles of love and charity. It is asserted by
the leading theologists of Siam that the Lord Buddha
never expressed the idea that his religion would be
universal, "that he was but as a transient gleam of light,
indicating the path of truth. His religion was but as a
stone thrown into a pool covered with floating weeds;
it cleared an opening through which the pure water
was seen, but the effect would die away and the weeds
close up as before. The Lord Buddha saw the bright,
the exact, the abstruse, the difficult course, and but for
the persuasion of angels would not have attempted to
teach that which he considered too difficult for men to
follow." As a fact that he did not care for a universal
religion he taught that as the existence of this world
was unsatisfactory and miserable the cessation of the
renewal of the species was not a matter to be deplored,
annihilation meant happiness. Nearly the entire East
accepted his teachings with a blind idolatory, but most
of his creed was afterward overshadowed by the monasticism of the monks, as has much of Christianity been
rendered obscure by the fabrications of priestly crafts-
men during the dark ages. The great question ever
uppermost in men's minds was as pertinent then as now:
"If a man die shall he live again?" the higher life; and
Buddha attempted to answer it in his first recorded
sermon, which is translated from the Pali text in the
so-called Sutra of the Foundation of the Kingdom of
Righteousness, among the very oldest of the Buddhist
records, as follows:

"There are two extremes which the man who has devoted himself to the higher life ought not to follow — the habitual practice, on the one hand, of those things whose attractions depend upon the passions and especially of sensuality (a low and gamma-pagan, way of seeking gratification, unworthy, unprofitable and fit only for the worldly minded); and the habitual practice, on the other hand, of asceticism (or self mortification), which is not only painful, but as unworthy and unprofitable as the other. But the Tathagata (the Buddha) has discovered a middle path, which avoids these two extremities, a path which opens the eyes and bestows understanding, which leads to peace of mind, to the higher wisdom, to full enlightenment—in a word to Nirvana. And this path is the noble eight fold path of

Right views,	A harmless livelihood,
High aims,	Perseverance in well-doing,
Kindly speech,	Intellectual activity, and
Upright conduct,	Earnest thought.

"Birth," said the Teacher, "is attended with pain, and so are decay and disease and death. Union with the unpleasant is painful and separation from the pleasant; and any craving that is unsatisfied is a condition of sorrow. Now, all this amounts, in short, to this, that wherever there are the conditions of individuality, there are the conditions of sorrow. This is the First Truth, the truth about sorrow.

"The cause of sorrow is the thirst or craving which causes the renewal of individual existence, is accompanied by evil, and is ever seeking satisfaction, now here, now there—that is to say, the craving either for sensual gratification, or for continued existence, or for the cessation of existence. This is the Noble Truth concerning the origin of sorrow.

" Deliverance from sorrow is the complete destruction, the laying aside, the getting rid of, the being free from, the harboring no longer of, this passionate craving. This is the Noble Truth concerning the destruction of sorrow.

"The path which leads to the destruction of sorrow is this Noble Eightfold Path alone—that is to say, right views, high aims, kindly speech, upright conduct, a harmless livelihood, perseverance in well doing, intellectual activity, and earnest thought. This is the Noble Truth of the Path which leads to the destruction of sorrow."

To understand this sermon a person should be well versed in the mythology of the East and it loses much of its force in the translation. It is an attempt to suggest to the Buddhist the course he must pursue, to point out to him the obstacles that he must meet in his progress along the Noble Path. The Eight Divisons of the Path show the qualities of the mind that he should seduously cultivate so that he can successfully contend against the Ten Fetters: Delusion of Self, Indecision, Dependence on the Efficacy of Rites and Ceremonies, Bodily Passions, Ill Will towards Individuals, the Highest Fruit, the Supression of the desire for a future life with a material body, the Desire for a future life in an immaterial world, Pride, Self Righteousness, the last but one to be broken, the most difficult to conquer and to which superior minds are peculiarly liable, Pharisees; and lastly is placed Ignorance. When all else has been conquered this will remain, the thorn in the flesh of the wise and good, the last enemy and bitterest foe of man. As the Eight Divisions of the Noble Path show him his duty so the Ten Fetters point out to him what he should most earnestly contend against, thus from the two combined the reader can get an idea of the state of mind called in Buddhist writings Arahatship, or the Fruit of the Noble Eightfold Path, the state of a man made perfect, the Noble Path traversed, all the Fetters broken, the mind purified and Nirvana attained.

The doctrines of Buddha are now receiving more attention from the western nations than ever before, they are being shorn of much of the superstitions that have hitherto surrounded them and as a late English writer, T. W. Rhys Davids, truthfully says:

"The fact is, that in spite of the general belief to the contrary, Christianity is at heart more pessimist even than Buddhism. To the majority of average Christians this world is a place of probation, a vale of tears, though its tears will be wiped away and its sorrows changed into unutterable joy in a better world beyond. To the Buddhist such hopes seem to be without foundation, to indulge in them is only possible to the foolish and ignorant; while thus to despair of the present life, thus to postpone the highest fruit of salvation to a world beyond the grave is base, unworthy and unwise. Here and now according to the Buddhist we are to seek salvation, and to seek it in right views and high aims, kindly and upright behaviour, a harmless livelihood, perseverance in well doing, intellectual activity and earnest thought."

Among the many books that the Buddhist has hitherto relied on as orthodox is the "Traiphome," the standard work on Siamese cosmogomy, which is a collection of chapters from the ancient Vedas, various extracts from the Sutras, parables, proverbs and fables, which were collected together by the monks, at an early day, and furnished one of the Kings, a convert of Buddha, as the actual work of the great Teacher. The people, being uneducated, accepted the "Traiphome" as it came from their hands as living truths, with all of its fabulous stories. Among others I select the following in regard to transmigration:

"In the sacred books we read of a certain rich merchant who was not a Buddhist, whose death-bed thoughts were only about money. The result of his merit and demerit caused him to be born a puppy in the very house that had belonged to him when a man and of which his son was master. One day, as Buddha passed the house collecting alms, the puppy ran to the gate and barked and the Lord called to it 'Tothai, Tothai,' and it ran and laid down at his feet. Then was the son very angry at the insult he considered to have been cast against his father by giving his name to a dog and he remonstrated with Buddha. Buddha asked him 'Have you yet found the money your father buried during his life?' He answered 'only a part of it.' 'Then if you would know whether or not this puppy is Tothai, the merchant, treat him with great respect for several days and he will show you.' And the young man did so and the dog indicated the place where the treasure was hid and from thenceforward the son of Tothai followed the teachings of the Lord Buddha."

Buddhists believe that every act, word or thought has its consequence, which will appear sooner or later in the present or future state, that merit and demerit is the law of nature or guiding power with which they supply the place of God, which the Siamese called Kam, sometimes translated fate or consequence. Evil acts will produce evil consequences—that is a man will have misfortune in this world or an evil birth in hell or as an animal in some future existence. Good acts will result in general good. There is no God who judges of these acts and rewards recompense or punishment; but the reward or punishment is simply the inevitable effect of Kam, which works out its own results. The meritorious and demeritorious Kam, which living beings have caused to exist by their own acts, words, or thoughts, are whether their fruits be joy or sorrow to be classed under three heads.

The first, is the Kam of which creatures will have the fruits at once in their present state of existence. The second is the Kam with which creatures will have the fruits in the next state of existence. The third, is the Kam of which creatures will have the fruit in future states of existence from the third onward.

Merit or demerit will cause a tendency of the soul in one direction sometimes as many as seven births and deaths, which will be followed by a relapse in the opposite direction for six or less times; such is the way of the soul. The merit of a single act of charity or the demerit of the slaughter of a single ant will be followed by one of these three Kams. These Kams are divided up into a number of lesser Kams covering almost every transaction of life.

The question being asked of Chao Phya Thepakin, author of the "Kitchanukit," a book explaining many things, "If a man believes in a future existence, governed by Kam, how shall he make merit to save himself from future misery?" The answer: "By following the teachings of Buddha, the holy and omniscient one; the teaching which praises kindness and compassion, and pleasure in the general happiness of all beings, and freedom from love or dislike to individuals, and which forbids hatred and jealousy, and envy and revenge; the religion that Than, or almsgiving; Sin, or rules of morality, and Bhawana, or simple meditation; which, with fidelity and other virtues, are the merits of an ordinary class; and the firm observance of the rules of the priesthood, which is merit of the highest class."

Comparing the commandments of Buddha with the laws of other religions he observes that "theft, adultery, lying and the destruction of human life (with exceptions) are regarded as sins by all people; that intoxication is only forbidden by Buddhists, Brahmins and Mahometans, and that the destruction of life, other than human, is regarded as sin by none but Buddhists and Brahmins, believers in the Buddha Avatar." In regard to the vice of intoxication he says: "It is a cause of the heart becoming excited and overcome. By nature there is already an intoxication in man caused by desire, anger, and folly; he is already inclined to excess and not thoughtful of the impermanence, misery and vanity of all things. If we stimulate this natural intoxication by drinking it will become more daring; and if the natural inclination is to anger, anger will become excessive and acts of violence and murder will result. Similarly with other inclinations. The drunken man neither thinks of future retribution nor present punishment. Again, spirituous liquors cause disease, and short life; and the use of them, when it becomes a habit, cannot be dispensed with without discomfort, so that men spend all their money unprofitably in purchasing them and when their money is gone become thieves and dacoits. The evil is both future and immediate.

"As for the argument that it is customary to make offerings of spirituous liquors to the Dewa angels and that that practice tells in favor of spirit drinking, I can only say that we have no proof that the angels consume these offerings; and the only foundation for such a supposition is the statement of some ancient sages that the Asura angels of Indra's heavens got drunk, which, after all, only amounts to the assertion that the Dewa (or sensual) angels resemble men in their taste for liquor. In the present age many Americans have declared spirit-drinking to be an evil, a cause of much immediate mischief and of no future good. The Jews used not to consider spirit-drinking a sin, but Mahomet declared that Allah had ordered him to forbid its use on the ground that if they went to heaven they would smell so offensively that the angels could not endure their vicinity."

Speaking of the third commandment, lust, he says: "The religion of Buddha highly commends a life of chastity. Buddha stated that when a man could not remain as a celibate, if he took but one wife it was yet a kind of chastity, a commendable life; Buddha also censured polygamy, as involving lust and ignorance, but he did not absolutely forbid it, because he could not say there was any actual wrong in a man having a number of wives properly acquired." After remarking that women as well as men can enjoy the highest pleasures of heaven and that there may be a change of sex with a change of state, he gives his views of the common sensual idea of heaven:

"The Hindoos, who live in countries adjoining the Mahometan countries, believe that in heaven every male has tens and hundreds of thousands of female attendants, according to what their teachers of old taught them concerning the riches of heaven and their ideas are akin to that of the Mahometans, who have held out great inducements to men, representing the pleasures that would result from their religion; and the Hindoo teachers, fearing that their people might be excited by this most promising new doctrine, themselves introduced it into their own teaching. If we must speak the truth as to these matters, we must say that the world of heaven is similar to that of man, only differing in the greater amount of happiness enjoyed. Angels there are in the high places with all the apparel and train of their dignity, and others of lower station with less surroundings. All take up that position which is due to their previous merits and demerits. Buddha censured concupiscence; Buddha never spoke in praise of heaven; he taught of but one thing as worthy of praise 'the extinction of sorrow.'

"All this incoherent account of heaven is but the teaching of later writers, who have preached the luxuries and rich pleasures of heaven in hopes thereby to attract men into the paths of holiness and the attainment of sanctity. We cannot say where heaven and hell are. All religions hold that heaven is above the world and hell below it, and every one of them uses heaven to work on men's desires and hell to frighten them with. Some hold forth more horrors than others, according to the craft of those that designed them, to constrain men by acting on their fears and making them quake and tremble. We cannot deny the existence of heaven and hell, for as some men in this world certainly live well and others live ill, to deny the existence of heaven and hell would be to deprive men's works of their result, to make all their good deeds utterly lost to them. We must observe that after happiness follows sorrow, after heat cold; they are things by nature coupled. If after death there is a succession of existence, there must be states of happiness and of sorrow, for they are necessarily coupled in the way I have explained. As for heaven being above the earth or below it I leave intelligent people to come to their own conclusions, but as to future states of happiness and sorrow I feel no doubt whatever."

Speaking of the many religions and disputes now in vogue as to which is the best, he says it "is hard for men to relinquish their first ideas, even the devil worshippers, the lowest of mankind, have faith in their own belief and will not hear those who would teach them differently." Some seem to change their belief for personal protection and benefit, others for protection, as is the case of the French Catholic converts in Siam; some who have listened to teaching and become enlightened. On this subject he quotes a Sutra, supposed to be one of the sermons of Buddha, as follows:

"On a certain occasion the Lord Buddha led a number of his disciples to a village of the Kalmachon, where his wisdom and merit and holiness were known. And the Kalmachon assembled, and did homage to him and said many priests and Brahmins have at different times visited us and explained their religious tenets, declaring them to be excellent but each abused the tenets of every one else, whereupon we are in doubt as to whose religon is right and whose wrong; but we have heard that the Lord Buddha teaches an excellent religion, and we beg that we may be freed from doubt, and learn the truth.

"And the Lord Buddha answered, 'You were right to doubt, for it was a doubtful matter. I say unto all of you, do not believe in what ye have heard; that is, when you have heard any one say this is especially good or extremely bad, do not reason with yourselves that if it had not been true, it would not have been asserted, and so believe in its truth. Neither have faith in traditions, because they have been handed down for many generations and in many places.

"'Do not believe in anything because it is rumored and spoken of by many; do not think that it is a proof of its truth.

"'Do not believe merely because the written statement of some old sage is produced; do not be sure that the writing has ever been revised by the said sage, or can be relied on. Do not believe in what you have fancied, thinking that because an idea is extraordinary it must have been implanted by a Dewa, or some wonderful being.

"'Do not believe in guesses, that is, assuming something at hap-hazard as a starting point draw your conclusion from it; reckoning your two and your three and your four before you have fixed your number one. Do not believe because you think there is analogy, that is a suitability in things and occurences, such as believing that as there must be walls of the world, because you

see water in a basin, or that Mount Meru must exist,
because you have seen the reflection of trees, or that
there must be a creating God, because houses and
towns have builders.

"'Do not believe in the truth of that to which you
have become attached by habit, as every nation believes
in the superiority of its own dress and ornaments and
language.

"'Do not believe because your informant appears to
be a credible person as, for instance, when you see any
one having a very sharp appearance conclude that he
must be clever and trustworthy; or when you see any
one who has powers and abilities beyond what men
generally possess, believe in what he tells. Or think
that a great nobleman is to be believed, as he would not
be raised by the King to high station unless he were a
good man.

"'Do not believe merely on the authority of your
teachers and masters, or believe and practise merely
because they believe and practise. I tell you all, you
must of your own selves know that this is evil, this is
punishable, this is censured by wise men, belief in this
will bring no advantage to one, but will cause sorrow.
And when you know this, then eschew it.

"'I say to all of you dwellers in this village, answer
me this. Lopho, that is covetousness; Thoso, that
is anger and savageness, and Moho, that is ignorance
and folly, when any or all of these arise in the hearts of
men, is the result beneficial or the reverse?'

"And they answered, 'It is not beneficial O Lord.'

"Then the Lord continued, Covetous, passionate,
and ignorant men destroy life and steal, and commit

adultery and tell lies, and incite others to follow their example, is it not so?'

"And they answered, 'It is as the Lord says.'

"And he continued, 'Covetousness, passion, ignorance, the destruction of life, theft, adultery, and lying, are these good or bad, right or wrong? Do wise men praise or blame them? Are they not unprofitable, and causes of sorrow?'

"And they replied, 'It is as the Lord has spoken.'

"And the Lord said, 'For this I said to you, do not believe merely because you have heard, but when of your own consciousness you know a thing to be evil, abstain from it.'

"And then the Lord taught of that which is good, saying, 'If any of you know of yourselves that anything is good and not evil, praised by wise men, advantageous, and productive of happiness, then act abundantly according to your belief. Now 1 ask you, Alopho, absence of covetousness; Athoso, absence of passion; Amoho, absence of folly, are these profitable or not?'

"And they answered, 'Profitable.'

"The Lord continued, 'Men who are not covetous, or passionate, or foolish, will not destroy life, nor steal, nor commit adultery, nor tell lies, is it not so?'

"And they answered, 'It is as the Lord says.'

"Then the Lord asked, 'Is freedom from covetousness, passion and folly, from destruction of life, theft, adultery and lying, good or bad, right or wrong, praised or blamed by wise men, profitable and tending to happiness or not?'

"And they replied, 'It is good, right, praised by the wise, profitable and tending to happiness.'

"And the Lord said, 'For this I taught you not to believe merely because you have heard, but when you believed of your consciousness then to act accordingly and abundantly.'

"And the Lord continued, 'The holy man must not be covetous, or revengeful or foolish, and he must be versed in the four virtuous inclinations (Phrommawihan), which are Meta, desiring for all living things the same happiness which one seeks for one's self; Karuna, training the mind in compassion towards all living things, desiring that they may escape all sorrows either in hell or in other existences, just as a man who sees his friend ill, desires nothing so much as his recovery; Muthita, taking pleasure in all living things, just as playmates are glad when they see one another; and Ubekkha, keeping the mind balanced and impartial, with no affection for one more than another."

From another Sutra he extracts the following passage. "Can you respect or believe in religions which recommend actions that bring happiness to one's self by causing sorrow to others, or happiness to others by sorrow to one's self, or sorrow to both one's self and to others? Is not that a better religion which promotes the happiness of others simultaneously with the happiness of one's self and tolerates no oppression?"

Much of the "Kitchanukit" was inspired by the late King Monkut, who had been a monk for twenty-seven years, entering the priesthood at the age of twenty, during which time he perfected himself in the English language and made the religions of the world his special study, bringing to bear upon them an able and vigorous mind, hence the "Kitchanukit," or Modern Buddhist, is considered as the views of a deep thinker and close reasoner, typifying the primitive creed as taught by the Buddha, shorn of most of the superstitions and fables injected into it by designing men. It is an extensive work and enters into all the details of the writer's researches and seems to have been written to answer some of the arguments advanced by the missionaries with whom the King and Choo Phya Thepaken held many conferences in regard to the merits of Christianity and the teachings of Buddha, and the author acknowledges that he has received much valuable information from them, but in answer to their arguments he tells them "that Buddha taught a morality as beautiful as theirs and a charity that extends to everything that has breath." When they speak of faith, he answers "that by the light of the knowledge that they have helped him to he can weed out his old superstitions, but that he will accept no new ones."

The following significant passages sum up the theory of the Buddhist's belief concerning the unseen God: "What is this unseen God, personified by the Theists (Keks) as God, The Creator, the Divine Spirit, and the Divine Intelligence? It seems to me that this Divine Spirit (Pra Chitr) is but the actual spirit of man, the disposition, be it good or evil, and I think that the Divine Intelligence (Phra Winyan) which is said to exist in the light and in the darkness, in all times and in all places, is the intelligence which flies forth from the six gates of the body, the faculties of sight, hearing, smell, taste, touch and knowledge, whose intelligence exists in all places and at all times, and knows the good and evil which man does. And God the Creator (Pra phu sang) is the Holy Merit and

Demerit (Pra Kusala a-kusala), the cause and shaper of all existence. Those who have not duly pondered on these matters may say that there is a God who exists in all places waiting to give men the reward or punishment due to their good or evil deeds, or they may say that prosperity and adversity are the work of angels or devils; but to me it seems that all happiness and misery are the natural result of causation (Kam) which influences the present existence and will determine the nature of the next existence.

"How can we assent to the doctrine of those who believe in but one resurrection—who believe in a man being received into heaven while his nature is still full of impurity, by virtue of sprinkling his head with water or cutting off by circumcision a small piece of his skin? Will such a man be purified by the merit of the Lord Allah or of the Great Brahma? We know not where they are. We have never seen them. But we do know, and can prove, that men can purify their own natures, and we know the laws by which that purification can be effected. Is it not better to believe in this which we can see and know, than in that which has no reality to our perceptions?"

In concluding his review of the modern Buddhist Mr. Alabaster says "The religion of Buddha meddled not with the beginning, which it could not fathom; avoided the action of a Deity it could not perceive; and left open to endless discussion that problem which it could not solve, the ultimate reward of the perfect. It dealt with life as it found it; it declared all good which led to its sole object, the diminution of the misery of all sentient beings; it laid down rules of conduct which have never been surpassed, and held out reasonable hopes of a future of the most perfect happiness. Its proofs rest on the assumptions that the reason of man is his surest guide and that the law of nature is perfect justice."

With all of their adoration of Gautama Buddha, his followers have never regarded him as a God, he is only the ideal of what any man can become, and this is what the late King of Siam attempted to fix in the minds of his people, and the adoration given to the supposed relics of the Teacher, the teeth or the footprints, as well as the statues, is only to recall the memory of him who trod the path that leads to deliverance. The veneration of the memory of Buddha is perhaps hardly distinguishable among the ignorant from the worship of a God; but in theory the ritual is strictly commemorative and does not necessarily denote idolatry any more than the blossoms laid on the tomb of a loved one by the hand of affection. The strict Buddhist believes that by the exercise of virtue, austerity and science men may acquire power sufficient to make the gods quake on their thrones. The Siamese have no fears of the missionaries making any encroachments on their religion, they encourage missionaries to come among them, and with the peculiar tact of the Asiatic make as much out of them as possible, and they are particularly anxious to have the Board of Missions send them physicians to attend their sick and furnish medicines free. Prince Dumrong, when informed that if he should send some young nobles to America to study medicine that they would have to associate with Christians and possibly partake of the tenets of our creed, replied, "That is of but little consequence, what religious ideas that they may pick up would be forgotten in a month after they return." And so it would. The teachings of Buddha are peculiarly adapted to an oriental people and the missionary labors on stony ground and his harvest is a meagre one.

To King Monkut are the Siamese indebted for a more liberal and progressive idea of Buddhism; he is the Luther of a reform in that religion. For twenty-one years he was a recluse in a monastery, its chief priest, during which time, after much study, he arrived at the conclusion that it was folly for him or the priests to longer attempt to prove the genuineness of the 85,000 volumes of sacred books which were regarded canonical. With a boldness unusual in a son of the sunland he enunciated his belief of their fabulous origin and his desire to purge the sacred literature of fables and restore the church to its former purity. He soon found himself at the head of a new school, which rapidly increased in popularity, numbering among his followers most of the advanced thinkers and prominent men of his age. After a thorough investigation he was astounded at the mysticism and priestcraft that had been the prurient growth of the monasteries; he and his followers rejected thousands of the old school books as unorthodox, especially those that could not be made to harmonize with the cosmography of the universe as now held by the scientific world. This new school was far more enlightened, liberal and expansive than the old and is to-day the ruling doctrine of the entire kingdom. When it was thought that the Prince was leaning toward Christianity he wrote to one of the missionaries, "You must not think that any of my party will ever become Christians; we will not embrace what we think is a foolish religion." On the day of his death he wrote a farewell address to the priesthood, the spirit of which was that "all existence is unreliable, everything mutable, that he himself would presently be obliged to submit to that stern necessity, going a little before them." Just as his spirit was trembling on the threshold of the unseen he said to his sorrowing attendants, "Do not be surprised or grieved by my thus leaving you, since such an event must befall all creatures who come into this world, and is an unchanging inevitability" and thus passed away one of the most profound scholars and philosophers of the East, who did much for his people, the Luther of Buddhism.

As an evidence of the liberal toleration of King Chulalongkorn, in regard to religious matters, in 1870 he issued a proclamation concerning the morals of his people and closed with the following noble sentiments which, at the time, was regarded as an advanced step in religious matters: "In regard to the concern of seeking and holding a religion that shall be a refuge to yourself in this life, it is a good concern, and exceedingly appropriate and suitable that you all—every individual of you—should investigate and judge for himself according to his own wisdom (what is right and what is wrong). And when you see any religion whatever, or any company of religionists whatever, likely to be of advantage to yourself—a refuge in accord with your own wisdom,—hold to that religion with your own heart. Hold it not with a shallow mind—with but slight investigation—with mere guess work, or because of its general popularity, or from mere tradition, saying that it is the custom held from time immemorial, and do not hold a religion that you have not good evidence is true and then frighten men's fears and flatter their hopes by it. Do not be frightened and astonished at diverse events (fictitious wonders) and hold to and follow them. When you shall have obtained a refuge, a religious faith that is beautiful and good and suitable, hold to it with great joy and follow its teachings, it will be a cause of prosperity to each one of you."

Each priest carries a spoon shaped fan which he holds before his face shutting out from his sight objects which might disturb his thoughts. It is one of the rules of the monks that when he walks abroad he must keep his eyes fixed on the ground within a plough length of his feet. Some of the strict ascetics make a circle about eighteen inches in circumference on the floor and steadily keeping their eyes on it for hours at a time do not allow their thoughts to stray from that small circle, a type of the Chokra, a quoit like weapon, emblem of the power of Indra, King of the Angels, known as the "wheel of the law," which is supposed to be ever turning and represents the continual existence of transmigration. This mystic wheel is stamped on the coin of Siam, is found sculptured on the walls of ruined temples of a forgotten era, and its wings or spokes are called Nedanas or the twelve causes and effects of life, the circle of existence. The favorite expression "turning the wheel," means to teach the law. Some of the northern Buddhists have a wheel to which is attached a box full of texts, which they revolve at pleasure; others fasten them on miniature water wheels and place them in a running stream thus praying by machinery.

XXIII.

A TRANSLATION FROM THE PONGSA-WADAN,

OR HISTORY OF THE KINGS OF SIAM.

In the year of the cock 1019 (=A. D. 1658) a French ship captain came with merchandise in his vessel to Siam to trade. About that time the King of Siam was building a large ship. When it was finished and all ready to launch, he commanded his interpreters to ask the French merchant how they launched large vessels most successfully in France? The Frenchman being a man of intelligence, and having great experience in ship carpentry, answered, that he would volunteer to launch the vessel himself; and immediately prepared a tackle and capstan with which he drew the vessel out into the water with the greatest ease. The king was much pleased and rewarded him bountifully. Soon after this the king made him an officer of Government with the title Looang Wich'a-yen, and gave him a house and ensignia of office, and allowed him to do the king's business. Looang Wich'a-yen was very faithful in all his duties and thereby found favor with the king. He was afterward promoted and received the title of P'ra Wich'a-yen. Some time after this, when he became more skillful in business, the king promoted him again, and gave him the title of P'raya Wich'a-yen.

One day the king asked him what kind of valuable

The High Priest of Siam.

you are a man of considerable intelligence, I will send you as an embassador to France to see the wealth of the king, and to find out if the story of P'raya Wich'a-yen is true. *Nai Pan* bowed himself and consented to go on the king's business. He retired from the royal presence, and began to prepare the ship and make preparations for the journey. He sent out to find men that were skillful in the various magic arts to accompany him. He found a teacher who was learned and skillful in the various cunning and magic arts, and was a drunkard, who consented to accompany him. *Nai Pan* was greatly rejoiced at this. He then engaged some Frenchmen and others for officers and sailors for his ship.

When everything was in readiness, he besought his brother Kosa to conduct him into the king's presence, that he might take leave of his Majesty. The king then commanded to prepare a royal letter, and appointed *Nai Pan* as principal embassador, with others to convey the royal letter and some presents to the king of France, and make a treaty of friendship.

On a favorable day *Nai Pan*, with his attendants, took leave of their friends, and conducting his whole company on board the ship set sail for France.

When they had been out at sea about four months, they came upon a large whirlpool in their course, near the mouth of a river on the coast of France. There arose a storm of wind which carried their ship into the midst of the whirlpool, in which place it kept whirling for three days. All on board the ship were wailing with loud noise on account of the danger of their lives; because every ship that came into the whirl must be lost. Not one had ever yet escaped. *Nai Pan* the first embassador alone had presence of mind, and consulted with the magician teacher thus:—Our ship has fallen into the whirlpool and has been whirling for two or three days; what plan can you devise to get it out in safety, that we may all escape death? The magician teacher then comforted the heart of the embassador saying, fear not. I will most certainly bring the ship out of all danger. The magician teacher prepared some offerings, lighted papers, and dressed himself in white robes and sat down to meditate (Samat'i Chamron P'ra Kamt'an Tang Wayo-krasin), that is, fixed his mind exclusively on counting his breath. Presently there arose a great wind which lifted the vessel and carried it beyond the whirlpool. They were all greatly rejoiced at this and thence sailed safely into the mouth of the river of France.

They then sent word to the officers of that place that a vessel had arrived bringing a Siamese embassy, with a letter and presents, and that they desired to make a treaty of peace with the French king. The Governor of that town forwarded the news up to the capital.

The French king then dispatched an officer with a boat to receive the Siamese embassadors and bring them up to the city, and allowed them to lodge at a hotel. They were afterwards admitted to the presence of the king, and presented the letter with the royal presents. The king then commanded the interpreters to ask them about their voyage, whether they came safely or not. When the king heard that their vessel had been in the whirlpool for three days, and had escaped in safety, he did not believe it, because never before had a single vessel escaped from that whirl of water. The king, to be certain, commanded to ask them again. The chief embassador affirmed that it was true; but the king did not yet believe it, and called the Frenchmen who had come as officers of the ship and inquired of them. They assured the king that it was true. His majesty thought it very miraculous. The king then asked them how they managed to get the ship out of the whirlpool? The embassador answered, I besought the merit and power of their Majesties, the kings of Siam and France to assist, and not suffer the treaty about to be formed, to be destroyed. It was this power and merit of both Sovereigns, in which we trusted that caused the wind to arise, which lifted our vessel out of the whirlpool.

When the king of France heard this he believed it, and remarked that the king of Siam had the same amount of merit with himself.

Some time after this the king sent for the embassadors to come into the royal presence. He then ordered a company of 500 soldiers—all good marksmen, to be drawn up and placed in two ranks, directly facing each other—250 on a side. They fired simultaneously, and each man on either side lodged his ball in the barrel of the gun in the hands of the man opposite to him, without a single failure. The king then asked them if they had any as good soldiers—sharpshooters as these in Siam? The chief embassador answered that the king of Siam did not esteem this kind of skill in the art as worth much in war. When the king of France heard this he was displeased, and asked them what kind of skill in soldiers did the king of Siam value? The embassador answered, the king of Siam admires soldiers who are well skilled in the magic arts, and such as, if good marksmen like your Majesty's soldiers here, would fire at them, the balls would not touch their bodies. His Majesty the king of Siam has some soldiers who can go unseen into the midst of the battle, and cut off the heads of the officers and men in the enemy's ranks, and return unharmed. He has others who can stand under the weapons of the enemy to be shot at, or pierced with swords and spears and yet not receive the least wound or even injury. Soldiers skilled in this kind of art, the king of Siam values very highly, and keeps them for use in the country.

The king of France did not believe this story, and remarked that the Siamese embassadors were boasting beyond all reason. The king then commanded to ask them if they had any soldiers skilled in this kind of art along with them in the ship? and could they give a specimen of their art?

The embassador remembering the feat of the magic teacher in lifting their ship out of the whirlpool, answered, the soldiers we have along for use in the vessel are but common soldiers; but we can give your Majesty a specimen of their skill. The king asked, what can they do? The embassador said, I beg your Majesty to arrange this company of 500 soldiers, sharp-shooters, in a position far off, and near as they please, to fire at my soldiers, and they will ward off the bullets, and not suffer a single one to touch them.

When the king of France heard this proposal, fearing lest his soldiers would kill the Siamese, and thereby destroy the treaty of friendship about to be formed between them, was unwilling to make the trial. The embassador then answered, your Majesty need not fear in the least. My soldiers really have an art by which they can ward off the bullets, and not suffer one to touch them. If it please your Majesty, then to-morrow let them prepare a platform here, having an awning of white cloth, and surrounded with flags, and place upon the platform some refreshments and wine; then spread the word and let all the people of the town come to witness my feat.

The king then prepared all these things as was requested. The following day the embassador requested his magic teacher to select and prepare sixteen persons and clothe themselves entirely with the panoply of figures for making the person invulnerable, the teacher and altogether seventeen persons. When every thing was ready they came into the presence of the king, and took seats upon the platform. He then addressed the king,—if it please your Majesty let these 500 sharp-shooters shoot these seventeen persons seated upon the platform. The king then commanded his soldiers to fire.

The French soldiers then fired several rounds, some at a distance, and some near, but the powder would not ignite, and their guns made no report. Those seventeen persons uninjured, partook of the refreshments on the platform without the least fear or confusion. The French soldiers were wonderfully surprised and startled. The magic teacher then said, "Don't be discouraged. Fire again. This time we will allow the guns to go off. The soldiers then fired another round. Their guns went off but the bullets fell to the ground, some near where they stood, some a little distance farther, and some fell near the platform, but not a single man was injured.

When the king of France saw this, he believed all the Siamese embassadors had said, and praised their arts very much, remarking he had never seen anything to equal it. He then presented the Siamese soldiers with money and clothes as a reward, and also feasted them bountifully. From this time forward the king believed every thing the embassador said. He did not doubt a single word.

Sometime after this the king commanded to ask the embassador if they had any more soldiers in Siam as skilled in the magic arts as these, or were these all? He answered, these are but common soldiers for going in ships, and have very little skill in the arts. The soldiers for guarding the royal capital are much better skilled in the magic arts than these. When the king heard this he believed, and feared the skill of the Siamese very much.

The Siamese had observed that when the French king sat upon his throne in the morning, the appearance of his person was of a reddish color; in the middle of the day it was green, and in the evening of a whitish color. They were very anxious to know the cause of this.

One day the king asked the embassador, if, in his own court he was an officer of high or low rank?—and when the king of Siam wished to favor any officer very much how he showed his favors? I wish to favor you in the same manner. The embassador being desirous to come near to examine the king's person to know the secret of the various colors morning, noon and night, now saw his opportunity, and answered, I am but an officer of low rank whom the king sends to trade with different nations, and I have but little wisdom; but there are many high officers in our country who have great wisdom and experience who serve his Majesty the king of Siam. It is also the custom, if his Majesty wishes to favor any one more than another, to allow them to come near to his person, and crouch even at his feet. The king of France believed this, and then granted to the Siamese embassador the same privilege of coming near, even to his foot stool. The embassador then saw, that in the morning the royal throne was strewn with rubies, at noon with emeralds, and in the evening with diamonds; and that the reflection from these precious stones caused his person to appear of different colors.

Upon a certain day the king appeared in state riding upon a beautifully caparisoned horse decorated with precious stones, and having a large ruby about the size of a betel-nut with the hull on, hanging about the horse's neck. The reflection from the ruby gave them both a reddish color, and very beautiful. The king then commanded to ask the embassador if they had many precious stones as large as this in Siam. The embassador answered, I am only an officer for the outside provinces, and am not accustomed to visit the royal treasury, and I am therefore afraid to say whether there are many or few lest it should not accord with the truth. But I remember on one occasion when the king of Siam rode in state upon a white horse, his Majesty had a ruby (Tap-t'im) suspended to the horse's neck about the size of this one of your Majesty's.

When the king of France heard this he was pleased, and praised the embassador for his eloquent speech as worthy of imitation, and commanded to note down his words for future reference.

Sometime after this, when in the king's presence the embassador said, formerly there was a merchant from this country came to Siam to trade. In speaking with the king of Siam, he praised the wonderful things of this country, and said that in your Majesty's palace were more beautiful things than were to be found elsewhere in the world. The king of Siam wishing very much to know if this was true, has sent your humble servant, bearing a royal letter, and presents from my lord, to form a treaty of friendship with your Majesty. When the king of France heard this, he commanded an officer to conduct the embassadors in to examine the interior of the royal palace that they might report to the king. The officer of the palace then conducted them through the palace. The Siamese took note of every thing they saw, and found that it exactly corresponded with the story of P'raya Wich'a-yen.

When they had seen every thing they returned to the king's presence and praised the great wealth in the royal palace, saying it was equal in beauty with the celestial mansions of angels.

The king was very much pleased with the Siamese embassador, and believed all he said. His Majesty was also very desirous of retaining his offspring in the country, and for this purpose secured him a wife, and gave him clothes to dress himself as a Frenchman. The king also had his portrait painted, and all his wise sayings carefully noted down.

When the Siamese embassadors had been in France about three years they came to take leave of the king to return. The principal embassador committed his wife and children to the care of the king. His Majesty then gave them money and clothes, and many precious and valuable things, and a letter and presents to carry back to his Majesty the king of Siam. When they took leave of the king, he sent an escort of boats to accompany them to the ship.

On a favorable day they set sail, and arrived at their native land in safety. *Nai Pan* was admitted into the king's presence, and presented the royal letter and presents from the king of France, and related everything he had seen.

The king was very much pleased, and praised the wisdom of *Nai Pan*, and rewarded him well for his faithfulness.

According to the Siamese History, from which the above was translated, that most extraordinary man, Nai Pan, returned safely to Siam about A. D. 1663, and was received with high honors by Somdet P'ra Narai, who was then King of Siam, and was subsequently made Minister of Foreign Affairs in the place of his elder brother who was removed by death.

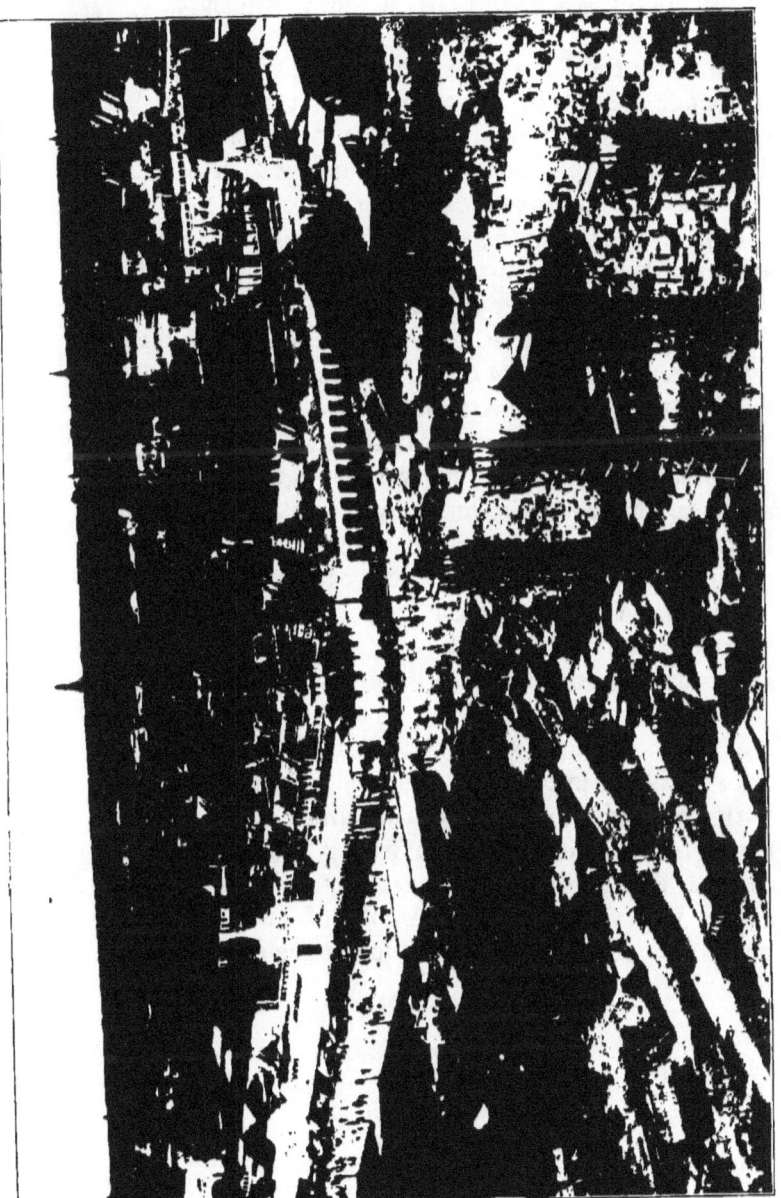

Bird's-eye View of the Palace Grounds and Wall.

XXIV.

"TAUT KATIN" OR WAT VISITING.

Annually the King visits the various wats adjacent to Bangkok and in fact every wat throughout his realms is either visited by himself in person or by deputy during the month of September. Taut Katin means the laying down of a pattern to cut patchwork, and this is generally the time of year that the priests are furnished with robes for their next year wear, being donated by the King and his suite and others who are desirous of making merit, the robes having been made by the devout believers in the teachings of the Buddha, some of them of rich material, but the larger portion of cotton cloth dyed yellow, the outcast color adopted by the priestly Gautama in his wanderings, all of which are torn into four strips and then sewn together, thus imitating patched robes, as a token of humility, the example having been set by the great teacher.

The principal attraction to the foreigner in wat visiting is the processions by land and water, which are gorgeous in the extreme, the latter of which I have portrayed in the description of a "royal flotilla." In the city the wats visited were Wat Ratahpradit, Wat Chakkrawat, Wat Samphang-napong and others, all of them within reasonable distance of the palace. The avenues through which the procession passed were lined with seamen, who do duty as marines, dressed in white and armed with rifles to the number of two thousand, making a good show as they stood at regular intervals the whole distance on each side for over a mile from the palace. Behind them, at the junction of the avenues, a large body of police in full uniform were formed in line, but only for show, as there appeared to be no need for them. Most of the stores and residences along the route were appropriately adorned with red and white streamers and altars on which were displayed offerings, some of them very beautiful and costly; but flowers, fruit, candles and incense sticks formed the greater part. In a number of instances the portrait of His Majesty was the central feature. The greatest order prevailed as the procession passed along, though there was much less of the abject kow-towing that formerly prevailed when the King went abroad, the usual accompaniment of oriental royalty, but which was abolished when His Majesty came to the throne; yet there was no lack of dignity in the pageantry, which was imposing and grand.

The approach of the procession was announced by mounted heralds, blowing trumpets, in advance of the lancers, who made a fine appearance, about two hundred, mounted on Australian horses, four deep, and ably handled by their officers. A detachment of artillery with six guns followed, veteran artillerists, then came the royal band playing European airs, leading the infantry column, comprising several regiments, which were followed by another band and more infantry, then the fasces bearers or lictors, and spearmen or tumruots, who defiled on each side of the road, leaving the center clear. A long line of nobles came next, preceding the palanquin of the King, who graciously acknowledged the salutations of the foreigners and others with his usual grace and dignity. He was dressed in a white tunic and colored silk panung, without any of the symbols of his high office beyond the usual decorations, his helmet surmounted by a plume of white feathers. Immediately following came the chairs of the royal children attended by their suites, and then came the Princes of the royal household, closed on either side by a detachment of the palace guard with retainers leading four caparisoned ponies. Each palanquin was accompanied by the usual royal umbrella, significantly borne and appropriately adorned, denoting to the uninitiated the rank of those that it covered. II. R. H. Prince Ong Noi, brother of the King, followed in advance of the royal palace band on horseback, which was escorted by the royal guard in double file, numbering about five hundred; then came another band heading a detachment of artillery with four Maxim guns and eight rifled field guns of the latest pattern, then another company of infantry appeared escorting the princes and nobles of state, then more music, and the rear of the procession was formed by detachments of seamen, from the various men of war in the harbor, under the command of their respective officers, both foreign and native, in full uniform.

Arriving at the wats His Majesty was met by the bishops and abbots and escorted into the building where services were held, consisting of reading the lessons of Buddha, a sermon was then preached, prayers offered up and the presents distributed. It was a solemn and interesting sight, the large temple filled with squatting natives, the altars a blaze of light and flowers, the statues of Buddha newly gilt, outside waving palms, the hum of the multitude, and through the ever changing foliage shimmered a stream of gold, a Danai shower. To the denizens of the Western world one can hardly realize the devotion that the followers of Buddha pay to his teachings, the groundwork of which is humility. The King is the head of the church, but he bows himself as low as the humblest when the bishops ask from the gods that blessings be vouchsafed his people. The ceremonies over, the royal retinue return to the palace, the priests place their robes away and the populace, ever eager to enjoy a holiday, return to their homes with no fear of the morrow.

XXV.

GRAND DISPLAY OF THE ROYAL FLOTILLA ON THE MENAM.

In days agone the sparkling waters of the Adriatic amorously kissed the prow of the beaucentaur and reflected back from its pellucid depth the silken banners of the Doge of Venice and his accompanying cavaliers when he cast into the opaline flood a jeweled ring, wedding the Queen of the Lagoons to the tideless tide, whose white-lipped waves spent a wealth of kisses on barge and gondola, mirroring chivalry and beauty on each swelling billow, a gleam of glory that must ever flash from the annals of the sea-born republic like a ray of sunshine through some ruined cloister window. Turn back the tide of time, forget the centuries fled and look out on the fast flowing Menam, glittering under an orient sun, and behold a hundred barges proudly floating down the stream with pavilions of cloth of gold and floating from prow and stern white horse-tails, each manned by from forty to seventy oarsmen who simultaneously lift their paddles from the water with a rhythmic motion, uttering a weird chant, the crested waves reflecting the brilliant colors of the boatmen's uniforms while drops of water fall from upraised paddles, a cascade of jewels. Onward sweeps the royal flotilla, past palaces and temples, beneath the graceful bamboo and towering banyan tree and emerald fern, with soft sounds of flute and trumpet floating out on the ambient air, making up a pageant akin to that pictured in the pages of the past when the Doge wedded the Adriatic.

The barges in advance were filled with soldiers and police, then the nobles, and in each barge the occupant reclined on a dais under a showy canopy, and before him was spread out the insignia of his rank: full sized solid gold tea-pot, cuspidor, betel box, ewer, plates, goblets, etc. About the center of the flotilla, the barges two abreast, came the king in his *rua prateenang*, barge of state, elaborately carved and gilded, preceded by a gold-covered barge with a pagoda filled with valuable presents and musicians blowing large ivory horns, accompanied by two barges with life-sized images of Buddha on their prow, also filled with presents.

The pavilion in the King's barge was festooned with curtains of cloth of gold and crimson silk, and the seventy oarsmen, clad in scarlet uniforms, swept the royal vessel along with a majestic motion, the oars being heavily plated with gold. The royal barge was one hundred and fifty feet in length, the prow and stern rising about ten feet out of the water, the whole shaped somewhat like one of our Indian canoes, the hull carved out of an immense teak tree. The prow and stern were a mass of carving and inlaid with mother of pearl and gold, and from them streamed an embroiderd cloth of its owner's rank, and three bunches of horse-tails bleached to snowy whiteness.

The *rua prateenang*, or royal throne boats, are characteristic of Siam of the past as well as of the present. For the most part constructed out of one single tree, being literally "dug outs," they give a fair idea of the size of the trees of the country and the skill of the native builders. They are apparently from about 120 to 150 feet in length, and ten to twelve feet beam at the center, tapering towards the stem and stern, which are each in order adorned by a towering beak and a lofty curved and decorated stern. The galleys at present used by His Majesty, the King, in these royal processions as indicative of supreme control and order in Siam are three in number. The first and largest is the *rua prateenang* proper, which bears a gilded throne or seat in its centre, and it is emblematic throughout. Its stem or beak is turned back as if pointing to the throne, and the boat is altogether a marvel of carving and gilded decoration. This galley is manned, as is also the other two royal boats, with uniformed royal boatmen wearing red tunics and caps, their order and number being fifteen on either side forward and ten on either side abaft the throne, or in all 50 rowers. The galley has no rowlocks or tholepins, but is propelled by hand paddles.

It is a beautiful sight to witness the progress of these boats, as the skill, order and regularity displayed by the rowers, and the ease and rapidity with which they control the great vessel is hardly to be equaled anywhere else than in this country. The whole power of the paddle rower is thrown into his stroke by a method which is not generally understood. Each man faces forward and can see the man before him, though the time is given by two regular time beaters, one before and one behind the central pavilion, who keep raising and lowering a decorated lofty bamboo stick, significantly adorned by regular size graded tufts of horsehair, after the fashion of the royal umbrellas, and letting it strike upon a sounding piece of wood. At the sound of the falling stick each rower plunges his paddle into the water and with the full swing of his arms inverts it in the air. The galleys have no rudders, but are steered by stern oars, and these are, if necessary, assisted by additional ones forward. The perfect discipline and thorough understanding between the commander of the galleys and the boatmen make it apparent that one mind controls all the workings of the boat, which at the word of command is made to remain perfectly motionless, turn in its own length, go ahead or astern, fast or slow by the action of the paddles in the hands of the rowers. The place of the throne boat in the procession is directly in front of the galley which bears His Majesty. The center of this boat is taken up with a beautiful pavilion, open at the sides and front, though closable by royal hangings at will, in which the King himself is seated with his courtiers, and probably one or more of the royal children. The covering of the pavilion is the royal red with a broad gold border, which is significant of His Majesty's government boats in the procession, though bearing only subordinate officers. The royal galley itself is distinguished more particularly from others by its color, which even below the water line is golden yellow, while its attendant boat, though approaching to the royal barge in decoration, has its color different. Colors and forms have all a significance in Siam. While visiting the wats near the Palace and where the relics of His royal predecessors are preserved, the color used was for the most part black. Again, when visiting other wats under royal protection gold color was predominant, and on another occasion white was extensively used.

The third royal galley in the procession, which,

however, generally keeps a position side by side with that containing the King, is for the accommodation of those near to His Majesty, though it was said that the Chow Fa or heir apparent to the throne goes with the King in person on most of these occasions. The announcement of the embarkation of His Majesty is made by signal gun, and the procession down the river is heralded by bugle sounds, the waterway being kept clear in consequence. The boats of the navy flotilla head the line and clear the way. As many as thirty *rua-dang* boats, each manned by from 50 to 75 men, dressed as usual among men-o-war's men in the tropics, *i. e.*, in white throughout, and commanded by their regular naval officers, who occupied the pavilions in the center of each boat, were in the procession, either preceding or following the royal throne boats. The bugle sound, giving the order to advance, was varied at intervals by the music of the bands, the sounds of the conch blowers, or players on Siamese wind instruments, and once in a while by a chant sung in unison and in good style by the whole crew of the *rua-phrateenang*. The boats kept their exact position in the line without varying the distance between each other a perceptible fraction of an inch, and as they proceeded down the river two by two they formed a sight worth going miles to behold. After the royal boats manned by seamen of the navy to the number of fully 2,000 men had passed came the private boats of the Princes, nobles and officers of Siam, each boat having its owner's degree displayed in the embroidered cloth and accessories hanging from the stem and stern, and each manned by the personal retainers of the owner in his own livery or uniform. The line of boats, mostly two and two, extended more than a mile on the river, while in motion, and on the landing of His Majesty at any of the wats the boats kept their order in the procession without difficulty.

The Princes' barges were also handsome affairs and decorated with horse-tails and embroidered cloths which were followed by the barges of nobles, soldiers and river police, a magnificent flotilla, truly oriental. This was kept up for two days, the King visiting the various wats on the river and canals that come under his immediate jurisdiction, Prince and noble vying with him, merit making, in the liberality of their donations to the wats and the yellow-robed followers of Buddha who live solely off the charity of the people, and it is to the credit of the Siamese that they do not allow them to suffer.

The temples of this people are very handsome and the residences of the priests adjacent are used as schools where the youths are taught the rudiments of a common education. Wats can be seen every where, surrounded by groves of the sacred Bo trees, their white and gold phrachedas and small tapering spires telling the wanderer that a place of rest was nigh. Adjacent to each temple is a sala, an open house, for persons to stop in should they desire to do so, virtually a place of rest.

When the King, with his flotilla, comes down the river from his palace, the various consulates, palaces and shipping display their flags; police boats patrol the stream and canals and a general holiday prevails. I was informed by a young lady, a native of Bangkok, that in the early days when the King went to visit the wats, foreigners were not allowed to witness the ceremony, in the bow of the royal barge servitors were stationed with balls of mud which they would let fly from a sling at the peeping Toms along the line of travel. The law is very rigid in regard to accidents happening to the royal barge, the penalty death, but should one occur the steersman in charge has only to break his paddle during the excitement and it thus being deemed unavoidable he escapes the full penalty, especially as the King is very humane. Among the many legends of Siam and its rulers is the account of the execution of the steersman of a King's barge, which took place during the reign of the ruler known for his ferocity as the Tiger King. While the barge was going at full speed through one of the canals, upon turning a sharp point it ran into a tree that had blown across the klang, breaking off the effigies and gilding on the bow of the barge, toppling his Majesty off of his dais and shaking things up generally. As soon as the boat struck the tree the man leaped into the water and swam ashore, sat down and awaited his doom. The King, knowing that the accident was unavoidable, pardoned him on the spot, holding him guiltless, but the boatman would not accept it, declaring that the law must be carried out, that if he accepted a pardon it would be establishing a bad precedent, all he asked was that a sala be erected on the spot where he was executed. Remonstrances proving unavailing, the King, with tears in his eyes, gave the order, and the boatman, true to the laws and his allegiance, was decapitated, a Siamese Brutus, whose name will ever live in the traditions of his land. His remains were cremated with special honors, his family ennobled and the sala erected to his memory, as the

Siamese are not parsimonious in well-doing for a friend, or one that adds a luster to their annals. These barges are only used on state occasions and are then taken out of the water and carefully housed, some of them doubtless a hundred years old. I regarded the pageant of "wat visiting" as the handsomest display of barbaric grandeur that I had witnessed in this land of orientalism.

XXVI.

THE MARRIAGE CEREMONY AMONG THE AFFLUENT.

From a Siamese manuscript I condense the following in regard to the marriage between a couple of young people in the higher walks of life. Elsewhere I spoke of the ceremony in general. The first step is to secure an elderly woman, a friend of the family, whom the parents of the young man consult in regard to securing a suittable wife for their son, she arranges a meeting of friends at the house of the parents of the young woman whom she has selected; the day having been declared favorable by the astrologers, betel is brought out and the conference commences by an appeal to the parents of the girl, assuring them that the desire of the young man was the happiness of their daughter, that he regarded her as the only one with whom he could be happy, to comfort him in sickness and care for him in death, and then ask: "What wilt thou father and thou mother say to us?" The parents reply "Our daughter we love much, the son of the respectable parents you represent to us is one they also love, we must rely on the ancient proverb: 'Move slowly and you will gain your object; a prolonged effort will be likely to result prosperously;' hence we must counsel with our relations before we can give you an answer." When another favorable astrological day has come the parents of the young man call their friends together and request that they again go to the residence of the girl and ask what will be the answer of her parents. They do so and if the proposition is favorable they are told: "We have counseled with our kinsmen and find them of the opinion that if the young man truly feels that he can confide in our daughter to take care of him in sickness and pay suitable attention to his body after death, that then his confidence should be allowed to grow and flourish." Then comes the question in regard to the ages of the respective parties, they must not be born in years antagonistic with one another; for instance the year of the rat and the year of the dog, the cow and the tiger, the tiger and the rabbit, or the dog and the monkey, each of them couplets and regarded as antagonizing; the husband born in one year and the wife in the other of the couplet would, in the course of nature, quarrel and fight. The parents respectfully request that some fortune-teller be consulted in regard to the times of their respective births which will allow them to live happily together. This matter settled, the delegated friends are again sent to the parents of the young woman, who has not been consulted, and ask concerning the property or money that they propose to give to assist the young couple to go to housekeeping, who reply: "We can not devote much of our effects for that purpose, but how much will the parents of the young man give?" To this the friends reply: "It is left entirely to you to say what you think would be suitable." They reply: "If such be the case, we would suggest a hundred ticals to build a house, to be made of wood, and a thousand ticals for mutual trade; also, that they contribute betel and cakes for the wedding, at least one hundred salvers or dishes, will they be willing to do this?" They reply: "We must report first, but allow us to inquire how much will you give maa ch'in (the bride) as her portion?" They answer. "Should the honorable parents of the young man do as we propose we will give our daughter as her toon (dowry) one thousand ticals and two or three slaves." This done and all the arrangements perfected, the bridegroom is taken to the residence of the bride, so that he can pay his respects to her parents, prostrates himself on the floor before them and craves their permission to see their daughter and that he may be allowed to call from time to time as he may desire, which is granted, and from that time on he is regarded as one of the family. The bridegroom then commences the erection of his house adjacent to and aided by his father-in-law and other friends. The astrologers are now consulted as to when an auspicious day will arrive for the ceremony, and it being determined the relatives and friends soon complete the building and then the parents of the two parties select five friends to receive the money and two white garments, presents to the parents of the bride, with the wedding cakes and betel, according to the agreement. These things are conveyed in a procession headed by a band of music and are presented to the parents of the bride, who bring forth the dowry and slaves, publicly giving them to the bride.

After this ceremony they all repair to the new house and are duly seated, the white raiment is exhibited and the money brought by both parties spread out on the floor and counted; the two sums are then mixed together, fragrant oil and flour and a little paddy scattered over the heap, symbolic of blessings asked for, that their rice, oil and perfumery may ever abound. The money is then handed to the mother of the bride to hold as trustee for the purpose it was given. This ceremony generally takes place at midday. A rich feast is then spread after which the friends disperse and return again in the cool of the evening with several priests who hold religious services. Prior to this the bride sends out a youth handsomely dressed with a waiter of betel nut inviting the bridegroom and his attendants to come in and be seated in the wedding hall, which is handsomely decorated with ferns and flowers, she and her attendants being screened by a curtain stretched across the hall. When the religious services are closed the curtain is lifted and certain elders proceed to administer the holy water of blessing. The young couple are seated close together, the chief elder takes up the vessel of holy water, pours a little on the head of the man and then on the head of the woman, pronouncing a blessing as he does so. The bride then retires and changes her dress for one more brilliant and at the same time a finely dressed boy presents, on a silver salver, a handsome suit to the bridegroom, a present from the parents of the bride, called Pa hawihaw, which he proceeds to don. In the meantime the priests are quoting texts from the works of Buddha, then refreshments are served, tea, sweets and ices, and the priests receive yellow robes. The special guests are then invited to partake of a banquet prepared by the family of the bride, after which further proceedings are adjourned till next day, all repairing to their respective homes but the bridegroom, who remains in the new dwelling where he assembles a band of musicians, and he and a few of his friends keep up a revelry all night, thus serenading the bride.

Early next morning the friends of both parties assemble at the new home and vie with each other in feeding the priests and themselves. Nothing preventing and the astrologers announcing that the day was propitious, the nuptials will be closed that evening by the selection of a middle-aged couple, friends of the bride, who have been blessed with a numerous progeny, to arrange the bridal chamber and marriage bed. This is done under the belief that such service performed by so meritorious a couple will secure like blessings on the happy bride and groom. At 10 o'clock P.M. some of the elders conduct the bride ceremoniously to her new abode where she is received by her husband; they remain with them an hour or so, giving them the best counsels and exhortations of which they are capable, and then, beseeching from the fates the highest blessings of the marriage state to rest upon them, they retire and this closes the nuptial ceremonies.

After two or three days the bridegroom takes the bride to visit his father's family, when she prostrates herself before them, carrying with her a few presents for the different members of the family in the form of cakes, bouquets, etc. Her father-in-law then makes her some valuable presents, generally jewelry. A few days after this the bride will conduct her husband on a ceremonial visit to her parents, at whose feet he will bow down when he will receive some valuable presents in silver or gold. At the time of the birth of the first child, the toon, which was committed to the care of the parent of the bride, is brought out and delivered over to the young mother. Up to this time they have lived upon her parents, from thence onward they will have to care for themselves. The birth of the first child is celebrated by the relatives on both sides in bringing presents for the child, intended as a peace offering to make its spirit bold and courageous, denominated tam-k'wan There are many varieties of wedding ceremonies in vogue among the natives, but they all partake of the character of the one described, some being more elaborate than others and the presents more costly, while those of the lower classes arrange to have the ceremony concluded in one day. It is thought bad form for a man to take a wife without some kind of public ceremony to sanction the union, but many of the peons do so.

The Laos have a form of marriage which is in most cases performed and recorded by the Nai, magistrate, of the district it happens in. A divorce may also be obtained by the parties if they are not comfortably suited to each other, but it must be by mutual agreement, except in severe cases of inconstancy on the part of the bride. Then they are separated by consent of the husband. A young aspirant to the hand of a female begs for the flower in her hair. If she gives it to him, he knows that his suit is a favorable one; but if it is refused him he knows to the contrary. One great mark of honor, to be placed to their credit, is that a young couple engaged to be married have every confidence placed in them by the parents of the bride, and it is a rare case that it is ever violated, the Laos women being generally virtuous.

A Nobleman and His Family.

XXVII.

THE ATTAP PALM, TONG YANG AND OTHER TREES.

One of the most peculiar growths of Siam is the Attap Palm, a cross between a tree and a fern, found only in the alluvial lands at the head waters of the gulf and along the rivers entering therein. Its leaves are held in high repute by the natives as a thatch for covering their houses. Its center or trunk is a large bulb, from two to three feet in diameter, from which shoot from thirty to forty immense leaves, somewhat resembling the cocoa palm, which stand out with singular uprightness and then curve outward like a gigantic lily, generally having an undeveloped leaf in the center that stands from eight to twelve feet in height. The full-grown leaf varies from twenty to twenty-five feet in length and resembles a monster fan. It is found along the banks of rivers and canals and when undisturbed forms an almost impenetrable jungle. The leaves are cut in three-foot lengths and fastened on the roofs by being tied to bamboo slats that extend across the rafters; formerly the strings were made from the midrif of the talliput palm which is very flexible, but now imported twine is used in the towns. The attap comprises both genders in the same tree and at times is full of sap which the natives obtain by tapping the tree similar to the way the maple is tapped in America, and convert the sap into sugar as they do that of the Palmyra palm, the monarch of the palms. Frequently the sap will flow for a month or longer. The blossom is cylindrical, about four inches long and very fragrant even after it becomes dry, and its fruit grows in clusters of from eighty to one hundred on a single stem, forming a globe about one foot in diameter, which when ripe are of a glossy purple hue and have a hard hull. It begins to bear from its fourth year and has annually from four to eight clusters, requiring six months to mature. The stems that bear the fruit and blossoms are made into brooms and brushes resembling a horse's tail after they are hackeled, some of the unfolded leaflets are used for cigarette wrappers. It is a tree almost unknown in Europe or America.

The Ton Yang or oil tree is another of the peculiar trees of this peculiar land. It grows in all parts of Siam and is one of the largest and most imposing trees found in the tropics; it grows very straight, like the betel, and reaches a height of from one hundred and eighty to two hundred and thirty feet, free from knot or limb, and is used for the immense pillars required for the premains or temples for royal cremations. Its leaf is similar to the basswood of America and its remarkable characteristic is its oil-bearing quality. The oil is obtained by tapping the tree, cutting a large notch two or three feet from the ground, the base of the notch being made so that it will form a basin capable of holding a half-gallon to catch the drip, but the tree will not yield readily till the notch is charred thoroughly. A large tree twelve feet in circumference can be tapped in several places and each notch will yield a gallon or more in twenty-four hours. At first the oil is milky and thin, but it soon becomes thick and brown by exposure. It is then brought to market in large jars and sold for the purpose of oiling boats and other purposes. By mixing it with finely pulverized rosin a cement is made with which the natives fill the seams of their boats, they also mix a small quantity of rosin with the oil and varnish the bottom of their boats which when it becomes dry is hard, glossy and impervious to water. This tree has almost entirely disappeared from the vicinity of Bangkok and can only be found in the distant jungles.

The Betel tree, the Aureca palm, attains great perfection on the plains of Siam and throughout the Strait's settlements; its maximum height is about ninety feet, its trunk is very slender and straight and is only from six to ten inches in diameter near the root which continues with but little change until the top is reached, having no limbs, and is crowned with a tuft of long lace-like leaves, six or eight in number, which branch like blades of corn from the stalk, each leaf being six or seven feet in length, curving gracefully outward as they bend before the monsoon. Betel trees are extensively cultivated and commence bearing from the third to the fifth year and continue to do so for nearly forty years, when they decay at the root. The fruit grows in clusters from three to five in number at a time, each cluster having an independent stem on which is suspended from one hundred and fifty to three hundred nuts. The clusters are attached to the tree a little below the insertion of the leaves, hanging in the shade, two or three leaves lopping over them. When ripe the nuts are about the size and shape of an egg plum and exchange their deep green color for that of a reddish yellow and look like small oranges. The outer part of the fruit is a tough hull a quarter of an inch thick. When stripped of its hull it is about the size of a large hickory nut, has the consistency of a peach kernel and is considered one of the essentials of life; all chew it. When the nut is in a dry state it is broken into small particles and mingled with a vermilion-colored lime paste and a little ceri-leaf makes a mouthful that renders the chewer hideous. The natives prefer it in its unripe state, and the girls and women prepare it in the most dextrous manner. Notwithstanding the practice of betel chewing is very filthy, it is universal among the people, causing the users of it to expectorate large quantities of blood-red saliva, distorts their lips, blackens their gums and teeth, causing the sockets of the teeth to become calloused so that many of their teeth fall out at an early age. Chewing betel has obtained greater power over the Siamese than tobacco over other nations, and it is extremely rare that a man, or a woman, or even a child, over ten years of age, can be found who is not addicted to it or some of its substitutes. They would sooner go without their rice than their betel. It is to the Siamese what the pipe of tobacco is to the American Indian, and it is considered a breach of hospitality if betel is not handed round to their guests; marriages can not be perfected without this token of friendship, in fact the Siamese word for marriage is Kenmac—a basin or salver of betel.

The ceri-leaf, which always goes with the betel, is a member of the pepper family, the plant is reared on poles or trellises, and the leaf is a bright green with a pungent taste, the fruit resembling the long pepper. It is for its pungent qualities that it is used with the betel and sometimes a pinch of tobacco is added. The other ingredient of the betel compound is red lime paste, which is made of newly burnt lime, and before it is slacked a decoction of tumeric root is poured on it which causes it to form a paste taking a fine vermilion color. While in this plastic state it is brought to market and sold up and down the river by hucksters, who retail it in little earthen pots holding a half a pint, twenty of which they sell for a fuang or a bucketful for a salung. This red lime is spread on the ceri-leaf with a wooden spatula and then rolling the lime up in the leaf it is placed in the mouth with a piece of betel, then the mastication commences and soon the red saliva is ejected in a stream. It is one of the filthiest practices that the Siamese are addicted to.

The Cocoa Palm is another valuable tree and found in all tropical countries; its average height is about eighty feet, and, like the betel, runs up a staff till near the apex, when it branches out into a crown of about twenty pinnatisect leaves about fifteen feet long by six feet wide. Each leaf has nearly one hundred leaflets set two inches apart on either side of its spine, which are generally about three feet long by three inches wide. Immediately beneath the leaves hang clusters of fruit, each having from six to eight nuts attached, and as they bear perennially ripe fruit and blossoms can be seen on the same tree, it requiring about six months for the nuts to mature. The nut proper is encased in a husk of fibrous nature which has to be cut off. When the nut has attained its medium growth it can be easily cut with a knife and it then contains about a half pint of fluid, cooling and nourishing as a drink, and they are sold in the bazaars for that purpose at a cent a piece. Travelers through the jungles drink nothing else if the nut is obtainable. It is very useful for a dipper, for culinary purposes, to measure rice, it being the standard measure of the kingdom for that purpose, the T'anon or one and a half pints; its meat is used in cooking and enters into most Siamese dishes, especially curry; large quantities of oil are also extracted from it, sold by the gallon, and is an article of export, much of it being used in illuminations and, in fact, until petroleum was introduced was the only illuminator that they had, it being frequently pressed into candles, hardened by a chemical process. The trees are also tapped for sugar, same as the betel, but the sugar is better and larger quantities are made, as is also from the Palmyra palm. This tree is the largest of its species, sometimes reaching the height of one hundred and eighty feet, tall and slender, and its crown consists of from twenty to thirty leaves, each leaf describing a circle, with a radius of three feet, shaped like a fan that opens both ways till the two handles meet, leaving the folds of the fan slack, three or four feet in length, which being round on the under side and grooved on the upper form a conductor for rain or dew to the parent stem. Like the cocoa, they bear at all times and have more blossoms during the dry season than the wet, which is the time that the natives select for obtaining the sap and making sugar. The fruit is smaller than the cocoa nut and each hull contains three nuts about the size of a goose egg which, before it matures, is filled with a delicious fluid. The chief use for the Palmyra palm is its sugar bearing, the natives making large quantities from it, and it is asserted that from thirty to forty millions of pounds is made annually, the province of Petchaburee alone furnishing over ten million pounds upon which a tax of forty thousand ticals ($20,000) is collected. The Teak, the wood of commerce and general use, is mentioned elsewhere. The woods of Siam are many and some very valuable, especially Padoo, Rose, Ebony, Sapan, Agilla wood, etc., many of them unknown to the commercial world.

XXVIII.

HOLIDAYS AND FESTIVALS

T'EEP CH'ĬNG CH'A HOLIDAYS.

These always occur on the 7th and 9th waxing moon of the second month. On each of these days a large procession is made for the Chief Minister of the Rice Department, by which he is carried in great pomp to the place called Sou ch'ing ch'a (pillars for swinging). A brick platform, carpeted with white muslin and tastefully curtained, having been prepared for him, he ascends it, and stands on one foot attended by four Brahmin priests, two on his right and two on his left hand, until three games of the swinging have ended, which occupy usually about two hours. If he venture to touch his raised foot to the floor before the games are ended, the Brahmins, it is said, are allowed to strip him of his property and otherwise dishonor him. When the games are over the swingers (persons belonging to the Brahmin priests) dip up with bullocks' horns water made holy by Brahminical ceremonies, and sprinkle it upon all about them. This is the Brahminical mode of calling blessings down upon the people of the land. The ceremonies of the first day being finished, the Chief Minister is escorted home by a procession like the one that brought him. This is all done in the forenoon. The ceremonies of the second day are performed in the afternoon. The King does not usually grace them with his presence. But they are attended by many of the princes and officers of government, and crowds of people.

KROOT CHEEN HOLIDAYS.

January 22d, 23d, and 24th. These three days are universally observed by the Chinese as their New Year holidays. The 23d of January is the first day of their year. Nearly all their ordinary business stops during those three days, and it requires at least three days more to recover themselves from the dissipations of that season. As the Siamese are intimately connected with them, the derangement of business extends throughout all their affairs also.

SEASON FOR VISITING P'RA HAT

January 29th, and February 6th, inclusive. This is the season which the Buddhists of Siam very generally spend in visiting P'ra Hat, about 100 miles north of Bangkok, where tradition affirms Buddha once placed his foot on a rock, and left there a clear imprint of it, even to all the peculiar and characteristic marks on the sole, to be a standing testimony to all his followers that he did indeed once live on earth, and visited Siam, and was, what their sacred books declare him to be, the All-knowing Teacher.

KROOT T'EI HOLIDAYS.

March 21st, 22d, and 23d. These are the Siamese New Year holidays, when almost all the Siamese, Laos, Cambodians, Peguans, and Burmans engage in performing extraordinary works of merit. Nearly every family makes a peculiar cake appropriate to the season. Fruits of all kinds then in market are procured and presented to the priests. On the third day the temple doors are thrown open, and the people, more especially the women and children, enter, attired in their best clothing, and bow down before the idol, and make offerings of flowers, etc. Many of the more wealthy families have on each of those days special prayers and preaching by the priests at their houses, when they feast them, and make offerings of yellow robes and other articles necessary to them as priests.

The religious services are usually completed by the end of the second day; the third day is almost universally devoted to games of chance. Men, women and children all join in it with all their hearts, as the laws of the land give them a gratuitous license to gamble on such occasions.

The King keeps these holidays with much ceremony, and with extraordinary religious services, and has companies of priests stationed on the top of the city walls in regular order surrounding the whole city, to perform exorcisms in concert. On the night of the first day, the 14th of the Siamese moon, guns, large and small, are fired from the tops of the walls from all points of the compass, at intervals of about twenty minutes throughout the night. Each gun, it is said, is fired 36 times. This is done for the purpose of expelling the evil spirits from the precincts of the city, and thus preparing the way for health and happiness to all within the city walls. In this custom is manifested about the same wisdom and power that we see in the natives, at the times of the eclipses, when guns, crackers, gongs and other instruments of rattling and confusion innumerable are brought into requisition to frighten the fabulous monster *Rahu* from his effort to swallow the sun or moon. As the people, living outside, desire to participate in such blessings and sports, many of them join in the concert of firing, so that guns may be heard from many parts of the suburbs all that night. The effects of this universal dissipation do not cease for many days after the holidays are past. This ceremony is fast falling into disrepute and will shortly be entirely abolished, but few guns being now fired.

THE CEREMONY OF T'U NAM.

March 24th, 3d of 5th waxing moon. This is the day established from time immemorial for all the Siamese Princes, Lords, Nobles, and people, to take their first semi-annual oath of allegiance to the King. At that time they assemble at the King's palace, and drink and sprinkle their foreheads with water, in which has been dipped swords, daggers, spears, guns, and other instruments by which the King may execute vengeance upon those who rebel against him, and thus they invoke the royal vengeance by these instruments upon themselves, and their families, if they shall be found unfaithful to the King. The priests are excused from this service by virtue of the sanctity of their office. But the chief priests of the temples in and about the city meet on that day and perform appropriate religious services at the temple attached to the royal palace.

The governors and people of distant provinces renew their oath of allegiance on another day quickly succeeding this day. They do it by having a portion of the same "water of vengeance" sent to the residence of the governors, who then require all persons of standing and influence within their jurisdictions to assemble and perform the ceremony.

SONGKRAN HOLIDAYS.

These are four successive days occurring generally

soon after the Siamese New Year, but sometimes a little before. It is not fixed to a certain month and day of month, because it is ruled by the sun, and not at all by the moon. It is observed at the time when the sun passes from the zodiacal sign *Manyarasee* over into the sign *Matesarasee*. When the Brahminical astrologers have made up their minds as to the day when that event will take place, they inform the King. The calculations are usually made by the day of the great congregation to renew the oath of allegiance. At this time the King issues a proclamation that the "*P'it'a t'a nom t'a p'isake*" will be observed at the royal palace on such and such a day. He also invites the priests generally to assemble at his palace on that day for a royal festival.

As to the laity, they very generally have special religious services, feast the priests and one another, and play at their games of chance much as on their New Year holidays. The women draw water and bathe the idol, the persons of the priests, the elders of the people, and their grandparents and other aged relatives. They do these things thinking to call down blessings upon those for whose benefit they profess to perform them; but more especially upon themselves and their families by way of recompense,—a central idea of self-righteousness.

BIRTH, INSPIRATION, AND DEATH OF BUDDHA.

May 3d, 4th, and 5th. These three days are to celebrate three great events in the existence of Buddha on earth, which all took place, it would seem, on the same day of the same moon, viz., the 15th day of the 6th waxing moon. Those events are, first, his birth; second, his most wonderful self-originated inspiration to see and know all things with perfect clearness; and third, his death, which then completed 80 years of life on earth. These anniversary days are observed by the Siamese very generally with great veneration. On the second day especially are they all alert in performing works of merit, as giving alms to the poor, making offerings to the priests, and to the idol, and in hearing prayers and preaching. In the evening of that day they usually have a display of lighted candles, lanterns, torches, etc.

RAAKNA HOLIDAY—BEGINNING OF SEED-TIME.

The Brahmin astrologers seem not to be able to determine long beforehand exactly on what day the sign will be the most favorable for the ceremonies of the occasion. It usually falls on a day in the former part of the sixth month, corresponding to the first half of May.

The Chief Minister of the Rice department is regarded as king during the day, because he is the King's proxy to hold the plow, break up the ground, and sow the first rice of the year. The custom from time immemorial has been that the people wherever he goes on that day shall honor the King through him by shutting up their shops. In case a shop-keeper be found exposing his goods for sale, he renders himself liable to suffer confiscation of all the property thus exposed. Consequently it is generally somewhat difficult to make purchases in the market on that day. It should be stated that His Majesty, through the Minister of Foreign affairs, declared this custom to be null and void from the beginning of his reign. But notwithstanding that, many of the people regard it as being still in power.

The Minister is escorted by a public procession to the field where the first "breaking of ground" is to take place. In the present reign, that place is within the city walls; formerly it was without. A shed having been there prepared for the ceremony, the Minister enters it, attended by a company of Brahmin priests. They then perform a variety of religious acts on a pair of oxen, to prepare them for the plow. They are decorated with flowers and fastened to the plow, which is likewise adorned. The Minister then holds the plow, while the oxen draw it over the field for about an hour. Then four elderly females, officers in the king's palace, take paddy and sow it over the plat plowed, where it is left uncovered. Then various kinds of grain most important for the sustenance of the people are so exposed that the oxen may eat them when liberated for that purpose. Of whatever kind they eat much, that kind, it is thought, will be scarce in the course of the year; and that of which they eat little or none at all will be abundant.

There is still another way by which they prognosticate about the next harvest. It is by observing the p'anung of the Minister, which is so adjusted that it is liable to hitch up too high or sag too low. Now if while he is holding the plow, his p'anung sags low down near the ankles it is an indication that the rain in the course of the year will be scarce, and the water so low that it can be waded without pulling up the p'anung at all. But, on the other hand, if his p'anung hitch up near his knees, it denotes that there will be much rain, and the country inundated. Both these conditions are looked upon as extremes, and threaten the ruin of the rice crop. The p'anung abiding midway between the ankles and the knees is regarded as the most propitious of all conditions.

K'ÒW WASÚ HOLIDAYS.

July 18th, the 15th of the Siamese 8th waning moon. All Buddhists who have much veneration for their religion anticipate this season by making special provision in behalf of the priests to serve them for a term of three months on which they then enter, and during which they are deprived of the privilege of traveling so far from the temples to which they belong as to make it necessary to spend a night away from them. For their comfort during this term of confinement, all classes set themselves to provide for them parched rice and corn, flowers that never fade, both natural and artificial, silvered and gilded trees, figures of birds and various animals beautifully constructed, and made to stand daily before them in their dormitories. On the day of the 15th, they are formally presented to them. Of these the priests take a part and offer them to the idol, and place them in order at his feet to stand there for three months. Another part they present to their teachers and elders, and aged priests residing in the same temple. Having done this, the priests then assemble together and pledge themselves to the idol, and to one another, that they will not sleep out of their dormitories until the expiration of the three months.

THE SECOND SEMI-ANNUAL OATH OF ALLEGIANCE, T'Ú' NAM.

This takes place August 29th, the 13th day of the 10th Siamese waning moon. The ceremonies for administering and taking the oath are the same as the first time on the 24th March.

THE AWK WASA HOLIDAYS

occur on the 29th and 30th September, and 1st October. The 15th waxing of the 11th moon is the day when Buddhist customs allow the priests to come out of their confinement in the temples and travel as far away from home as they please. To provide for them suitable clothing during their wanderings, extraordinary efforts are made by the laity, from the highest to the lowest, in anticipation of these days.

The King, especially, takes care to have innumerable bales of white cotton shirtings cut up into small pieces, and then sewed together into large priest robes to imitate apparel made up of patchwork (for Buddhist priests in the beginning clothed themselves with rags, to show their self-mortification). These robes are afterward died yellow. They are not all, nor the greater part, presented to the priests on either of those days. A whole month is required to finish the offerings. There is on those three days a general devotion to works of merit making.

The King of Siam has on each evening a public exhibition of his own personal offerings made with particular reference, it is said, to Buddha's footprint near the sea-shore in a distant country unknown, which can only be reached by water conveyances. Consequently the offerings are made on the river. They consist of little skiffs and plantain stalk floats; some in pagoda form, towering ten or twelve feet; some bearing images of birds and beasts, real and fabulous; with other varieties innumerable; all splendidly illuminated with wax candles. These offerings are floated off in regular succession, one by one, by the ministration of His Majesty's servants, he himself being present in his royal seat on the river. The offerings float down with the ebb tide, beautifully illuminating the river for several miles before their lights burn out. After this, many of the naked floats are captured by the people, and each skiff is returned by the man who had charge of it.

This part of the ceremony being finished the King then ignites a match to the fire-works arranged in boats, in the midst of the river, when a new scene breaks forth. Fire trees are seen standing in the river; and by their powerful sulphurous blaze illuminate much of the city. Presently the glory of these departs, and then a line of flowering shrubbery made by fire appears, and develops their varied flowers, continually changing their hue. After this, rockets and squibs of great variety are let off from boats.

The people generally make their own family offerings, on those three evenings, an hour or two before the King comes out of his palace. You may see them all over the city, on the rivers and canals near their homes. They consist of little arks made of the inner layers of the stalk of the *scilla maratima*, illuminated by wax candles, and squibs innumerable flying in the open heavens, and frolicking in the water. The prevailing notion among the common people seems to be that these fire-works are offerings to the goddesses of the land and water, to expiate for the sin of polluting their domains with the excrement and filth of man and beast, as they have done, during the twelve months which are then about to close.

All the time onward thence to the first day of the

12th waning moon is regarded as being peculiarly propitious for making offerings to the priests, and worshiping the idol. About the beginning of the 12th month the King makes his appearance in his best estate, being escorted by vast processions by land and water, carrying yellow robes to present to the priests with his own hands, at the many temples dedicated to them. Fifteen days are almost wholly occupied in this way, passing in great pomp from temple to temple. Three or four of the temples are usually visited daily.

Other temples not dedicated to the Kings are in the meantime visited by large parties of Buddha's followers, who unite together, in processions by water, and carry yellow apparel, fruits and other things to their priests after the fashion set them by their sovereign.

About the same time, many parties get together evenings, and make a great show of lanterns, gongs, and trumpets on the river, in bearing to temples yellow garments and fruit, suspended on bushes fixed in their boats. Having arrived at their destination, the priests come out and pick them off from the bushes, according to their several wants. This custom is said to have originated in the fact that Buddhist priests in olden time lived in the woods, and satisfied their daily wants by gathering wild fruit and old cast-off clothing. Such self-mortification was highly praised by Buddha.

THE KING'S SECOND FIRE-WORKS.

October 28th, 29th, and 30th; the 14th and 15th of the 12th waxing, and 1st of the waning. On these three days the King has extraordinary religious services in his palace, and late in the evening of each day makes offerings of fire-works publicly on the river, much as on the former occasion, but more complete and beautiful. This is the better time of the two to witness these displays, as the weather is almost sure to be fine. His Majesty has made many innovations of these customs, and the fire-works are not as interesting as they have been wont to be. I have mentioned the celebration of the King's birthday elsewhere.

XXIX.

CUSTOM OF THE SIAMESE FOR THE DYING AND DEAD—CREMATIONS, ETC.

The late Dr. D. B. Bradley, one of the early missionaries that went to Siam and who had free entree into the palace of King Monkut, wrote a series of articles for his calender, and to it I am indebted for much of the following account of the ceremonies attending the death of a high noble or King, he being in attendance when the late King was cremated.

When a Buddhist prince is found to be at the point of death, his or her attendants, wishing to give the departing spirit as good a passport into the spirit world as it is possible for surviving friends to do, suspend every other care, and address themselves to the one work of fixing the thoughts of the dying man upon Buddha. To accomplish this object, they take their turns in enunciating as clearly as possible one of the names by which it is known the dying man was accustomed to speak of his god when in health. P'ra Arahang is one of the names of Buddha, and is one generally employed among the Siamese Princes when they speak of him. It is uttered as often as eight or ten times in a minute; consequently you can hear at such times scarcely anything else. They do this hoping that the departing spirit will thus be helped to think of Buddha, and that that will accumulate a large fund of merit to his credit, which will become of vast service to him in the spirit world. It is continued

from ten to fifteen minutes after the pulse has stopped its beating and the lungs their heaving—even until the body is cold and stiff in death.

When all evidence of hearing is gone, the attending friends will raise their voices almost to a stunning pitch, hoping that they may force the departing spirit to hear the name P'ra Arahang. When the most loving friends have ceased to have any lingering hope that the dying man can by any means hear them longer, then the continuous and deafening sound of P'ra Arahang are exchanged for the most uncontrollable wailings; and these are so loud that they can be heard at a great distance. Then all the members of the family, including the slaves in the house and out of the house, within hearing, join in a general outburst of crying and sobbing, with every evidence that their hearts mourn for the departed.

Dr. Bradley, an eye witness of several such scenes in the Royal palace, states that the most remarkable was at the time of the demise of the first Queen Consort of King Monkut. The King himself labored hard to make the dying Queen hear the dear name P'ra Arahang, and when he became weary in his utterances of it others took it up, and kept the enunciation of it agoing unbroken for an hour or more. And such weeping and wailing he had never before seen, as he heard then all about the royal palace. The King of Siam did not think that it was beneath his dignity to weep on that occasion the most bitter tears.

When a Prince of high rank has just departed this life, the King visits the house of mourning and bathes the corpse with simple water, doing it with his own hands. After him other Princes, in the order of their rank, step up one by one, and pour a dipper of water upon it. Then come the nobles and lords according to their rank, and perform each the same kind office for the remains of the departed. When all the chief princes, nobles and lords present shall have had an opportunity to show such respect, certain officials in the royal palace concur together in dressing the body for a sitting posture. For this purpose they put on it a pair of short pantaloons tightly fitted, and a jacket also made to fit snugly. Over these they apply a winding sheet, wrapping the body in it as firmly as possible. Being thus prepared, the corpse is then placed in a copper urn in a sitting posture, and then this is put into one made of fine gold. The inner urn has an iron grating for its bottom, and the outer one an outlet at the most pendant point, with a stopcock from which the fluid parts of the body are daily drawn off until it becomes quite dry.

The King usually remains until the corpse has been seated in the urn, and then graces the ceremony of placing the golden urn on an elevated platform, ascending by three gradations to the height of five feet. The conch shell blowers and trumpeters and pipers perform their several parts with the greatest possible harmony of such instruments, while the urn is being elevated to its place. This act is denominated Ch'o'n p'ra sop k'u'n p'ra t'aan—literally an invitation to the corpse to be seated on the platform.

When thus seated, all the insignia of royalty which the Prince was accustomed to have about him in life are brought and arranged in due order at his feet. They also place on the platform his more common personal utensils, as the golden platter in which he was accustomed to have his changes of raiment brought to him, his gold betel-box, his cigar case, his golden spittoon, his writing apparatus, etc. The band of musicians above named now perform a funeral dirge; and it is arranged to have them assemble daily at early dawn, and at noon, and when the day is just merging into night to perform in concert with a company of mourning women, who bewail the dead and chant his virtues and excellencies. These spend about half an hour each time in these services. In the intervals of these hours, there is present a company of Buddhist priests, four at a time, sitting on the floor, a little distant from the platform, reciting moral lessons and chanting incantations in the Pali language in loud, clear and musical intonations, in perfect harmony as to matter and tone.

This service is continued day and night, with only the intervals for the performance of the dirges, and the wailing of mourning woman as above stated, and a few minutes once every hour for one company to retire and another of four to come in and take their places. This is kept up from week to week and month to month until the time appointed for the burning of the corpse has arrived, which may be from two to six, or even eight months. The remains of a king are usually kept from eight to twelve months.

On the death of a king, as was the case with his late Majesty, his successor to the throne immediately begins to make arrangements for the erection of the P'ramëne, which is the splendid temporary building, under which the body is to sit in state several days on a throne glittering with silver, gold and diamonds, and then and there to be committed to the flames.

The building is intended to be in size and grandeur

according to the estimation in which the deceased was held. Royal orders are forthwith sent to the governors of the four different provinces far away to the north, in which large timber abounds, requiring each of these to furnish one of the four large logs for the center pillars of the P'rämëne. These must be of the finest timber, very straight, from two hundred to two hundred and fifty feet long, and proportionately large in circumference, not less than twelve feet. There are always twelve pillars, a little smaller in size, demanded at the same time from governors of other provinces, as also much other timber needful in the erection of the P'rämëne and the numerous other buildings connected with it. As sacred custom will not tolerate the use of pillars that have been used on any former occasion, consequently new ones must be obtained for every new occasion of the funeral obsequies of a king. Those four large pillars are very difficult to find, and can be floated down to the capital only at seasons of the year when the rivers, where they are found, are full.

They are hauled to the banks of the stream by elephants and buffaloes. The great difficulty of procuring these pillars is one main cause of the usual long delay of the funeral burning for a king. When brought to the city, they are hauled up to the place of the P'rämëne chiefly by the muscular power of men working by means of a rude windlass and rollers under the logs. They are then hewed and planed a little, just enough to remove all crooks and other deformities, and finished off in a cylindrical form.

Then they are planted in the ground thirty feet deep, one at each corner of a square not less than one hundred and sixty feet in circumference. When in their proper places, they stand leaning a little towards each other, so that they describe the form of a four-sided truncated pyramid, from one hundred and seventy to two hundred feet high. On the top of these is framed a pagoda-form spire, adding from fifty to sixty more feet to the height of the structure. This upper part is octagonal, and so covered with gilded and tinseled paper as to make a grand appearance at such a height; but it would not well bear inspection at a close view.

At each of the four corners of this pyramid they erect by means of the twelve smaller posts mentioned above a wing extending out from the main pillars about forty feet. Each of these has also a pagoda-form spire of the same general form and appearance as the center one, but not as tall by thirty or forty feet. The large as well as the smaller pillars are handsomely papered, as are also all the halls of which they form the boundary. Between each of these corner buildings is a splendid porch looking to each cardinal point of the compass.

Surrounding the P'rămĕne there is a new fence made of bamboo slats in an upright position, ten feet high, the paling being so closely set that you can not see through it. It encloses a large square of ground, and has only one gate midway on each side. In close contiguity with this fence on the inside are numberless and indescribable buildings mostly made of bamboo, fantastically papered and painted, for the accommodation of priests, princes, noblemen and others. One side of the square is chiefly occupied with buildings for the King's own accommodation while attending the ceremonies of the royal cremation. These are distinguished from all others by having their roofs covered with crimson cloth, and by the peculiar curved horn-like projections at the two ends of their ridges, and the golden drapery suspended in front and tastefully gathered up to the several posts of the halls. The whole area occupied by houses and other fixtures is curiously and neatly covered with bamboo wicker work; the slats of which the woof and warp are made being about an inch wide, forming thus one unbroken bamboo carpet, giving great elasticity and squeaking to the steps of all who walk upon it. There are placed here and there upon this bamboo floor multitudes of standards peculiar to the Siamese. Some are like the Sawe-krachat, one of the insignia of royalty, or, in other words, the royal umbrella of nine stories, several inches apart, connected by one common staff. These stories become smaller as you ascend; the uppermost one being less than a foot in diameter, and the one at the bottom four feet or more. Some of these are seven stories, and some only five. There are several other indescribable standards and fixtures thickly studding the floor, some of them tinseled, some of them gilded, some with machinery exhibiting a variety of little paper figures in perpetual action, some imaginary angels, some devils, and some suffering souls in hell. Here and there you will see a niche with rude landscape views of the lower series of the Buddhist's celestial worlds, and of princely dwellings there, with delightful pools and groves, and many other sensual luxuries, which the mind fancies a heaven of happiness must give its inhabitants.

Outside of the bamboo walls are various buildings designed for the accommodation of princes, officers of government, and others who can not find sufficient room within the enclosure. There are also numerous play-houses for theatrical performances, puppet shows, masquerades, turning summersaults on rods highly elevated, wire dancing, leaping through hoops from aloft, lying on the points of spears, sword and cudgel sham fighting, wrestling, etc.

There is also one other place outside of the P'rămĕne gates more interesting to many than those already alluded to: and this is the great victualing establishment for all classes above the peons, presenting a large variety of dishes and fruits, well prepared, and very tempting to the appetite, all freely offered without money and without price, at all hours of the day.

If there be a second king, he has a temporary palace erected for his accommodation out of the enclosure, on the north side, which is distinguished from all other buildings by a crimson-colored roof, royal horns, and golden drapery like that of the first king.

The real P'rămĕne is erected in the center of the whole, in the great hall directly under the loftiest spire. This is a most splendid eight-sided pyramid, fifty or sixty feet in circumference, its base sitting on a floor twenty feet above the ground. It diminishes by right-angle gradations upward some thirty feet to a truncated top, and on its top is placed the golden urn, containing the remains, most superbly decorated with gold and diamonds and other precious stones. Some ten or fifteen feet above this is suspended from the lofty ceiling a rich golden canopy. And far up above that is a tasty white circular awning overshadowing the whole. Immediately under the golden canopy hang the sweetest and whitest flowers, arranged in the form of a large chandelier.

The body of the pyramid is made indescribably brilliant by the tasty arrangement on its several steps of the most showy articles of porcelain, glass, alabaster, silver and gold artificial flowers, and artificial fruits intermixed with real fruits; little images of birds and beasts, of men, women, children, angels, etc. For illuminating the hall, splendid chandeliers are suspended from the ceiling in the four corners of it, being assisted by innumerable lesser lights on the angular gradations of the pyramid.

At the time appointed for placing the royal remains in state on the lofty throne, nearly all the princes, chief nobles, and rulers in the kingdom assemble at the royal palace just after break of day, to escort "the sacred corpse" to its last earthly throne on the summit of the new P"rămĕne. The golden urn, already most brilliantly decked with diamonds, is placed upon a high golden seat in a kind of Juggernaut car, drawn by a pair of horses, assisted by hundreds of men. This vehicle is preceded by two other wheel carriages. The first is occupied solely by the high priest of the kingdom, sitting on a high seat, reading a sacred book of moral lessons in Pali, called app'it'am. The second carriage is occupied by a few of the most favored of the children of the deceased. A strip of silver cloth six inches wide is attached to the urn, and loosely extended to the seats of the royal highnesses in the second carriage, and to the thighs of the high priest, over which the other end lies, while the procession is moving. This forms the mystical union between the deceased and the sacred book and his children. The carriage next behind the one bearing the royal urn carries some fifty or sixty sticks of imported fragrant wood, richly gilded at the ends, with which the body is to be burned. Each of these carriages is drawn by a pair of horses, with scores of men to assist, all pulling at a rope in front of the animals.

Both in their front and rear are figures of elephants, rhinoceroses, lions, tigers and fabulous animals of many kinds, utterly defying description. These are all made of bamboo wicker work, covered with paper, and painted to suit the prurient fancies of Buddhists. These all go in pairs, and are all drawn on small wooden wheels. Each of the figured animals have on their backs a large receptacle for priests' robes, which are well filled with this article, neatly folded, ready for offering. In front of these and in their rear are hundreds of men dressed in white, purporting to be angels, wearing white turbans with pagoda-form spires or crowns eight or ten inches tall. These walk four abreast, and carry glass imitation lotus flowers.

The moment the procession begins to move, the shells, trumpets and pipes are sounded, and the death drums are beaten with a slowly measured stroke, until the royal hearse reaches the P'rămĕne. Having arrived, the golden urn is removed from the hearse, and placed upon a kind of railroad bridge fifty or sixty feet long, one end of it resting on the ground, and the other on the top of the P'rămĕne, at an angle of forty degrees or more. On this, the urn is drawn up slowly by ropes and pullies with much ceremony and placed on the splendid throne, to remain in state at least fifteen days before the burning.

Having placed the royal urn on the top of the P'rămbencha, or P'rămĕne pyramid, they then take the strip of silver cloth, which had been the mystic communication between the deceased and his children and the sacred book while in the procession, and extend it from the lid of the golden urn down the eastern and western sides of the pyramid, and thence on a Brussels carpet, protected by white muslin, nearly to the flight of steps on the east and west sides of the building. It is about noon when this is completed.

Then the chief priests of the city and from nearly all other parts of the kingdom begin to assemble, a hundred or more at a time, on the floor of the P'ramēne, in sight of the royal urn, and rehearse in concert lessons in Pali, called P'ang-sŏŏ-k'oon, which are in substance "reflections on the brevity and uncertainty of human life, the certainty of death and transmigration, the sorrows inseparably connected with every state of mutability, and the blessings of Nipp'an, where there can be no more change." Having uttered audibly these short lessons, they continue in a sitting posture with downcast looks a few minutes, reflecting silently on the condition of the living and the dead, and then retire, giving place to another hundred or more, to recite the same lessons, and to exercise their moral natures with similar reflections. Thus they come and retire, until thousands of the chief priests and others of lower rank have had the privilege and honor to engage in this exercise, and this is repeated every day the corpse sits in state, and three days afterwards.

All the princes and nobles, and officers of government taking a part in the funeral solemnities are dressed in white, as are also the royal servants, and most of the servants and slaves of the princes and nobles. Every Siamese subject, whether prince or noble, governor or plebeian, men and women, rich and poor, bond and free, must then out of respect to the deceased have his head entirely shaven, thus showing to all his neighbors that he is truly in mourning for the dead. This differs from the European custom of *putting on* mourning, in that it requires the *putting off* the natural and pleasant clothing of the head, and putting on entire baldness and desolation, and the putting off all their usual dress of figured apparel, and putting on the plainest white muslin, which they regard as being entirely devoid of show, and therefore a fit emblem of sadness of spirit.

It is arranged that there shall be four common priests rehearsing Pali, every hour of the day and night, as when before the corpse was brought to the P"ramëne, and for this purpose the four corners of the P"ramëne hall are reserved for four companies of four each, to sit down and perform this service; but only one company at a time, continuing the exercise nearly an hour. Then the next four in order take their turn for the same length of time, and so on for twenty-four hours, at the expiration of which another band of sixteen, divided into four companies, come and take their places and serve in the same way twenty-four hours; and then these are relieved by another band of sixteen, and so on day and night. No company who have served twenty-four hours are called to that service again. These services are continued from fifteen to nineteen days; that is, until the protracted meeting breaks up.

These priests, together with the multitudes of other priests, are sumptuously fed from the royal bounty early every morning and again between eleven and twelve o'clock A. M. Extraordinary attention is paid to the priests by all parties, from the King down to the slaves, as that is accounted the most ready way to obtain great profits in merit making. The King himself spends a large portion of each day of the ceremonies in distributing to the priests yellow robes, which he has caused to be prepared for them at the expense of his private purse. To every chief priest he gives a complete suit of clerical apparel, and to every other priest presents some important part of a suit, if not the whole.

If the King be necessarily absent, he deputizes his eldest son to distribute in his stead. Besides the yellow robes, the King has also in readiness vast provision of bedsteads fully furnished with mosquito bars, mattresses, pillows, towels, spittoons, betel boxes, cigar cases, rice kettles, lacquered trays and other dishes for collecting rice, lamps, candles, sampans, and boats with little houses on them, and other articles which the priests need in their daily calling. These things he distributes to them every day.

Twice every day, morning and evening, the King invites one of the chief priests to preach to him and the princes, nobles and others. The exercise is simply to read from Pali sacred book some of the lessons of Buddha. The priest does this sitting cross-legged in a large chair, in the hall of the P'rämëne, or in the audience hall of the King's temporary abode on the premises, while all his hearers sit bowed forward on their elbows, with the palms of their hands met before their faces, most reverently looking at the reader whose Pali not one in a hundred of them understands at all.

Sometimes the princes and nobles, in their desire to make as much of the occasion as possible to add to their stock of merit, arrange to have preaching in other places about the P'rämëne, on their own responsibility, and embrace the opportunity to make liberal presents to the preacher and other priests after the exercises.

At early candle lighting, the P'ramëne is most brilliantly illuminated within and without by electric lights, and wax candles, and cocoanut oil. Then sundry plays are initiated; the Nang cheen, the Nang k'aak, and the Nangt'ai—that is, leather theatrical figures moved about by the hands of men behind a thin white muslin screen lighted from behind by a blazing fire; and these are of Chinese, Malay and Siamese dramas. In another place before the royal hall you will see the figure of a huge fabulous animal, animated by a boy within him, walking hither and thither to catch what appears to be a large globe of fire, continually eluding the jaws of the monster, and sometimes almost swallowed by him. Also, the lantern dance, in which about fifty performers take part, each carrying a lantern.

About eight or nine o'clock in the evening, the fireworks come off, being occasionally ignited by the King himself. You first hear the crackling of the matches, then you see the sulphuric fire and smoke running up tall bamboo poles, and extending out into branches. Presently you see a dozen tall trees of fire, throwing an intense light over all the premises. These quickly burn out, and another flash brings into view beautiful fire shrubbery. In a minute or two they blossom roses, dahlias, oleanders, and other flowers of all hues, and the most beautiful, continually changing their color, like a chameleon, until they all fade out into darkness. Presently you are startled by the report of rockets sent up from various places in rapid succession, being altogether a hundred or more, showing clearly that the Siamese are not far behind the times in this art. Immediately after this, you will hear a terrible roaring like the bellowing of a dozen elephants, with an occasional crash like the bursting of a small engine boiler. They are fireworks called Ch'ang rawng, which means "bellowing elephants." This unearthly noise and confusion is kept up from ten to fifteen minutes, when suddenly you will hear innumerable fire-birds chirping, quacking, buzzing, and see them hopping in all directions. Some of them ascend high up in the air, and burst with a small sputtering report. Here and there on the top of a small staff are a kind of whirligig propelled by weak gun-powder; some revolving slowly, exhibiting puppit figures; some whirling rapidly, turning out showers of sulphurous scintillations. Having in about fifteen minutes, had enough of these things, they are exchanged for mimic volcanic eruptions, which, though on a small scale, are attended with great roaring and forcible jets of ignited sulphur and iron, ascending like water spouts, and falling in golden showers. It is well that only one crater is in action at a time, and that not exceeding a minute in duration; beginning with a low rumbling noise, and increasing in power, until it suddenly exhausts itself by a terrible belch of fire. Then the man in charge places another artificial crater into the same place, which almost instantly ignites, and acts just as its antecedent did. So they keep them going until fifty or more have been fired.

These plays and sports continue till about midnight, when the King leaves his temporary abode and retires to his home in the royal palace. This is received as a license for all others to retire who wish to do so; and accordingly the most go to their several abodes. But the priests, whose turn it is to watch and rehearse the Pali lessons all hours of the day and night, remain, as do also the keepers of the premises, numbering many hundreds.

There is one other performance usually more exciting than all the rest, and belongs to the latter part of the afternoon of every day of the funeral ceremonies. It is the scattering of money broadcast among the many thousands that have assembled there for the sport. The King takes personally a very lively part in it, though he has his own select company to favor by it, who are princes, nobles, officers of government, and European and American officials. The pieces of money used for the purpose are seven-and-a-half cent pieces of silver, and sixty cent pieces of gold, and sometimes gold rings. These are usually imbedded in little green limes, or small balls of wood of the same shape and size. The object of this is to prevent them from getting lost among the crowd. His Majesty standing in his temporary palace door, having bushels of limes at his feet, charged each with one piece of money, takes up a handful at a time, and throws them out among the large select audience before him, often so skillfully guiding his hand as that some peculiar favorite shall have the best chance in the game—some corpulent prince or minister whom he wishes to set into ludicrous motion by his efforts to catch the flying prize.

The money thrown to the common people is also put into limes and paper balls, and thrown by persons appointed by the King to do it in his name. The coins are first arranged like apples thickly set on eight trees, or what purport to be trees, standing on so many small mounds, here and there on the premises outside of the P'rămëne enclosure. These trees are called ton kappap'ruk, or ton karea p'ruk—literally trees that gratify the desires of man. They are intended to represent the four trees that are to be found one in each of the four corners of the city, in which the next Buddha is to be born ; which will bear, not only money, but every thing else that man shall need for his comfort under his reign.

Each artificial tree is thought to have hanging upon it about one hundred ticals worth of money in silver and gold ; and four men ascend each mound to pluck the fruit by handfuls, and cast them to the crowd of men who stand as compacted as it would seem possible for them to live. Every throw is instantly followed by a universal shout from the multitude, and a rush for the prize. And then they surge hither and thither like a forest swayed by a mighty wind. Thousands engage in this kind of sport. It takes but about fifteen minutes to pluck all the fruit from those trees, and then the game is over. It is a rare thing for a man to catch more than two or three limes.

There is still another mode of dispensing the royal gifts on such occasions. And that is, to divide them into lots with a slip of palm leaf attached to each lot, and a copy of each on another slip, which, being rolled up, and put into a paper ball or lime, is thrown out by the King to his favored audience. He sometimes adopts a similar mode in dispensing his favors to companies of the chief priests. But on arranging lots for the priests, he will take care of course that only such things as are suitable to them as priests shall be put into the lots, and usually the most costly articles are arranged for them, suits of yellow robes, bedsteads, sampans, and boats with covers. Lots designed for the laity comprise silver and gold pieces of money, finger rings of pinch-beck and gold; small silver and gold artificial shrubbery, some of which have on them the various silver and gold coins of the country; fans, napkins, wash bowls, goblets, etc.

The forenoon of every day is occupied by the laity, comprising princes, lords, masters and servants, in waiting upon the multitude of the priests at their breakfast and dinner; and helping them to betel, cigars and tea, together with nameless and innumerable little attentions; and in the meantime taking good care to feed themselves bountifully, as it were, from the second tables. The afternoons are spent in serving the priests to their tea, betel and cigars, conversing with them, hearing their preaching, looking at theatrical performances, sham fighting, boxing, wire dancing, somersault adventures, catching the King's gratuitous lottery tickets, and scrambling for the flying money. Every day appears to be a perfect copy of the one preceding it, until the afternoon of the burning.

Then the golden urn containing the corpse is removed from the top of the pyramid and the copper urn taken out of the golden one. This has an iron grating at the bottom overlaid with spices and fragrant powders. All the precious articles with which the pyramid was decorated are temporarily removed from it, and some eight or ten feet of the upper part of it is taken down to form a place of suitable dimensions for the burning. Then the fragrant wood is laid in order in cross layers on the platform, having a bellows attached to the pile. Precious spices and fragrant articles, many in kind, are put among the wood. A gunpowder match is laid from a certain part of the hall set apart for the seat of the King, reaching to a spot made particularly combustible in the pile of wood.

These changes are made with surprising rapidity. All being ready, the King takes electrical fire, which had been preserved for such purposes for a long time,* and touches it to the end of the match at his feet. This kindles a flame in the midst of the wood. Immediately the next in rank among the princes steps up and lays his large wax candle, lighted from a lamp burning with the same lightning fire, and lays it among the wood, or on the top of it, as it may seem to him the most convenient. After him the next prince in the order of rank does the same, and so on in that order, until most of the chief princes and princesses have shown the same sympathy. Then the nobles and lords out of the royal family bring each in quick succession his wax candle, being first lighted by the electrical fire, and lays it on among the wood. At first the order is according to rank, but this is soon lost in the hurry of the many who wish to contribute their candles before it shall be too late. There are many hundreds of wax candles, great and small, laid on the wood and cast into the flames ere the burning has advanced too far to admit of any more. To prevent the flames from becoming too intense for the purpose intended, and too great for the safety of the P'rămĕne and its appendages, there are several strong men armed with long handled dippers, dashing on water wherever and

---

* In the reign of P'ooti Yawt Fa, grandfather of his present Majesty, the royal audience hall was destroyed by lightning. It is commonly believed that fire taken from that conflagration has been kept constantly burning in the palace, and is used only on occasions like the above.

whenever it is required; and there are others armed with iron pokers, whose business it is to stir the fire occasionally.

The moment the pile of wood is fired, the usual funeral band strike up their dirge, and the company of mourning women set up their wailing. But this is continued only a few minutes. The time occupied in the burning is not more than one hour. The fire is extinguished a little before all the bones have been reduced to ashes. A few of the remaining parts of the bones are carefully collected and deposited in a neat and very precious little golden urn. By the time this is done the sun has set and the P'rămëne is consequently left in a despoiled state until next morning. Nevertheless the hall is lighted, and all the usual exercises go on through the night as before. Early next morning, the P'rămëne pyramid is restored to its original splendor, and the little golden urn of precious bones is placed on its summit; and all the ashes left by the burning are put up in clean white muslin, and laid in a golden platter. They are then ceremoniously carried in state to the royal landing, and escorted by a procession of state barges, attended by the funeral band; and being carried down the river about a mile, are there committed to its waters.

The funeral obsequies of a king are continued three days after the burning, and the ceremonies are almost precisely the same as those in anticipation of it, until the last day. On that day a royal procession is formed somewhat like that of the first day, to bear the charred remains in the little golden urn to a sacred depository of such relics of the kings of Siam within the royal palace.

Very soon after this, the servants of the King proceed to gather up all the articles which it is customary to preserve for future funeral occasions, the permanent silver and gold stands, the golden canopy, the ornaments of the pyramid, etc. But the timber of which the P'rămĕne and its appendages are made is taken down and converted to other uses.

It sometimes so happens that there are at the time of a burning for a king one or two more bodies of deceased princes of high rank awaiting an opportunity to be turned quickly to dust by fire. These are brought and burned under the same P'rămĕne; but it is first shorn of its kingly glory. In such cases they will be placed in state from three to seven days, and then burned with essentially the same ceremonies as obtained for the body of the King. If there be two or more bodies to be burned, they will be placed in state on the same pyramid, in separate urns, and burned at the same time, separately on the same platform.

When a P"rămĕne is built expressly for the burning of a prince next in rank to a king, the style of the buildings is much the same as those for a king, but much less imposing and expensive in money and time. Buildings erected for the funeral ceremonies of a nobleman of the first rank will in general style be the same as for a prince of the first rank, and but little inferior in the outlay of money and general appearance. The King usually attends the funeral obsequies of all the princes and chief officers of government who die in his reign. He has temporary rooms prepared for him at the place of burning, and always ignites the wood by a match of electrical fire, which act is denominated T'awáip'rap'long.

The grand object on all such funeral occasions is to feast the priests, listen to their Pali rehearsals and chantings, and make offerings to them.

The common people generally think that such honors bestowed on the priesthood, and through them upon Buddha, will surely accrue to the good both of those who bestow them and the departed spirit of the deceased whose funeral obsequies they celebrate. But the more intelligent of the new school party of Buddhists deny that any good thereby comes to the deceased, if his spirit shall have gone beyond the boundary of this world; to any one of the sixteen great hells or to any of their appendages. But if the spirit become a prate, or yak, or raska (which are the evil spirits of men roving about among men, and often come near to their surviving relatives, and witness the respect paid to them in the spirit world) they too will obtain great benefit by the respect paid to Buddha and his priests at their funerals. Their sufferings will be mitigated, and the term of their banishment shortened. All new school Buddhists affirm that the grand motive for these immensely expensive funeral services is simply to follow old and revered customs, of which nobody knows the origin, but which have become sacred by their great antiquity; and also to show to all about them that the friends of the deceased are not cold and niggardly in their regard for him; but contrariwise, most affectionate, noble and munificent.

People of but ordinary rank, in their funerals, follow essentially the customs of those above them. But for the want of money, they are obliged to burn their dead in P'rămĕnes of comparatively little show; still they have the form and fashion of the rich in an humble style.

To save the expense of erecting a P'rămĕne, they often employ a permanent one, built in connection with some of the larger temples: and by erecting a few sheds get along very well with all the ceremonies by the aid of the zayat, and other places on the premises. This class of people always have numbers of the priests to recite Pali lessons, preach, and receive their offerings of yellow robes, etc. They also have fire-works in the evening of one or two days. Their ceremonies usually terminate on the third day. The bodies of their dead are kept but a few days. Sometimes they do it by putting them in a tight coffin, filled in with lime and sawdust, and sometimes by burying them until they can have time to attend properly to their burning.

But the dead of the very indigent classes are carried by four men, on the very day of their death, together with the cushion or mat they died upon, to some temple, and burned on a small pile of wood, which they bring with them, or purchase on the spot. Sometimes they do it themselves, and sometimes employ a sexton called Sapparo, by paying him sixty cents for the cost of wood, the same sum for his trouble of burning the body.

It is almost a universal custom to bury all who die of small-pox, cholera, childbirth, accident, suicide, murder, fighting, etc., for a month or two, and then disinter and burn their bodies. The reason given for burying them first is the fear they have of a superstition that when their bodies are quickly burned their spirits will come and haunt their friends, and cause them to die some unnatural and speedy death; as they will be likely then to be very irritable and pugnacious, but will naturally get over that in a month or two, so that there will be no more danger in burning their bodies.

Some classes of criminals when executed are subjected also to the horrid treatment of having their bodies cast out in a desolate place, and left for the dogs and vultures to devour.

XXX.
PRACTICE OF MEDICINE—NATIVE DOCTORS.

The Siamese formerly believed that the human system is composed of four elements: water, wind, fire and earth; that disease is simply a disarrangement of these elements; hence if fire from without, the heat of the sun, for instance, enters the body in undue proportion fevers, small-pox, etc., necessarily follows. Each element is claimed by the physicians to have its regular seasons, similar to climatic changes. In the native books that they read they are told that during such a month that wind is prone to prevail and beget disease, another month fire. Appoplexy, they say, is caused by an internal wind blowing upon the heart with such strength as to rupture it. The theory of the native doctors is that all diseases are produced from an excess or diminution of one or more of the four elements. Wind, lom in Siamese, seems to be the leading element, and in nineteen cases out of twenty a sick person, when questioned, will reply as to what ails him, "pen lom," it is wind. They believe that it enters the system by inhalation and proceeds to the head as wind enters into a bellows; without it the blood would not flow, perspiration cease, bile stagnate, bowels inactive and the waste gates of the system remain closed. It is supposed that there are two divisions of wind, above and below the diaphragm. Rheumatism, epilepsy, etc., are caused by the wind blowing upward; colic, pains in the loins, legs, etc., by its blowing downward. It is seldom that a disease runs its course without all of the elements being called into play, water especially, as in cases of dropsy, which is caused by the fire not having sufficient force to dry up the water, as the sun does the mists and fog, and they think that fever and cholera are caused by the invisible mists and vapors that exhale from the ground, miasma. They also believe that spirits, good and evil, produce a multitude of human ills, and the people are in continual dread of them, conscious of the demerit that has accrued to them since the beginning of their existence, hence they perform many acts in the way of propitiating them. They have an idea that medicines have the power to counteract the element deranged and thus restore the body to health. The origin of medicine is claimed to be miraculous and they have nostrums for each and every ailment; for instance, a remedy for the head would be very different from that for the bowels. A snuff, a plaster to the temples or a wash for the eyes may calm the wind in the head, while something entirely different, taken internally, will dissipate the storm in that region upward or downward, or through the pores of the skin; wind may also be withdrawn by cuping, poulticing, etc., in fact that health may be restored by medicines which have the power to drive the surplus elements out of the system or to parts of the system that need it. Giddiness they attribute to a deficiency of wind blowing upward, hence a vacuum in the brain; their mode of treatment is to make the patient eat his fill and then go to sleep. For small-pox and cutaneous eruptions, they use a variety of medicated effusions of a cooling nature. If the disease is from the effects of too much water they will use drastic cathartics, if from a predominance of solids of the earth they will try to render the system more plastic by the use of fluids.

Their medicines are chiefly derived from the vegetable kingdom mainly indigenous to the country, but a small portion is imported from China by the Chinese doctors. Sometimes they employ articles that belong to the animal kingdom, such as tiger and other bones, teeth, sea-shells, fish and snake skins, urine, eyes of birds, cats and cattle, snake's bile and other such stuff; also saltpeter, borax, blue-stone, lead, antimony, salts, mercury, etc.; they also use aloes and gamboge, and of late years quinine has become very popular with them as a tonic. In Bangkok modern medicines are extensively used, especially pills. In the interior the old method still prevails and the native practitioner doses the unfortunate, who may be in his power, with the vilest of decoctions, as there is not a weed or shrub that grows that they do not put to some use. An American physician, who was conversant with their practice, assured me that in one of their prescriptions they had one hundred and seventy-five ingredients, to be taken in three doses, and they are sure enough doses, as the common way of paying a doctor is by the potful thirty to sixty cents per pot, each holding from two quarts to one gallon, and a dose is as much as a man can swallow at one time, frequently a quart. They also make pills, some of them of huge dimension, so large that they have to be cut up and softened in a cocoanut shell of water, then taken in a fluid state. Fifty years ago tonics were unknown until introduced by the western physicians, the native doctors accounting it a sin to use a drop of ardent spirits; but this dread has given away before the practice of drinking introduced by the Europeans, and now many of the Siamese partake of strong drink not only as a medicine, but as a stimulant.

The native doctors, as a general thing, are self-taught, but now the King has made arrangements to have a large class taught at Wang Lang hospital, where several eminent physicians lecture and take charge of the classes. Hitherto when a man was desirous of becoming a doctor he read one or two books or manuscripts on a special subject and practiced in accordance with what he had read. Sometimes he will read a number of books and manuscripts, and witness the practice of an older doctor and then in a year or so branch out as a full-fledged doctor. They make one or two diseases a specialty, none of them attempt to become a general practitioner of medicine. They know but little in regard to surgery and will send for miles to secure the services of a foreign physician. Doctors stand high in the estimation of the people; they look to them as their natural protectors, not only against the effects of disease, but the spells that the spirits may cast over them, and when a doctor fails of a cure he always attributes it to the spell of a witch or a spirit beyond the power of human skill to avoid, and thus retains the confidence of his dupes. The King always has a number of native physicians in his employ who live in or near the palace. He also has two regular physicians, Drs. Gowan and Hayes, the latter an American of the modern school, and he is doing much towards advancing the young men in the hospitals in the study of medicine and surgery, introducing all of the latest works and medicines. The princes and nobles now call in a foreign physician when they are needed, and several physicians are doing an extensive business in Bangkok and vicinity. Thus, in the march of progress they have learned to ignore the old custom of employing none but native doctors, since they have witnessed the remarkable cures effected and skillful operations performed by the American and other physicians. The Siamese are very generous to their physicians and frequently after the patient is convalescent he will send presents to him, the most beautiful and fragrant flowers, in the form of chandeliers and baskets, to be suspended in his room.

The fee for a "job of healing" is never less than eight or more than twenty ticals, but aside from this the law allows a special fee of three and a half ticals called k'wan kow-k'aya. This is divided into two parts, k'wan kow consists of a proffer of a tical and a half in silver, which is stuck on the bottom of a wax candle, then the candle is stood upright in a brass basin or some other utensil; a little rice, salt, pepper, onions, bananas, etc., is added and an incantory form recited over it by the doctor, an offering to propitiate the spirit of the great medical teacher Komara-P'at, who lived during the days of Buddha, beseeching him to exert his influence in the spirit world over the diseases of men. No doctor will ever undertake a case if this rite is overlooked. The kaya is two ticals, for the cost of the medicine, be the same little or much, but he can't claim it until the patient is restored to health. They also have another rite, an appeal to the spirits in behalf of the patient, which they do by moulding little clay images of men, women, cattle, or some other symbol of animated nature, which they place on a small float or stand made of banana leaf on which he puts the statuets together with some rice, salt, pepper, betel, ceri leaf etc., lighting it with a small taper and then carries it into the street or commons or sets it afloat on the river or canal, leaving it to care for itself. This is done in the hope that the offering may be acceptable to the spirits and that they will dispel the storm that is beating on the sick one. This is called krabon, and if successful the doctor receives a tical and a half. The native doctor has nothing to distinguish him from the common run except a box that he carries under his arm holding about a half bushel of pills, powders and other nostrums.

One mode of treating fevers is by water, medicated drinks and frequent bathing in tepid water, ablutions and fomentations. A common mode is showering the patient, the attendant nurse or a priest blowing the water from his mouth, which falls gently and agreeably upon the sick one like a warm spray. Some of the Siamese remedies are valuable, while others are ridiculous; for instance, the following for "morbific fever," as given by Bishop Pallegoix: "One portion of rhinoceros' horn, one portion of elephant's tusk, one of tiger's and the same of crocodile's teeth, one of bear's teeth; one portion composed of three parts bones of vulture, raven and goose; one portion of bison and another of stag's horn; one portion of sandal. These ingredients to be mixed together on a stone with pure water; one-half the mixture to be swallowed, the rest to be rubbed into the body; after which the fever will leave."

The following is an abstract of a recipe for the

worst type of small-pox, taken from a Siamese Mss. of the highest authority. It contains twenty-eight ingredients, to-wit: One portion of conch shell; two kinds of aperient fruit, one portion of each; one portion of asafœtida; one of borax; one of ginger; nine kinds of pepper, including the hottest spices, a portion of each; four kinds of cooling roots, a portion of each; two kinds of sour leaves, one portion of each; one of an astringent root; four kinds of drastic cathartics, including the fruit and leaves of the Croton plant, one portion of each; one of rhubarb, and one portion of Epsom salts. Boil in three measures of water until it be diminished to one measure of the decoction, then squeeze out the oily parts of it, dry and pulverize. A woman may take one salung's weight of it. A child may take a fuang's weight. It will purge off everything in the bowels."

The following are specimens of medical recipes taken from a Siamese Mss. on the treatment of snake-bites. The author states it as being an important fact to be taken into consideration in forming a diagnosis, that the bite of a venomous serpent, and indeed any other wound or sore on the left side of a female and right side of a male, are unfavorable to a cure, and that the reverse is favorable; and furthermore, that there is a difference in the curative capabilities of all wounds according to the day of the week on which they were inflicted, as there is also in the time of the day—the morning being much more favorable than the evening.

One of the prescriptions comprises nineteen ingredients, among which is a portion of the jaw of a wild hog, and one of a tame hog and one of a goat; a portion of goose bone and one of a peacock; a portion of the tail of a fish, and one of the head of a venomous snake. These, being duly compounded and mixed, form an excellent receipt for use in all cases where the venom has produced tetanus or lockjaw.

Another prescription is called a general sternutatory to be blown into the nose in cases of a venomous bite or other poisoned wounds. It comprises seventeen ingredients, as wood, bark, nutmeg, camphor, flowers, the bile of four kinds of venomous snakes and of a wild hog. This, it is said, may be used with much utility also by women who can not lie by the fire after childbirth, and in cases of epilepsy and asthma.

Another recipe is a compound to be taken internally, being briefly as follows. The bile of two kinds of buffaloes, of two kinds of hogs, of a goat, of a sheep, of a fresh water alligator, of a large tortoise, of a salt water alligator, of a sword fish, of a shark, and of thirty kinds of snakes—so much for the bilious part of it. Then there is to be added four kinds of stone, alum, and ratsbane; five kinds of iron, five kinds of bulbous roots, and borax; seven kinds of flowers and fruit; seventeen kinds of leaves; a little gum and resin; seven kinds of medicated water, etc., etc.; being in all one hundred and seventy-four different ingredients. These, being all intimately mixed, are to be divided into three doses. It is termed a large and excellent remedy for the bites of all kinds of venomous snakes.

Another is a snuff made of five kinds of lotus flowers, calculi taken from the livers of cattle, many kinds of animals' teeth, several kinds of roots, two kinds of ratsbane, being twenty-nine ingredients in all. When well mixed, rehearse over it some form of incantation thirty-seven times. Then add twenty-two other ingredients of equal parts. This is said to heal all kinds of poisoned wounds.

Then follows a recipe for an external application in the form of a paste or poultice, consisting of the eyes of vultures, crows and cats; and three kinds of animal deposition found on trees. These having been intimately united, then take nine wax candles, and place them on as many floats made of plantain stalk or leaf, each ornamented with flowers. Then the doctor is to take nine salungs (each equal to fifteen cents), nine handfuls of rice, nine ceri leaves, and nine betel nuts, and make an offering of them one on each float or altar to the Teacher of Medicine. Then he is to take the residue, rub together, dry in the sun, and make into slugs. Then gild the slugs and rub them up in a little water, and apply to the wound.

Following the above is a direction for an enchantment with a view to call the snake to suck out the poison of the wound which it has inflicted, viz.: Take proof spirits three bottles. Let the doctor officiating repeat the form of the incantation. Then let him drink one of the bottles of spirits and enchant over it. If the snake does not come, let him take a second bottle and proceed in the same way. If on drinking the third bottle, with an enchantment, the snake does not come, the patient must die. In case the snake comes, let the doctor take three cowries in his hand, and then rehearse one form of the enchantment, and then another seven times repeated for the purpose of charming the snake to come to the left side of the doctor; for if he comes to the right side a contention will ensue. Then let the doctor brush off the poison from the wound with a handful of meyom leaves seven times, when the form of incantation must be rehearsed over the three bottles. Then if the patient can eat betel he will get well.

SIAMESE OBSTETRICS.

Superstition has invested the whole subject of native midwifery with the most silly and ridiculous notions, and some very pernicious and cruel. In accordance with the teachings of Buddhism, the Siamese believe that there never have been any new creations of animal or intelligent beings, hence that all living creatures that ever have been, or ever will be born, are simply and only transmigrations from previous states of existence—that all mere animal beings, have once been in a higher state in some previous life, in the form of men or women on earth, or as angels in heaven or devils in hell, and that mankind have all transmigrated to their present state either from some of the many heavenly worlds, or from some of the many infernal abodes.

The native books on midwifery make an earnest business of teaching parents how they may know whence their new-born infants have come, and soberly state certain signs by which they may know whether their expected child is to be a son or daughter.

Their books say that there is great choice to be had between the different days of the week on which a child shall be born—Wednesdays and Thursdays being regarded as more favorable than any other day for the development of vigorous constitutions and bright intellects. Children born on Sundays are thought to be peculiarly liable to be careless and reckless all their days.

Besides these days of every week, they pay much

regard to other days, months and years, which their astrological books show to be the most auspicious for the birth of children.

There are a thousand other superstitious observances connected with this subject, which tend greatly to enslave and dwarf the mind of the mother. Happy should all other mothers be that they have not been brought up under such chains of ignorance and consequent misery.

The superstitions surrounding childbirth are peculiar and cruel. Those who practice obstetrics are generally old women, a doctor is seldom called in except on rare occasions, and the midwives endeavor to aid natural labor by means of domestic medicines, shampooing, etc., at times doing much serious mischief. The cruelest part of their procedure is immediately after childbirth, causing the mother to lie by a hot fire for a period of from five to thirty days. If it is the first child she is doomed to lie thirty days within four feet of a fire always uncomfortably warm, much of the time hot enough to blister, on a bare board without a mattress or the least thing to soften the hard plank. This must continue night and day, at the same time wearing nothing but a thin cotton cloth around her hips to shield her from the fire, and she is forced to keep turning constantly as the heat becomes too much for her to bear, in a climate where a fire is anything but pleasant to a person in good health, let alone an enfeebled woman, and this too in a small room without any chimney to carry off the smoke of the burning wood, so that the eyes of the patient are almost blinded as well as her body half baked. This is called "lying by the fire." The fire-place is a box about four feet long by three wide, from eight to ten inches deep, filled with clay, on the top of which the wood is piled and kept burning for the time required. The bench on which the woman lies is of the same height and is brought into immediate contact with it. No one knows the origin of this most pernicious custom, cruel in the extreme, but it is practiced by a number of the East Indian nations. Every effort has been made by the foreign physicians to abolish this practice, but so far without any signal success. In a few instances the wives of His Majesty and of some of the princes have dispensed with this barbarous custom, but the old midwives continue to have their way and the poor mothers are still systematically roasted.

The Siamese are rapidly advancing in their knowledge of anatomy. A few years since they absolutely knew little concerning the human frame; they had a vague knowledge of a few of the bones and tendons, but knew nothing in regard to the nerves, having no word to designate them. Concerning the arterial circulation they had the most novel ideas, imagining the pulse to be a conductor of wind. Ask a native when feeling his pulse what causes it to beat. As in other cases, he will reply "pen lom," it is wind. They formerly imagined that the chest and abdomen were one, which they termed bowels; that the passages to the lungs and stomach were one and that the heart could be reached through the esophagus. A foreign doctor had been called in to treat one of the princes who was suffering with palpitation of the heart. Ten royal physicians were in attendance, who had been physicing him on the supposition that there was a direct passage from the mouth to the heart, hence they had been administering cathartics for the purpose of expelling the wind that was supposed to be pent up in his heart causing the trouble. It was a new idea to them that there was no road to the heart except by way of the circulation of the blood or by the systematic influence of the nervous system. They regarded the liver as having so slight a fastening as to be liable to get out of its place, sinking down among the intestines and producing grave complaints by its erratic wanderings. Even up to the present time the students and native doctors at Wang Lang hospital could hardly be made to understand that there were kidneys in the human body, nor realize of what use they could be in the system. They know but little concerning surgery, they but seldom use a lancet, and treat cancers and tumors with a poultice made up of many ingredients, more injurious than beneficial. It was a long time before the natives would submit to a surgical operation; now that they have realized the beneficial effects of Western skill, they are not slow in catching on to a good thing, our surgeons and doctors are in demand, sometimes having to go hundreds of miles in the interior to amputate or set a limb. Thus it does not take long to break down the barrier of prejudice with them when they are to be benefited. It is well that the Siamese are inveterate bathers, otherwise the way that they live in filthy huts disease would run riot among them, the walls and floors of their rooms being stained with betel saliva and other filth. No wonder that cholera has here its abiding place the year round, its natural home, as it has come there to stay. Vaccination is very popular with the people, having been introduced into the kingdom by an American missionary in 1840, and now the King has instructed the native doctors to vaccinate the people at his expense.

One of the worst diseases in Siam and the Asiatic coast is leprosy. Hundreds of these miserable diseased wretches can be seen begging by the wayside for alms in all stages of the dread disease. Some with fingers and toes gone, others with noses and lips off, their blackened gums protruding in the most hideous manner, while many are a mass of hideous ulcers, barely able to crawl into the shade of a tree and point to the cocoanut shell that holds the few coppers tossed to them by the charitable. The native doctors never undertake to do anything for a leper; they say it is useless, and so far science has been unable to cure or alleviate the ravages of this worst of all human ills. It is impossible to tell the number of the lepers in Bangkok, but I have seen at least one hundred at Wat Kok soliciting alms, and to the credit of the Siamese they contribute liberally to these unfortunates whom they think the spirits have persecuted for some misdemeanor committed in another period of their existence. While it is asserted that the disease is not contagious, it would be well if these unfortunates were housed and cared for, as their appearance is horribly repulsive. It is generally supposed that there is a large number in the city that no one sees but their relatives, those at the wats being paupers whose only chance for subsistence is what is given to them. Outside of the lepers there are but few beggars in Siam, only those who are deformed, crippled or otherwise objects of charity, and they are generally found around the temples.

XXXI.

SIAMESE PLOUGHS, OX-YOKES AND HARROWS.

A native plough is not worthy of the name. They are of two kinds, one designed to be drawn by a single buffalo, and the other by a yoke of oxen. The difference between them is mainly in the length of the beam. The plough for a single buffalo has a beam only about four feet long; but the beam for a yoke of oxen is from 10 to 12 feet in length, proceeding forward from the handle with an upward curve, then downward, and then again upward to a slender and graceful point which is seen above the heads of the oxen, and 18 or 20 inches ahead of them. This long beam saves the necessity of having any rope or chain to draw the plough. The yoke is attached to it by means of a rope passing through an auger hole in it and around wooden pins in the plough beam some three feet from its anterior end. The end where it curves above the heads of the oxen serves an important purpose aside from mere fancy. Cords passing from the nostrils of each ox is made fast to it, with sufficient tightness to keep the heads of the cattle quite elevated, making them, it is said, much more manageable than without such an expedient. But for it, they could not be kept in the track marked out for them, as they lose all recollection of duty in their hunting for something to eat as they plod along. Such appears not to be the weakness of the buffalo, and consequently needing no

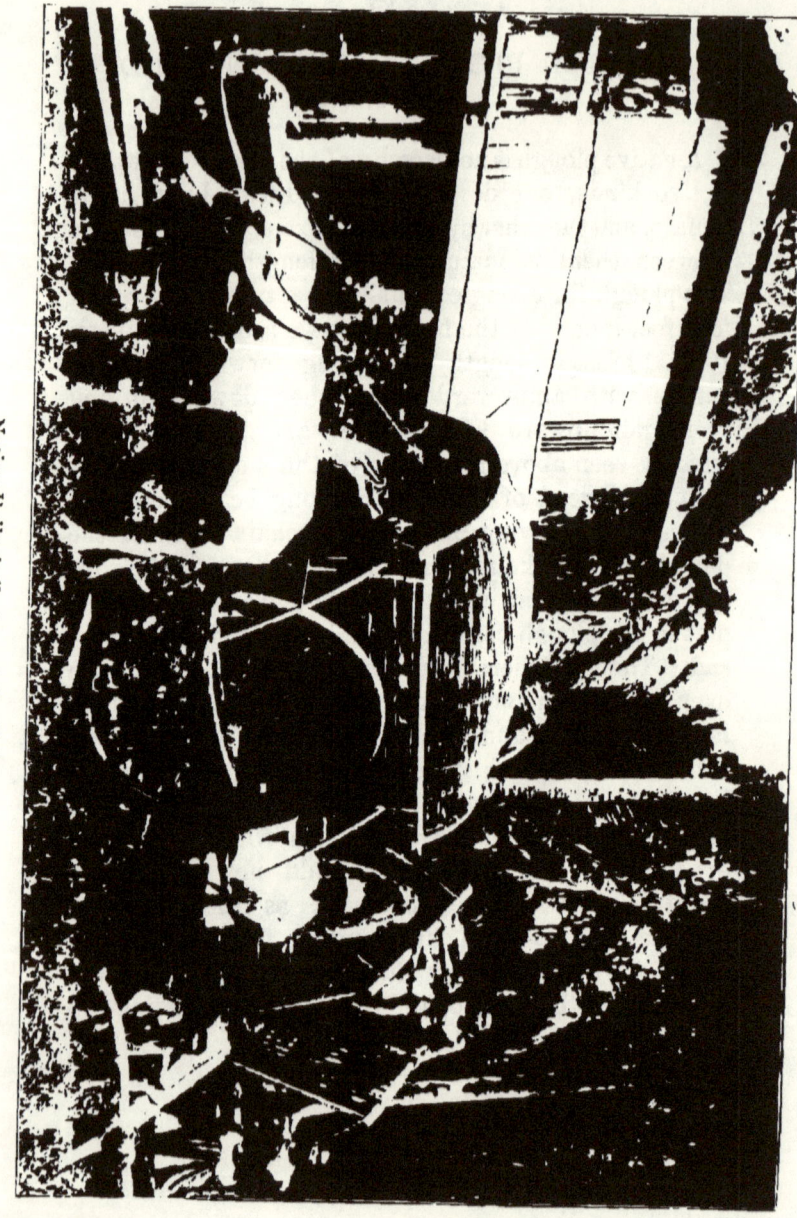
Native Bullock Carts and Ox Yokes.

such martingales to keep his head up, he is hitched to a plough with a short beam and draws it by means of rope traces passing from a rude whippletree to a wooden yoke fixed on his neck by a rope in place of our ox bow. The yoke is in the form of a crescent with its extremities curving a little outward forming a small knob. To these knobs the traces are tied. You will see the buffalo going along with great apparent carelessness, always holding his head near the ground, snapping up here and there a mouthful of grass, and yet never losing the furrow by which he is to walk. The only trouble seems to be that he will halt a little to get what he wishes to eat. He, as well as the oxen, is guided by reins fastened to his nostrils.

A yoke designed for a pair of oxen is often a simple straight and rounded stick 2½ inches in diameter and 3½ feet long. Some of them are more tasty by having a slight bend downward in their middle with a little enlargement there for an auger hole for the rope of the plough or the tongue of a cart to be attached, a slight curve upward and then downward for the necks of the oxen, ending in a little curve upward. The neck of each ox is confined to its place by means of two straight wooden pins three-quarters of an inch in diameter and a foot long, passing through the yoke in the place of a bow, being less open at the top than at the bottom; and then small cords, passing under the neck tied to the upper ends of the pins, complete all the purposes of an ox-bow.

The two kinds of ploughs are about equally strong, but neither of them strong enough to stand a hard pull from a yoke of ordinary western oxen. The one for a buffalo would not usually weigh more than 30 lbs. Its runner and mould board is a natural crotch being one and the same stick, the shorter branch of the crotch serving for the mould board, and the longer branch for the runner. The latter is about two feet long by 10 inches round. It comes to a small point at its nose fitted for the socket of the ploughshare. The latter, but a little larger than a large human hand, is made of cast-iron the shape of half of a large ovate leaf cut square off in the middle. Its upper plane is flat, inclining a very little to the right hand when in its place. It bulges out on the under side to form a flattened socket to receive the nose of the runner. It is never fastened in its place excepting by a close fit, their owners wishing to have them so that they may be knocked off at night and carried home to secure them from thieves.

The mould board, if such it can be called, is only of the same width of the runner, but made thinner, curving backward and upward about 12 inches. It has a slight inclination to the right hand to favor the turning of the clods to that side rather than the other. Being a natural branch of the runner it needs nothing to strengthen it. The hinder end of the beam curves down and is framed into the back end of the runner. The handle of the plough (for there are never two) is a natural crook forming a large segment of a circle four feet long, passes through the beam just behind the mould board, and is framed in the runner near the acute angle made by the two.

Now such is all there is of a Siamese plough, the wood part costing only 75 cents, and the iron 16 cents. It cuts a furrow 2 inches deep and from 5 to 6 inches wide. We should judge that only about half of the clods it breaks up are turned over by it. It does its work very imperfectly at the best.

The natives plough in the same way as we do in America, going round and round a part of the lot or the whole, if it be but small, until it is all cut up. The teams always have rope reins fastened to their nostrils, and these the ploughmen take in their left hand while they hold the plough with the other.

The harrow is simply a large wooden rake, consisting of a rounded stick of tough wood 3 inches in diameter, having 10 or 12 teeth. It has a hoop shape handle for the convenience of lifting it up to shake off grass and stubble that get entangled in its teeth, and for bearing down to give it more execution when needed. Its tongue is made of two small bamboos and extends far enough ahead to admit of tying to it the cords from the nostrils of the oxen and forcing them to hold up their heads. The pitch-fork used in handling rice and grass has but one prong, yet they get along rapidly with it. American hatchets, hoes and axes are coming into use and find ready sale in the bazars.

XXXII.

BRIEF SYNOPSIS OF SIAMESE HISTORY.—A TRANSLATION.

The history commences with a Laos king who reigned in Chieng-rai, at that time the capital of the kingdom. The neighboring king of Sa-tawng invaded his country and took the capital and carried away many captives. On the capture of Chieng-rai the king with many of its inhabitants fled and took refuge within the boundaries of Siam. Crossing the river Po, they came to the ancient city of Paap then in ruins. This city and Kam-p'aang-p'et were situated on opposite sides of the river. The king being endowed with extraordinary merit, P'ra-In, assumed the form of an ascetic and presented himself before him as he was riding on his elephant. He counseled him to found his capital there, being an auspicious place, where he would be safe from all enemies. He then vanished. The king, being delighted with this apparition, said, this ascetic is assuredly P'ra-In, who has assumed this form in order to give me this advice. He therefore encamped and there he built his capital with walls, forts, gates, towers and trenches all complete. When his royal palace and dwellings for the nobles and people were completed, he called it Trei-trung, because its sight had been designated by P'ra-In. In this city he and his descendants reigned for four generations.

At that time there was a very poor man, whose

Scene on the Canal.

whose body was covered with tumors, on which account he was called Nai Saan Pom, or the man of a hundred thousand tumors. This man had a small garden on the river's bank a day's journey south of the city in which he cultivated egg-plant, pepper and other vegetables as a means of subsistence. One of these egg-plants, standing near his house, was watered daily from his own person, it therefore bore fruit of extraordinary size and beauty. The king's daughter, at that time desiring some egg-plant, sent her maids to buy some. Attracted by the beauty of these large ones offered for sale by Nai Saan Pom, she purchased them. She carried them to her mistress, who partook of them, and was consequently found to be pregnant. When her father became aware of it, he made inquiry, but could not learn that she had in any way violated her chastity. At the end of ten months she brought forth a son perfect in all his parts and distinguished for his great beauty. All the royal family aided in nourishing the child till it was three years old. Its royal grandfather then thought that he would then endeavor to discover by divination its father. He made a proclamation commanding all the males of the city to assemble in the grounds of the royal palace, each person being required to bring with him some article of food. He then commanded the nurse to bring the child forth, with a prayer that if his father were present the child might be guided to him and eat whatever he had in his hand. Passing by the inviting portion in the hands of the rich and the great, he made his way straight to Nai Saan Pom who had only a lump of cold rice. Embracing him round his neck, he took this and ate it, to the great astonishment and indignation of all present. A feeling of shame predominated in the breast of the king; he, therefore, gave both his daughter and her child to Nai Saan Pom, and had her put on a raft to be floated out of the city. When they arrived at the garden of Nai Saan Pom, he led them up into his hut. In consequence of the great merit of these three persons, P'ra-In assumed the form of a monkey, and presented to Nai Saan Pom a celestial drum. At the same time he told him that he had only to strike that drum and whatever he desired should be immediately granted. The monkey then vanished from his sight. Knowing that it was the gift of a celestial being, he was greatly delighted, and instantly struck it with the desire that he might become beautiful in form and handsome in appearance. His tumors all immediately vanished and he became distinguished for his extraordinary beauty. He brought the drum to his house, and told his wife all that had happened. She was much rejoiced and struck it again, desiring that they might receive gold of the first quality sufficient to make a cradle for their boy No sooner done, than the gold was theirs and from that circumstance the boy received the name of P'ra-Chow-oo-t'awng

In the year 681 Siamese era, or about A. D. 1320, the father of Chow-oo-t'awng again struck the drum and a large splendid capital sprung into existence with walls forts, towers, gates and trenches all complete, together with a royal palace. He called the city T'ep-na-k'awn because it was accomplished by the power of the t'ewada. The people then encouraged each other to take up their abode there, so that it was soon filled with a large population and the father of Chow-oo-t'awng, whose fame reached to Siam, reigned there under the title of Somdet P'ra-Chow-see-ch'ei Ch'ieng Saan. He was a prince of distinguished merit and great power. He reigned twenty-five years, and died in the year 706— A. D. 1346. At his death the celestial drum also disappeared. He was succeeded the same year by his son—

P'ra Chow Oo-T'awng. He made a great burning for his father's remains, and reigned in T'ep-na-k'awn, his father's capital, six years. Desiring to found a new one, he sent his officers to search for a place where fish of every kind was abundant. Coming south they found such a place and reported it to the king. He came down to it with all his people. They pitched their tents in a place called Weeang-lek, and immediately commenced leveling the ground, and preparing materials for building a new walled capital, which he called Kroong t'ep'a-maha-nak'awn bawawn t'a-wa-ra wadee see-a-yoot'aya ma-ha-dilok-p'op nop'a-archa'a-t'anee booree-rom oodom rach'a-ni-wet maha sat'an—alias Ayuthia.

While building the city in the year 712 on Friday the 6th day of the fifth waxing moon, at nine minutes past nine in the morning, they found under a mulberry tree a shell whose spiral whorl is sinistral or from right to left. Regarding that as an auspicious omen, he caused three royal audience chambers to be erected on that spot. P'ra-Chow oo-T'awng began to reign at the age of thirty-seven under the title—

I. Somdet P'ra Rama T'ibawdee the 1st. He appointed his queen's elder brother governor of Soop'-an-booree, under the title of Somdet P'ra Bawroma-Rach'a-T'irat, and made his own son P'ra Rame-sooan governor of Lop booree. There were at that time sixteen provincial cities tributary to Siam, viz.: Malaka,

Ch'awa, Tanow-see, Tawai, Maw:-tama; Maw:-lam lo'ng, Nak'awn-see-t'ama-rat, Songk'la, Chant'a-booree P'ra-p'itsa-noolok, Sook'ot'ei, P'ich'ei, Sawank'alok, Kamp'aang-p'et-P'ichit, Nak'awn-sawan.

The king built two temples during his reign. He also sent his son on an expedition against Cambodia, Somdet P'ra Bawroma-Rach'a-T'irat leading the reserve force. They conquered the capital of Cambodia and brought back a great many captives to Ayuthia. This Somdet P'ra Rama-T'ibawće, the first king who reigned in Ayuthia, died in the year 731 or A. D. 1370 in the 56th year of his age and the 20th of his reign, the projenitor of the Siamese monarchs, and was succeeded by four dynasties, embracing thirty-nine kings, the present dynasty representing five kings. The three first dynasties reigned in Ayuthia, which was captured and destroyed in the year of 1767, after a three-year siege, they having been the monarchs of Siam for a period of four hundred and seventeen years. After the Burmese had sacked the capital and taken off thousands of the people prisoners a Siamese General, P'ra yah Lohk-Sin, of great celebrity, rallied the Siamese under him at T'onaburee and after a number of hard-fought battles, drove the invaders back and laid the foundation of Bangkok, since then the capital. He founded the present fourth dynasty, and after a reign of twenty-seven years was succeeded by his son P'ra P'utt'a Lo't-lah, who reigned fifteen years, and was succeeded by his son P'rabaht Somdetch P'ra Nang Klow, who reigned twenty-seven years, then his son P'ra baht Somdetch P'ra Paramendr Maha-mongkut, who reigned seventeen years and was succeeded by His Majesty King Chulalongkorn.

FAC SIMILE OF COPY OF HIS MAJESTY'S SPEECH.

เมื่อกาลเมื่อภายที่ท่านมิสเตอเยกอบกิไหล่ กงซุลกรุงอเมริกัน จะกลับไปจากสำนักนิวรอมเกษัยโดยเกษัณี ในกาลที่ท่านอยู่ในตำแหน่งกงซุลในสำนักนิวรอมเกษัณี เราได้เห็นความอุสาหเพื่อที่จะรักษาทางพระราชไมตรี โดยเรียบร้อยจงท่านมิปรากฎแก่เราเนื่อง ๆ ทำให้เรามีความเมตตาในตัวท่าน เราเกษัณสรเสรินูความประพฤติเช่นนี้ ในการที่ท่านได้ประกอบกับเสนาบดี ของเรา รักษาทางพระราชไมตรีให้สนิทยิ่งขึ้น เวลาท่านก็ได้อยู่ในกรุงสยาม ทั้งนาน พอที่จะได้เห็นเปนพยานการอุสาหของเราที่จะรักษาทางพระราชไมตรี เราที่จะบำรุงรักษาบ้านเมืองให้มุ่งเจริญสมกับที่คบหากับนานาประเทศ ณที่ท่านได้ก็สามาเมื่อก็นี้แล้ว

ในการที่สุดที่ท่านจะไปจากสำนักนิวรอมเกษัณี เราจะให้ท่านนำความมุ่งหมายอันดี เมื่อที่จะให้ทางพระราชไมตรีในระหว่างกรุงสยาม กับประเทศยุนิกิสเตกอเมริกา จะมีประโยชน์แก่เมืองเราอย่างยิ่งนั้น ให้มีความเจริญที่ยิ่งขึ้น กับตั้งความรักใคร่ปกกอกกันที่จะมงเจนยี่ ไปเร่งแก่ท่านประธานาธิบดี ของประเทศยุนิกิสเตกอเมริกาด้วย เราเราให้ท่านกลับไปบ้านเมืองโดยความภูมิสัสดิ์ทุกประการ

XXXIII.

Translation of His Majesty's speech in reply to Col. J. T. Child, Minister Resident.

AUDIENCE OF JANUARY 17, 1891.

We regret that you should be compelled to leave our capital so quickly. We have while you fulfilled the office of Minister Resident to our court received various proofs of your endeavor to maintain our friendly relations, and thus we are bound to you by love and must praise you for the spirit in which you approached all questions with our Minister in order to make our friendly relations still more close.

You have been long enough in Siam to bear witness of our solicitude to maintain in every instance the friendship between Siam and the United States and to increase the welfare of our country by closer relations with other powers to which you have just alluded.

On the point of leaving our capital we request you to assure the President of the United States of our anxiety to increase our friendly relations with the United States of America, which are of the highest moment to us, and we beg likewise that you will assure him of our personal esteem and friendship.

And now we wish you in every way a prosperous voyage to your home and country.

XXXIV.

HIS MAJESTY'S BIRTHDAY FESTIVITIES.

The festivities celebrating His Majesty's birthday lasts for three days, when the city of Bangkok is a scene of unrivaled mirth and jollification. This event occurs on the 26th of September, during which time business is virtually suspended and at night the city is illuminated in the most gorgeous manner, each one trying to outdo his neighbor in the display of lights. At noon on the third day the diplomatic body, the princes and nobles repair to the supreme palace to tender congratulations to His Majesty on the anniversary of his birth. The American Minister, being the dean of the diplomatic body, was required to deliver the congratulatory address to the King, which was listened to attentively by the large number of princes and nobles that were in attendance, the throne room being filled with courtiers, the King being attended by the Chow Fa, Crown Prince. His Majesty replied at some length, assuring his hearers that he would do everything that lay in his power to advance the interest of his people, that concessions for railways and tramways, as well as for the workings of mines, had been granted; that the same spirit that had prevailed in the past would be carried out in the future, that outlawry should be put down, etc. Congratulatory addresses were also made by the princes and nobles. The reception was a very pleasant one; the King and his nobles dressed in full uniform, flashing with jewels, together with the diplomats, most of whom wore showy uniforms, standing in the large audience chamber, made a picture of oriental magnificence, once seen it became indelibly photographed on the memory, but the grandest sight was the illuminations. The pearly skies had scarcely faded into ebon hues ere the whole place seemed to have been touched by the wand of an enchanter; miles upon miles of glittering lights gleamed everywhere, and tower and spire and dome were sharply outlined against the dusky canopy that night had thrown over the city, marvellous to behold to one unaccustomed to such scenic displays.

It had been my belief that the display in St. Louis during fair week was unrivalled, but it was nothing in comparison to that in Bangkok on this occasion. The majestic Menam was a blaze of light, all of the legations, large mercantile houses, club houses, noblemen's palaces and residences, boats and shipping were literally covered with lamps filled with cocoanut oil, the design of many being very elaborate, mottoes, coats of arms, etc., but the handsomest display was the royal palace and walls surrounding it, over two miles in extent, which was literally ablaze with parti-colored lights, the outlines of the buildings being sharply defined by rows of lamps that stretched from turret to foundation, lighting up the embrazures and towers along the battlements, while the large arsenal, palace of justice and government buildings along the esplanade, opposite the palace, about a mile in extent, were similarly illuminated, flashing as if studded with brilliants, the effect being marvellous. Immediately in front of the main palace gate a fountain throws its waters high in air and the liquid drops, catching the gleam of the electric lights that streamed through globes of colored glass, seemed like a shower of rubies, diamonds and emeralds; above it glowed a flaming scroll on which was emblazoned in large letters "Long Live The King." Inside the palace ground the illumination was still more elaborate. To add to the interest of the occasion several bands of music discoursed national airs. In the distance, springing out of groves of palm and banyan trees could be seen a number of palaces distinctly outlined, seemingly giant planets amid a world of lesser stars, which added no little to the beauty of the scene.

During the evening the King, accompanied by his nobles, steamed slowly down the river in his yacht to witness the illumination, and his passing was the signal for a display of rockets, bombs, etc., the upper deep soon becoming ruddy with the glare of the grand pyrotechnics, it being a triumphal trip and one that proved that His Majesty was very popular with all classes of people, foreign as well as native. In various parts of the city, Chinese theaters and Siamese lacons gave free performances, thousands atttending highly delighted, and on every side bazars and stands for the sale of fruits, sweets, food, tea, soda water and other refreshments, including liquors of all kind. On the evening of the third day a grand ball was given by the Foreign Minister, the Kromata, H. R. H. Prince Devawongse, at his magnificent palace, which was generally attended by the foreign residents of the city; but a feeling of regret prevailed when it was announced that, owing to the death of the uncle of the King, he would not be present, and thus the assemblage was debarred from a sight of royalty, but it did not detract from the enjoyment of the occasion; dancing was kept up till 4 o'clock and the heavens aglow with the coruscations of morn; the banquet was superb and champagne and other liquids flowed more freely than water. At the banquet it fell to the American Minister to offer the toast of the evening, "The health of His Majesty, King Chulalongkorn," which he did in a few remarks congratulatory, saying *en passant*, "In the future may nothing heaver fall on his brow than the lilies of time." To this the Kromata responded most happily, then the band played and dancing recommenced. To an American it was a novel affair and the magnificent room, lit with electric lights and filled with elaborately costumed, handsome women and gallant gentlemen keeping time to one of Strauss' popular waltzes, made a pleasing picture. One could hardly realize that he was at the antipodes, in a city almost unknown to most people, a terra incognita, but so it was. This annual ball is looked forward to with great interest by the foreign population of Siam's capital as the one event of the year, and they make the most of it. Upon this occasion diplomats, princes, merchants, skippers, engineers, in fact all classes who have received invitations to attend, put in an appearance and mingle on terms of social equality; at other times the etiquette of position is rigidly observed. During the evening wine, ices and other refreshments were passed around by well-trained waiters, and each one handed a fan as a souvenir; the ladies were also presented with a bouquet and a scarf of mogries to wear over the shoulder. In the sitting-rooms some of the gentlemen retired to smoke, play whist or billiards, and thus while away the hours, while others devoted the time to terpsichorean revels with the fair divinities who were there for enjoyment. Nothing was left undone to make it an enjoyable affair; all present pronounced it a grand success, and thus ended the festivities in honor of the reigning monarch. The politeness and attention of the Siamese towards their guests is proverbial, and upon this occasion it was evinced to the fullest extent.

XXXV.

THE MONEY STANDARD OF SIAM.

Silver is the standard of values in Siam, no gold being coined except a few pieces that the King distributes on coronation or cremation ceremonies. The gold pieces are similar in design to those of the silver coinage and possess twenty times their value. Their table of money and weights is as follows:

Fifty Biah make one Solot, two Solots one At, two Ats one See-o or Pai, two See-o one Seek, two Seeks one Fuang, two Fuangs one Salung, four Salungs one Baht or Tical, four Bahts one Tamlu'ng, twenty Tamlu'ng one Chang, fifty Changs one Hahp, one hundred Hahps one Pahrah. The biah or cowdery shell has been abolished. The Solot, At, See-o and Seek are copper pieces; the Fuang, Salung and the Baht or Tical are silver pieces. The denominations after Baht represent weight, the Siamese chang is equivalent to two Chinese catties and is the equal of two and two-thirds English pounds. No law of Siam affects the Chinese standard of weight. The catty can be no more nor less than what the law of China ordains. As the export trade is greatly in excess of the imports, large quantities of Mexican dollars are brought into the country and recoined into ticals and smaller currency The late King Somdetch P'ra Chaum Klow established the present law, making five ticals the equivalent of three Mexican dollars, Mexican silver being the standard of the Asiatic coast. The importer takes his dol-

Interior of the Throne Room.

lars to the mint and the officers there heat them red-hot to detect counterfeits, and if genuine, ticals are given in exchange. This law makes the par value of the tical sixty cents of a dollar, the salung fifteen and the fuang eight and a half cents, the tamlu'ng $2.40, the chang $48.00, the hahp $2,400 and the p'arah $240,000.

Previous to and during a portion of the reign of the late king the small change of the country consisted of sea-shells, known as the cowrie, and designated by the natives as the bi'ah; the purchasing power of the bi'ah was about fifteen hundred to the fuang or eight cents, notwithstanding the government attempted to fix their value at 800 for a fuang. At that time the coins were all round, almost bullet-shaped, millions of which are still in circulation, but the King improved the appearance of the coin by having it struck similar to that of other nations, instead of the round bullets, with two small stamps on them. The coins now issued have the profile of the King on them and are really pretty, showing that the Siamese are abandoning some of their old prejudices, one of which was that no one should make the profile of His Majesty for general circulation, as it was considered a gross violation of Siamese etiquette should it be multiplied and sold as foreign pictures were. The silver coins are the standard of weight in the lower provinces, the rupee in the Laos states. Occasionally one of the gold pieces can be purchased, but they are rare and bring large prices by coin collectors, being regarded as curiosities. There are a large number of counterfeits in circulation among the bullet-shaped coin, owing to the fact that a number of years ago the master of the mint, unknown to the King, manufactured an immense number of copper ticals, and being an adept in metallurgy plated them with silver, and put them in circulation. He was arrested, his property confiscated, and I was informed that he was still in jail, a prisoner, but demented. The Chinese have also put a large number of bogus coins in circulation. A couple of years since the Hong Kong and Shanghae bank commenced the issue of paper money and it grew rapidly in popular favor, as paper is so much easier carried than weighty silver, and it was no novel sight to see eight or ten coolies on their way to the banks or mercantile houses carrying large sacks of silver coin, and frequently boat-loads of ticals are seen on their way up the river to pay for teak and rice; and cart-loads, escorted by soldiers on their way from the interior, taxes to be paid into the royal treasury, frequently from ten to fifteen in the train, all heavily loaded, each drawn by a couple of bullocks.

XXXVI.

THE PRESS OF SIAM.

This is no land for newspapers, the history of the press of Siam is a novel one. There are now two English printed papers published there, the *Times*, simi-weekly, at $20 per annum, and the *Advertiser* weekly, at $24 per annum. They represent the two extremes, one favorable to the Siamese, the other in decided opposition. For a half century the missionaries have endeavored to keep pace with the times by publishing an annual calendar and newspapers. By their efforts several papers have been started, but they somehow have always been brought up in the consular courts charged with libel, on the most frivolous pretexts, and suspended. In 1864 a Mr. Chandler, an American, started the Siam *Times*, but General Partridge, our consul, not liking his style, the *Times* soon ceased to circulate. Dr. Bradley then started the *Bangkok Recorder*, but the American consul, who it appears did not like newspapers, at the conclusion of a libel suit brought by the French consul against the Doctor decided that he was libelous and must be fined because he had published a report current in the palace that the French consul had demanded the removal of the Prime Minister. As the paper was not paying and the Doctor had to settle the bill, he concluded that running a paper was not a part of his mission, and the *Recorder* slept the sleep that knows no awakening, not even issuing another number to record its demise. The *Siam Monitor* then sprung up, but the American consul having come to the conclusion that Bangkok was an unhealthy city for newspaper enterprise the *Monitor* went out with the mango showers. Rev. Sam J. Smith then stepped to the front and started the *Siam Weekly Advertiser*, which he continued to publish for seventeen years, more as an advertising sheet than a disseminator of news, but supposing that the era of libel had passed he was startled when he was brought up by a round turn and met the fate of his predecessors, for when he was called on to pay $1,500 by the English consul for publishing a communication that he had not written or even endorsed, not libelous in a general sense, he shut up shop and said the paper could go to a warmer place than Siam, that the proud privilege of running a paper was exhausting his exchequer and he would have no more of it, in fact it had never paid. This ended the efforts of the missionaries to keep up a paper.

Appreciating the power of the press, if properly handled, the Siamese officials endeavored to keep the *Advertiser* afloat by offering to subscribe for one hundred and fifty copies, provided that they would be allowed to exercise a censorship over its columns, but the proprietor had had enough of glory and the paper still remains with the honored dead. Then an eccentric genius, a cosmopolitan, as much at home in Paris as at Singapore, who had had some experience on the Hong Kong papers, drifted into Bangkok, stood in with the Siamese officials and now publishes, in fact, the first newspaper that has ever been published in the city. During its existence it has published more libelous articles than any of its predecessors, but it still lives. To counteract its influence a German, who had a grievance with the Siamese government, started the *Mercantile Gazette;* he made things hot all along the line, made his paper readable, but he was soon arrested for libeling the Siamese by publishing an article clipped from an English paper and other assaults on the King. He was tried before the German consul, fined and imprisoned; the *Gazette* then shortly followed the others, his speculation proved a failure, but another paper has been started with the same material, possibly to share the same fate.

The Siamese have, strictly speaking, no regular newspaper, only a Government Gazette, printed in Siamese, which contains court proceedings, proclamations, ceremonies, promotions, etc., containing no political or other news of importance, and has but a limited circulation. A native journal was started by Noi Plang, a well educated Siamese, who had passed a very creditable examination at the English bar and who acts as one of the advisors of the government. His paper was rapidly becoming popular, but his remarks were trenching on dangerous grounds, in fact he had commenced to advocate that the Chinese were becoming too numerous in Siam, which was something that His Majesty thought should be let alone, so his paper venture was nipped in the bud just as it was blossoming out into usefulness. Mr. Smith, the editor of the defunct *Advertiser*, edits and publishes a Siamese paper from his office which is interesting from the native correspondence appearing in its columns. It has no life in it and is but little read. A monthly journal is published under the auspices of one of the leading nobles, which aims at Western ideas in its endeavors to give the current news, but it receives but a meager support, having a very small circulation. The Siamese are great readers, but it is the most trashy stuff, strictly oriental and frequently of the most obscene nature, the native novels abounding in the filthiest stories told in the grossest manner; in fact all oriental literature is of that, nature, but highly poetical. This they read and it is in great demand. Thousands of novels of this character are printed in Bangkok which find ready sale at good prices. A collection of Siamese novels, histories and other works would form quite a library, especially their religious works. They are not far enough advanced to appreciate newspapers, caring but little for the news of the outside world.

XXXVII.

A VISIT TO PETCHABUREE, ITS PALACE— THE HOLY MOUNTAIN AND LAOS VILLAGE.

One of the most pleasant trips one can take, if time is no object, while on a visit to Siam, is to the ancient city of Petchaburee, capital of the province of that name. The route thither is by a series of canals and rivers, thence across an arm of the lovely gulf; the trip generally occupying two days, which is accomplished by means of a house-boat, the distance being about seventy-five miles. A portion of the scenery is grand, especially that on the coast of the gulf where small mountains and pinnacles stand out sharply against the bluest of skies, but most of it along the canals is monotonous, the wide stretches of rice-fields only broken in places by groves of palm and betel trees in which are nestled the whitest of wats and handsome salas. When the shadows of night fall the con ruas, boat boys, tie fast to some sala, prepare dinner, then the mosquito nets are stretched and as the darkness increases the trees around are illuminated by millions of fire-flies flashing their light together, apparently by some preconcerted arrangement; then again all would be gloom, seemingly the work of the genii of the forest. On this route you pass a village memorable as the birthplace of Chang and Eng, the well known Siamese twins. In many places monkeys can be seen playing in the branches of the trees, pelicans standing lazily along the canals and now and then a flash of gleaming color dazzles the eye as some bird of gorgeous plumage flies from tamarand to palm or nestles in the emerald foliage of the Bo tree.

At every village are canoes laden with fruit, rice, flowers, with other articles, for sale, the loud smelling durian being the favorite fruit, selling readily at from one to two ticals. At early morn, having drifted down the river, we raised a small sail and started across the gulf, the mouth of the Petchaburee river, with its fringe of attap palms faintly defined on the distant horizon. As the stars slowly faded away and the sun came up gilding the tremulous waves that rocked our boat gently, a cool breeze filling its sail, the blue outlines of the far-away Burmese mountains plainly visible, it made us realize that this was indeed a favored spot for the children of the sun, worthy of poet's pen or painter's pencil, our hearts filled to fullness as one of the party sang "Nearer my God to Thee," and as the words of the well-remembered hymn floated out over the waters we all appreciated the grandeur of the scene, that here nature had poured from her cornucopia many of man's choicest blessings, an Arcadian retreat of supernal loveliness.

Reaching the mouth of the river our boys rowed rapidly up stream and all were much pleased with the scenery along its meanderings, most of the time passing under the shade of majestic trees and flowering vines, the air heavy with its weight of perfume, while at every turn could be seen numbers of natives sporting in the sparkling water which was as limpid as a dewdrop. The sun had well-nigh reached its meridian ere we made the landing that led to the abode of the missionáries. Before we could step ashore we were met with a most cordial greeting from Mr. Dunlap and family, Dr. Thompson and wife, Misses Cort and Small, members of the Presbyterian mission at Petchaburee, the most active and efficient station in lower Siam. They have fine residences and lovely grounds, their compounds are a wealth of flowers, evincing great floral taste and skill. Belonging to the mission is a substantially built church, a number of school buildings, and Dr. Thompson has established a fine hospital, subsidized by the King. Since then Dr. Thompson and family have moved to Ratburee, farther into the interior, where he has established another hospital. The city contains about 20,000 inhabitants, is the home of the Governor, one of the most prominent of Siam's nobles, built like other Siamese cities, mostly bamboo houses, some handsome palaces, large filthy bazaars, ruined temples and a general air of apathy prevails throughout the whole place. The river passes through the center of the city, which is used for all purposes. Some of the modern wats are large and handsome, one containing a sleeping Buddha one hundred and forty feet in length, another over five hundred statues of the great teacher, of life size, standing and sitting, both of whom are worthy a visit.

The Governor, being notified that I was in the city, called on me with all the style and ceremony in keeping with these magnates and kindly placed at my disposal a carriage so that I could visit the holy mountain, the King's palace and a Laos village, the lions of the place, which was accepted in the most courteous manner, our party returning the visit of the Governor next morning at his palace where we were received most courteously; tea, cigars and cigarettes being tended us. A couple of days travel distant, on ponies, are a number of hot springs, which it was our intention to visit, but learning that a fatal fever was prevailing in the vicinity we were forced to give up the trip. The carriage having called at the mission for us, our party set out for the holy mountain, about two miles distant from the city, over a well-kept road shaded with palms and fringed with oleanders, the latter growing here from twenty to thirty feet high. The mountain is about two hundred and fifty feet in height, apparently an extinct volcano, hollow, with two apertures at the top, one of which is used as an entrance, a long flight of stone steps leading into the interior, known as the "Cave of Idols." This immense vault has been fitted up as a temple, its floor handsomely tiled and statues of Buddha placed everywhere within it, one for each day of the year, several of them of immense magnitude, five persons being able to stand at once on the thumb of one of them. In niches along the steps were placed life-sized figures of men, made of clay, flesh-colored, intended to represent the dead, with all of the agony of dissolution portrayed on their features and distorted limbs. Huge stalactites hang like pendants from the roof, which towers about two hundred feet above, the chamber is about an acre in extent with another not used branching off from it. The largest opening in the center of the roof lights it up magnificently, like the Pantheon at Rome. It is one of the most unique temples of this wonderful land. As it is a sylvan solitude, quite a number of priests resort thither for meditation and they can be seen squatting beside the clay figures, typical of man's dissolution, the living almost as callous as the dead.

Having spent several hours in this subterranean temple, we drove to the royal palace, situated on a lofty hill on the outskirts of the city, a long avenue sheltered with palms leading to it. Reaching the base of the hill we dismounted and walked over a wide brick-paved path to the top, a winding road, passing a number of salas used for the reception of the retainers of His Majesty while on a visit to this regal abode. In some of the salas were handsome vehicles in the last stage of dissolution, a number of rusty cannon, everything grown up with dank weeds, while on the stones large lizards lay basking in the sun, the place seemingly the abode of venomous serpents; but we saw none and were thus agreeably disappointed. The path terminated at the base of two steep stairways with massive stone balusters, which led to several two-story brick buildings; then came the private apartments of the King's nobles with wide paved terraces and extensive barracks. On the summit of the hill, as can be seen from the engraving, is situated the palace proper, comprising the royal audience hall, chambers, library, a wat and an observatory. The audience chamber was barren of ornaments, is about seventy-five feet in length by forty in width and twelve in height. At one end is a semi-circular dais, consisting of four marble steps, over it the royal umbrella. A few ordinary pictures hung on the walls, while a handsome chandelier was suspended from the ceiling. The palace was partially furnished, it only being occupied at long intervals. From the observatory a grand view can be had of the surrounding country. As far as the eye can reach is a vast ocean of paddy fields, and here and there stand out groves of bamboo and palm, islands in a waveless sea of verdure; to the west the Burmese mountains hemmed in the horizon, while away off to the South an orient sun was reflecting back its glory from the sparkling waters and turning into gold the lateen sails of the fishing boats that lazily floated on the rim of the faraway gulf, a panorama not to be excelled in beauty in any other portion of our planet. A scene lovely as a poet's dream, nature's choicest handiwork.

Tendering the polite seneschal of the palace a silver coin, we were soon on our way to the Laos village, a cluster of about twenty huts, occupied by slaves of the King, descendants of captives in war. The houses are unlike those of the Siamese; they are built of bamboo, two stories high, thatched with attap; the lower story is used for a stable and rubbish generally, the upper entered by a ladder which is drawn up at night, for all purposes and is but scantily furnished, in fact contained nothing but a few boxes and baskets with some matting to sleep on. The houses are of a peculiar cone shape, like the bark huts of some of our Indians, but much larger. A center pole is planted in the ground and the roof, that comes nearly to the ground, like a half-closed umbrella, comprises the outside of the house, looking at a distance like a huge straw stack. Adjacent to these houses were a number of sheds where the women did their cooking and kept their looms for weaving cloth, and they are very skillful, making handsome panungs and sarongs, raising their own silk and cotton. The Laos women wear a peculiar head-dress, and in the place of the panung they use a sarong, a garment similar to a petticoat, also large silver ear-rings. Some of their dresses are very handsome, embroidered most elaborately, and no Laos maiden is allowed to marry until she has made a full and complete stock of clothing for herself. They are more industrious than the Siamese, and are considered among the best subjects of His Majesty. Their language is somewhat similar to the Siamese, but the letters of their alphabet are entirely different. Since I paid this village a visit it has been entirely destroyed by fire, not a single house left; but I can never forget the kindness of its people nor the pathetic tales they told of the capture of their forefathers, yet they all expressed a deep devotion to the King, for whom they had no words but praise. Returning to Bangkok I took nothing with me but the most pleasant reminiscences of this trip into the interior, convinced that if King Chulalongkorn is allowed to carry out his plans of progress for the development of his kingdom, aided by his nobles, in a short time Siam will become one of the most prolific countries occupied by man, for it would seem as if the Omnicient has showered his blessings on this favored kingdom with a lavish hand, making it indeed The Pearl of Asia.

THE END.

www.ingramcontent.com/pod-product-compliance
Lightning Source LLC
Chambersburg PA
CBHW032011220426
43664CB00006B/211